Fighting the polar ice

Anthony Fiala

FIGHTING THE POLAR ICE

Painted by Russell W. Porter

"ON OCTOBER 15TH, OUR LUMINARY DIPPED BELOW THE HORIZON IN A GLOW OF SCARLET FIRE."

Fighting the Polar Ice

By

ANTHONY FIALA

Commander of the Ziegler Polar Expedition

Author of " Troop 'C' in Service"

With an Introduction by
W. S. Champ, and Reports by William J. Peters, Russell W. Porter
and Oliver S. Fassig

*Illustrations from photographs and sketches by
the author. Also nine, from paintings in colour
by Russell W. Porter and J. Knowles Hare*

NEW YORK
Doubleday, Page & Company
1907

Copyright, 1906, by Anthony Fiala
Published, November, 1906

Hast thou perceived the breadth of the earth? Declare if thou knowest it all

Where is the way where Light dwelleth? And as for Darkness, where is the place thereof.   Job.

To the Memory

OF HIM

WHO SENT THE EXPEDITION FORTH

PREFACE TO SECOND EDITION

THE scientific records of the Ziegler Polar Expedition and the results of the observations taken in the Franz Josef Archipelago during the years 1903, 1904, 1905, because of their length and volume, could not be placed within the pages of a simple narrative and were thus excluded from "Fighting the Polar Ice."

The task of preparing the scientific data for publication was taken up by Mr. William J. Peters during September, 1905, upon the return of the expedition. He was unable to complete the labour personally owing to his association on January 1, 1906, with the Department of Terrestrial Magnetism of the Carnegie Institution of Washington, when he was appointed Commander of the Magnetic Survey Yacht. In his absence, through the courtesy of Dr. L. A. Bauer, Director, the burden of the completion, computation, editing, and, publication of the results has been borne by Mr. J. A. Fleming of the Department of Terrestrial Magnetism, and acknowledgment is due to Mr. Fleming for his masterly arrangement of the matter in hand and his painstaking and faithful attention through the long series of computations in securing the necessary reductions. Acknowledgment is also due the Department of Terrestrial Magnetism of the Carnegie Institution, through its Director, Dr. L. A. Bauer, for his valued assistance.

The expedition is under great obligation for generous

assistance received from sources other than that of its lamented organiser and donor, Mr. William Ziegler of New York City. Mr. Ziegler was personally interested in every phase of the work. and in the hope of carrying out some of his last wishes, the executors of his estate are publishing these records.

Acknowledgment is due Mr. William S. Champ, the rescuer of the party, whose opportune arrival at Cape Dillon saved both the members and records of the expedition.

The National Geographic Society as a whole, and through its members individually, has given encouragement and assistance in many ways, both in the initiation and completion of the work of the expedition. It was to this organization that Mr. Ziegler extended the privilege of selecting the scientific leader and it was by the unanimous action of its Board of Managers that Mr. Peters was commissioned in this capacity. The scientific work accomplished conforms, in general, with the suggestions made by the Research Committee of this Society, of which Professor G. K. Gilbert was chairman.

Grateful acknowledgments are due Professor Geelmuyden, Director of the Christiania Observatory, who loaned a Repsold circle when at the last moment it appeared that one could not be obtained.

Mr. O. H. Tittmann, Superintendent of the United States Coast and Geodetic Survey, on the part of himself and the members of his Bureau, extended every possible help in the way of instruction and suggestion. Through his courtesy the expedition had also the use

PREFACE TO SECOND EDITION

of the instrumental outfit necessary for the execution of the magnetic work.

Professor Willis Moore, Chief of the United States Weather Bureau, supplied a number of instruments for use in the meteorological observations

General A. W. Greely, of the United States Army, extended assistance by many valuable suggestions as the result of his own wide experience in Polar work; he also arranged for the loan of some meteorological instruments from the United States Signal Corps.

Dr. L. A. Bauer, Director of the Department of Terrestrial Magnetism of the Carnegie Institution of Washington, devised the plan of observation best suited to the limited instrumental outfit and conditions to be encountered, which plan experience proved successful. He has further suggested the general scheme of reduction of this portion of the observations.

The volume of Scientific Records is to be published under the auspices of the *National Geographic Magazine* of Washington, D. C., and will appear about April 1, 1907.

February, 1907. ANTHONY FIALA.

(*Died May 24, 1905*)

INTRODUCTION

THE crowning desire of the late Mr William Ziegler was to link his name with some scientific achievement which would be considered great when compared with others of the 20th Century, and he thought there was no mystery, the solution of which would be so heartily welcomed by the world at large as the exact location of the North Pole and accurate information as to the conditions existing there.

In July 1901 he sent out an expedition consisting of the *America*, a vessel of 466 tons burden, the *Frithjof*, 270 tons, and the *Belgica*, under the command of Mr. Evelyn B Baldwin It has been said, and I believe truly, that no explorer had ever sailed under more favourable or promising conditions. Be this as it may, in the following summer the expedition returned unsuccessful. Mr Ziegler, although greatly disappointed at this failure, immediately decided to send forth another expedition, and in looking over the field for a competent leader, and after consulting with several gentlemen whose names are familiar in Arctic history, he selected Mr. Anthony Fiala of Brooklyn, who had served the first expedition as photographer so well, and the high regard in which he was held by all of the members had a decided bearing on Mr Ziegler's determining this all important problem.

Thus it was that in the spring of 1903 Mr. Fiala left for Norway to take personal charge of the fitting out of the ZIEGLER POLAR EXPEDITION which sailed from Trondhjem, Norway, June 23, 1903.

As the personal representative of the late Mr. William Ziegler it was my duty to attend to a very large extent to the financial and business end of both of these expeditions, and I want to take this opportunity to publicly acknowledge the great assistance rendered and uniform courtesy extended by both the Norwegian and Russian Governments, and also to Mr. Johannes H. Giaever former British vice-consul at Tromso. To the President, Officers, and Executive committee of the National Geographic Society is largely due the mapping out of the scientific work which was successfully carried out by their representative, Mr. W. J. Peters, who was afforded every opportunity for his work by the leader of the expedition, who speaks highly of his service and also of the service rendered by the members of the scientific staff.

Though the expedition failed of its object through an unprecedented experience of unfavourable conditions linked with the loss of the ship, it did not return without results and the records of its work. The valuable scientific instruments were dragged hundreds of miles over ice of glaciers and channels first in the accomplishment of duties and later to the relief ship.

Three attempts north were made and an opportunity was afforded for heroic and loyal devotion to the trust, in which the small body of volunteers who stayed at Camp Abruzzi through the second winter proved true.

One died at his post. Their names are given in the narrative by Mr. Fiala and I will not attempt to add to his story.

It is with a great deal of pleasure that I announce that this valuable scientific record is being published by the Estate of William Ziegler under the direction of Mr Gilbert H. Grosvenor, Editor of the *National Geographic Magazine*, Washington, D. C.

In conclusion permit me to introduce to the readers of this narrative Captain J. Kjeldsen of Tromso, Norway, a true Arctic hero, the man who safely navigated the S. S. *Terra Nova*, which effected a timely rescue of the members of the Ziegler Expedition. To him and his faithful Norwegian officers and crew the writer feelingly tenders this acknowledgment, and publicly expresses the heartfelt appreciation of the rescued.

WILLIAM S. CHAMP.

New York, Aug 14th, 1906.

CONTENTS

CONTENTS

LIST OF ILLUSTRATIONS

FAC-SIMILE OF STAMP PRINTED AND
ISSUED AT CAMP ABRUZZI, RUDOLF
ISLAND, IN 1905

FIGHTING THE POLAR ICE

FIGHTING THE POLAR ICE

CHAPTER I

THE PROBLEM

NAPOLEON is quoted as having once said that if he had three things he could conquer the world. The first of these was money, the second more money, and the third still more money.

If Napoleon's estimate of the power of money had been correct, Waterloo would have been a victory instead of a defeat, and his legions, better equipped then than in any previous campaign, would not have been hampered by conditions internal and external and the great commander would not have sighed in vain for his grand army of veterans whose bones strewed the trail from Moscow to Paris.

The Polar explorer needs money, but he needs other things more. While in the history of almost every polar expedition the sad story of imperfect preparations through lack of funds can be read, it is also true that conditions play an important part. The element we call Chance has much to do in the giving of success or failure, but the human elements of endurance and courage are the most important of all.

In the frozen zone there is not the stimulus to effort raised by numbers. The soldier in the excitement of battle, sustained and cheered by onlooking thousands, may become a hero; but the Polar explorer has a hard, cold, and lonely way in which patience, more patience, and still more patience seem to be the cardinal requirements. There are few to encourage him in his long fight against almost impossible conditions, and the highest qualities of Christian character in the personnel of his party are necessary to achieve any measure of success.

Beyond the geographical and scientific value of the discovery of the North Pole, and the solving of questions of popular curiosity, another reason exists to explain the ceaseless effort to reach that mystic point: The Spirit of the Age will never be satisfied until the command given to Adam in the beginning—the command to subdue the earth—has been obeyed, and the ends of the earth have revealed their secrets to the eye of man.

The conquest of the North Pole has a military as well as a scientific character. To reach 90° North Latitude from the northern limits of Greenland or the Franz Josef Archipelago, an expedition party would be obliged to make a forced march of at least one thousand miles from its base of supplies, the expedition column of men and animals subsisting upon provisions carried along.

From Rudolph Island, the northernmost land in the Franz Josef Archipelago, to the Pole is about five hundred miles, over fields of rugged, moving ice that drift continually. Allowing for pressure ridges and open water lanes, the distance of five hundred miles would be augmented instead of diminished by the general twist and zig-zag direction of the line of march. Of course the return distance of five hundred miles must be considered, for there would be little value in reaching the Pole unless the explorer returned. The rough character of the ice and the fact that it is moving and continually changing its form make it impossible to station auxiliary depots of supplies on the ice itself. Even if the ice were stationary it would be almost impossible to find a cache after a few days, for the wind sometimes obliterates a well marked trail in a few minutes, the flying drift covering everything with a solid hard blanket of packed snow.

A team of nine dogs, the unit of transportation in the north, consumes about nine pounds of food a day, or one pound of pemmican per dog, the human driver about three pounds, making a total of twelve pounds a day. If ten miles a day could be averaged—though it has never been done—in one hundred days the journey to and from the Pole could be accomplished. At twelve pounds a day the total amount of food required by a driver and dog team would be twelve hundred pounds. Through experience it has been found that the sledges go to pieces, no matter how well built, if loaded with more than six hundred pounds, which is the food allowance for only half the distance There is also to be considered the necessary dead weights of tent, sleeping bag, cooking apparatus, extra clothing, ammunition, firearms, nautical instruments, and kayak—the last a light boat for use on the return march when melting snows and ice, with the motion of the Polar pack, open great lanes of water across the explorer's path.

Dr. Nansen, in his record-breaking trip with but one man and three dog teams, left his ship at the high northing of 84 degrees and reached 86° 13' N. Lat. But, despite the decided advantage of a start from so high a base he was obliged on his retreat to Franz Josef Archipelago, to feed his dogs to his dogs, and in the end he and Johansen drew the two remaining sledges to land themselves.

Capt. Cagni, with a party from the expedition led by the Duke of the Abruzzi, broke Nansen's record by about twenty miles, reaching 86° 33' N. Lat. He started from a base on Rudolph Island and succeeded in making his splendid march by the use of supporting parties that were detached and sent back to the base camp as the main body advanced, each supporting party carrying food for the advance of the entire column and its own return. The first detachment of three men never found its way back to camp. The men probably starved to death while trying to cross the rough ice that separated them from their comrades on the Island. The rough ice was caused by the breaking into pressure ridges of the comparatively smooth newly frozen lanes over which the sledge column made its northward march.

The question of food then is important. A remark of General Grant's that "an army travels on its stomach" is now a maxim in text-books on military logistics and puts into few words a truth accepted ever since men went to war. If it is true of an army that operates in a cultivated or partially cultivated country that its progress is determined by the excellence of its commissary arrangements, and by the certainty and celerity with which the food supplies reach the individual soldier and animal, how much more true must it be of the Polar explorer who operates in a decidedly hostile and uncultivated territory, where there are no cornfields or henroosts along the line of march, but instead an active enemy in every wind that blows from the north, and opposition to advance in every pressure ridge and water lane that crosses his path.

CHAPTER II

IN AUGUST of 1902 the Baldwin-Ziegler Polar Expedition returned to Norway after an absence of a year in the Franz Josef Archipelago. The expedition ship, the steam yacht *America*, had wintered at Camp Ziegler on Alger Island, 80° 24′ N Lat. from where a large sledge party in the spring of 1902 transported about 40,000 pounds of pemmican to Cape Auk (81° 43′ N. Lat), the southwestern end of Rudolph Island, four miles south of the Duke of the Abruzzi's station at Teplitz Bay.

On the return of the expedition to Norway, the late William Ziegler, who had so liberally financed it, resolved to send a second party in seach of the North Pole. It was not until December of 1902 that a leader was chosen Mr. Ziegler then gave the command to me with instructions to equip and sail north in the following spring

Only a few months remained for preparation, a large store of provisions and an extensive equipment had to be purchased, and many things devised and manufactured. The steam yacht *America*, formerly the Dundee whaler *Esquimau*, after her year in the north, was in a condition requiring docking and extensive repairs before she could again be headed toward the ice fields of the Arctic Circle. Nothing remained of the large sledge equipment of the former expedition and only a small amount of food stores, so small that it could not be considered. Fortunately there were left 183 dogs, and five Siberian ponies on the small island of Trono, some miles south of Tromso, Norway, where they had been placed for the winter on the return of the *America* in 1902.

In addition to a large pack of dogs a number of Siberian ponies were taken on the 1901–1902 expedition. These little creatures behaved so well and proved of such value that I made provision to take more of them this time. The ponies had been used with success by Jackson and Baldwin and it seemed to me that they could be trained during the autumn and early spring to follow one another "in trace," one man in charge of several pony sledges, just as our pack trains travel in mining districts and in the army, for I realised that if a driver had to go with each sledge whether it was drawn by a team of dogs or a pony, the Polar problem must remain unsolved.

Dependence had also to be placed on a good pack of dogs, to be fed on the ponies as the latter's sledge loads disappeared, the ponies to serve as food on the hoof. With the ponies came the necessity of providing tons of hay in compressed bales. Hay could be purchased in America in bales only a quarter the size of foreign bales and weighing twice as much, so all the hay was transported from this side of the ocean for the sake of economy in space. There were also tons of oats to be purchased and transported to Trondhjem, which was to be our sailing port. Corn could be bought in Russia, one of the few countries in Europe that produce more than enough for their own consumption. Thirty-six tons of Spratt's dog-cakes were purchased and about 10,000 pounds of tallow as supplementary food for the ever hungry dogs.* The aggregate weight of our food supplies was about ninety-eight tons and the stores alone, exclusive of meats, occupied 7,200 feet of space.

In addition to the commissary stores for men and animals coal had to be provided and a large equipment of sledges, harness, clothing, furs, footwear, cooking apparatus, boats, explosives, tentage, lumber for a house, and the thousand little things necessary for the protracted stay of a large party of men and animals far from the shops and supply stations of civilisation. Before the numberless parts of the equipment had been received for shipment, many hours were spent in calculating the available space aboard the *America* and in measuring the cargo.

In the organisation of the party the question of personnel was a troublesome one particularly in view of the limited time at my disposal. That the party should be all American was the desire of the late Mr. Ziegler and myself, but it was not until nearly all the supplies were arranged for and the entire equipment ordered that we succeeded in finding a native American, Captain Edwin Coffin of Edgartown, Martha's Vine-

---

* It may be interesting to know what a body of 39 men need in a two years' expedition. Allowing 1½ lbs. of meat a day for each man—the U. S. Army allowance in a temperate climate—39 men dispose of 42,705 pounds, or over 20 tons of meat. For a cold climate, of course, more has to be allowed.

In the same period on the army plan, 39 men consume about 145 bls. of flour, 2,600 pounds of coffee, over 8,000 pounds of sugar, and so on down the list of vegetables and stores.

yard, Mass., to navigate the expedition ship. Capt.
Coffin, in turn, after much trouble, got together his
officers and crew, a number of them experienced
whalers. Because of the high price that whalebone
was bringing in the market, whaling, the last few years,
had been a lucrative business, and, as all who serve
on a whaler share in the profits of the cruise, it was
not an easy task to get able men to leave their favourite
hunting grounds for the field of exploration.

For the sake of organisation I had divided the expedition party into three departments, a Field Department, a Deck Department, and an Engine Department. Capt. Coffin, as Navigator and Master of the
vessel, was of course in charge of the Deck Department. In charge of our Engine Department was Henry
P. Hartt, a marine engineer of sixteen years' experience aboard steam whalers, who had passed nine
winters in the Arctic and had been with the Baldwin-
Zeigler party in 1901-1902. For the Field Department
I received numerous applications, many of the American
members of the last expedition wishing to go north
again. Where possible, preference was given to them,
for, having lived and laboured with them through the
trials of an Arctic voyage, I knew them as I could not
know others.

It was odd how quickly the Arctic lost its terrors
after the return to civilisation. During the long,
dark winter of 1901-1902, every night, after the working hours of the period we called day were over, we
would huddle together for warmth around a tiny
stove in the cabin of the *America* and talk of warmer
countries. Two of the men avowed their intention

of going on an expedition to the island of Borneo as soon as the *America* returned to Norway; two others stated that they were going to Mexico; another expressed a wish to explore Africa, and one of the doctors of the party said he meant to go to the equator and never travel farther than five degrees north or south of it the rest of his days. Yet on the eve of another expedition these men applied to go north once more.

The Field Department comprised the members of the Scientific Staff and those of the expedition company not signed on the ship's articles. Among these were the Surgeon, Assistant Surgeon, Assistant Surgeon in charge of the dogs, a Veterinarian, a Quartermaster, a Commissary and a number of assistants.

William J. Peters of the U. S. Geological Survey and representative of the National Geographic Society, was chosen as Chief Scientist and Second in Command of the Expedition. Russell W. Porter, First Assistant Scientist and Artist of the Expedition, was commissioned Third in Command while in the field. The following is a list of the members of the expedition:

1. Anthony Fiala, Brooklyn, N. Y., Commander of the Expedition.
2. William J. Peters, Washington, D. C., Chief Scientist, and Second in Command of the Expedition.

Field Department

3. Russell W. Porter, Springfield, Vermont; First Assistant Scientist and Artist.

THE EXPEDITION'S DOGS AT TRONO, NORWAY

4. R. R. Tafel, Philadelphia, Pa., Second Assistant Scientist.

5. Francis Long, Brooklyn, N. Y., Weather Observer.

6. George Shorkley, M. D., Camden, Maine, Surgeon.

7. Charles L. Seitz, M. D., Evansville, Ind., Assistant Surgeon.

8. J. Colin Vaughn, Medical Student, Forest Hill, N. J., Second Assistant Surgeon in charge of the dogs.

9. H. H. Newcomb, D. V. S., Milford, Mass., Veterinarian.

10. Chas. E. Rilliet, St. Louis, Mo., Quartermaster in charge of equipment.

11. John W. Truden, Pittsfield, Mass., Commissary.

12. Jefferson F. Moulton, Sergeant Troop G, 2d Cavalry, U. S. A., detailed by courtesy of the War Department to serve in the Expedition. He served as Assistant Quartermaster in care of the ponies.

13. Spencer W. Stewart, Brooklyn, N. Y., Assistant Commissary.

14. John Vedoe, Boston Mass., Assistant Quartermaster.

15. Pierre LeRoyer, Three Rivers, Quebec, Canada, Assistant in care of dogs.

Deck Department

16. Edwin Coffin, Edgartown, Mass., Master.
17. Edward Haven, Lynn, Mass., First Officer.
18. James W. Nichols, New Bedford, Second Officer.

Crew

19. Peter L. Tessem, Trondhjem, Norway, Carpenter.
20. Franklin Cowing, New Bedford, Mass.
21. Allen W. Montrose, Lowell, Mass.
22. Wm. R. Myers, Boston, Mass.
23. Chas. Kunold, New York, N. Y.
24. Harry Burns (Harry Paxton), Dunkirk, N. Y.
25. D. S. Mackiernan, Dorchester, Mass.
26. Alfred Beddow, London, England.
27. Elijah Perry, New Bedford, Mass.
28. Gustave Meyer, New York, N. Y.
29. William Ross, New York, N. Y.
30. John J. Duffy, Waltham, Mass.

Engine Department

31. Henry P. Hartt, Portsmouth, Va., Chief Engineer.
32. Chas. E. Hudgins, Norfolk, Va., First Assistant
    Engineer.
33. Anton Vedoe, Boston, Mass., Second Assistant
    Engineer.
34. George D. Butland, Brooklyn, N. Y., Fireman.
35. Augustinsen Hovlick, Trondhjem, Norway, Fire-
    man.
36. Sigurd Myhre, Trondhjem, Norway, Fireman.

Steward's Department

37. Bernard E. Spencer, Boston, Mass., Steward.
38. Clarence W. Thwing, Boston, Mass., Cook.
39. James Dean, New Bedford, Mass., Cabin Boy.

The *America* had been left through the winter at
Tromso, a town above the Arctic Circle in the north
of Norway, a place noted as a depot of supply for many
a Polar expedition. Her American crew left New

"WE CROSSED THE ARCTIC CIRCLE, AND ALL MEMBERS OF THE EXPEDITION WHO HAD NOT CROSSED THE PARALLEL BEFORE, WERE SEIZED BY THEIR COMRADES WHO HAD, AND INITIATED AS POLAR EXPLORERS BY BEING THROWN OVERBOARD WHILE THE STEAMER WAS IN MOTION, THEIR SAFETY FIRST INSURED BY A LONG LINE MADE FAST AROUND THEIR WAISTS."

York for Tromso in March. 1903.   As nearly all meat
and food supplies and equipment had to be shipped
from the United States, the stores were ordered early
to allow at least a month's time on freighters from
New York to Hamburg, from which point they were
forwarded to Trondhjem.

The mixing of the cargo had troubled us considerably on the last expedition, and, to obviate a similar
confusion this season, I had a number of conventional
signs made into stencils, and had the cases of supplies
marked on all sides, so that a glance would reveal the
contents, no matter in what position the box might
be.   For example, a red star signified that the case
contained pemmican; a red maltese cross meant preserved or canned meat; the crescent designated commissary stores; a red crescent, condensed food; a
blue crescent, breadstuffs or flour; a green crescent,
vegetables; black always denoted equipment; the
horseshoe surrounding a cross was the sign of the
Veterinary Department; and so on.

In Trondhjem, where the cases were unloaded from
the freight steamers for customs house inspection before
loading aboard the *America*, the Norwegian freight
handlers had no difficulty in arranging the cases according to the signs.   When the marking was completed, the boxes had a curious appearance looking
much like a number of enormous playing-cards; but
the value of being able to tell at once the contents of
a case in the dimly lighted place between decks or in
the hold of the ship, can hardly be overestimated, and
many times during the voyage we had occasion to
test and recognise the value of the signs.

CHAPTER III

WE SAY FAREWELL TO AMERICA

THE early days of the expedition were characterised by many departures and farewells. My wish had been to have the *America* brought over the ocean from Tromso to New York City to be repaired, and to receive her cargo on this side of the water, but the limited time at my command would not allow of it. So all members of the expedition, except three men engaged in Trondhjem, were sent over the Atlantic on the passenger steamers to Norway.

The Chief Engineer left in January 1903, for Tromso, for which port the officers and crew sailed from New York City on March 10th. Two days later I left for the same port, via England, Germany, and Denmark, for the purpose of purchasing supplies in all these countries. I reached Tromso March 31st in a snow storm. I was glad to find that my American crew had arrived some days before. The expedition ship was anchored out in the fjord, her decks covered with snow, and although a force of men had been busy cleaning her during the spring she still had a dismal, desolate air, her ice worn planking, paint denuded sides, and ragged rigging showing the need of much overhauling before she would be seaworthy again. The only cheerful place was the engine room, where I was glad to find that Engineer Hartt had put the engine together and was ready to turn on steam. A French-Canadian, Pierre LeRoyer by name, who had acted as guide in the north Canadian woods for Mr. Ziegler in many hunting and camping trips, and who accompanied Mr. Champ on the Relief Expedition in 1902, had been left aboard the *America* as a watchman during the winter. I had written him to use all the heavy furs aboard, left from the previous expedition, in the manufacture of one-man sleeping bags and had also instructed him to make mittens and footwear of fur. I was glad to find that he had improved the time and could show me twenty-five complete sleeping bags in addition to a number of articles of wearing apparel. Furs suitable for clothing could not be purchased in Norway or Sweden. All the garments offered to me by the fur merchants of those countries were too heavy, being made of the fur of the adult wild deer, useless for the purpose of a sledge expedition on account of its weight, the hides being too thick and the fur too long. So I was obliged to order them from Russia and over 800 fawn skins, of from two to five months old deer, of the domesticated variety were purchased. I had to be content with skins tanned in the regular commercial way, very beautiful to look upon, but not as durable by half as the skins tanned by the native Samoyede. To have secured the latter it would have been necessary for me to make a journey along the Siberian coast for the purpose of trading with the Samoyedes, and for that there was not time. Fortunately, through Mr. Bruno Paetz, the British pro-consul at Archangel, I was enabled to secure a number of Samoyede coats made of the skins desired.

There was not a dry-dock in Tromso large enough for the *America*, so, manned by her American crew, with Capt. Keldjsen for pilot, she left for Trondhjem, where she was to be repaired and loaded, and from where she was later to sail on her voyage north.

On my return to America in April, arrangements were made for the departure of the members of the Field Department from New York City for Trondhjem.

[Copy of order sent to Field Dept. members of the Expedition]
ZIEGLER POLAR EXPEDITION
60 Liberty Street
NEW YORK, May 9th, 1903.

GENERAL ORDERS NO.I.
SIR:

You are hereby ordered to report at the Astor House, New York City, on the afternoon of May 25th, ready for sailing the morning of the 27th of May for Norway.

2. Accommodations have been arranged at the Astor House and you are to report immediately upon arrival there to Mr. William J. Peters, Second in Command, who is to conduct the expedition party to Norway.

3. Transportation is provided on the Steamship *Helig Olav*, sailing from Pier, foot of 17th Street, Hoboken, N. J., May 27th. Mr. Charles E. Rilliet, Quartermaster, will arrange for transportation and baggage.

4. Members are expected to carry all their baggage, outside of hand-bags, etc., in two trunks—one steamer trunk to be carried aboard expedition steamer *America*—the other to be left in storehouse at Tromso, with supply of clothing until return of expedition.

5. Clothing has been provided for the use of the members after August 1st, 1903, but it is advised that each man provide himself with two blue flannel Army shirts, two pair of heavy shoes, of larger size than usually worn, three suits of medium weight underwear, a supply of socks and handkerchiefs, and several suits of old clothing, and a small sewing and darning outfit.

6. Every man should be careful to see that his teeth are in good condition before leaving.

7. This order to be acknowledged immediately on receipt.

The Commanding Officer presents his compliments to the members of the Field Department of the expedition, and wishes them a pleasant trip across the ocean, regretting that necessity for an earlier departure prevents his accompanying the party to Trondhjem.

ANTHONY FIALA, *Commanding.*

The last shipments were made from the United States and eleven days later I was once again at sea on my way to Norway. On arrival at Trondhjem, I found that the repairs on the ship were almost completed, and she was moved to a dock to receive her coal and stores. Leaving the *America* again I hurried by rail across Norway and Sweden to Stockholm, and from there by steamer to St Petersburg, and then by the slow moving Russian railroad made my way to Archangel, to inspect the furs that had been ordered and to assure myself of their suitability. On return to Trondhjem I found the storehouses and dock filled with cases, bales, barrels, and bags. The great shipment of stores from six countries had arrived and the work was well under way. An interested crowd of Norwegians watched us load the vessel and several ship captains there volunteered the information that they believed it would require two ships to transport all our supplies In addition to this great cargo we purchased lumber with which to construct a house on some Arctic shore for our winter quarters.

For the reception of the thirty ponies we were to take along I ordered a stable built on the deck amidships. The floor was raised and slatted to keep the ponies' hoofs dry, and stalls were built so as to protect the little animals from accident during the voyage On the roof of the pony stable a dog pen was constructed as all space had to be utilised.

The *America's* appearance now offered a pleasing contrast to the last view I had had of her. With rigging taut, spars cleaned and painted, and a new smokestack, I hardly recognised the old ship. Under the direction of First Officer Haven the cargo was soon stowed and the great mass of supplies and stores went down between decks and into the hold. When at last the decks too were laden it took quite a degree of agility to move from one end of the ship to the other.

The members of the Field Department arrived in Trondhjem in early June and helped the crew in the loading of the ship. By noon of June 23 everything was aboard. Mr. William Champ, Mr. Ziegler's secretary, who was to accompany us to Archangel, came aboard, and, at six P. M. we steamed from the dock at Trondhjem followed by the cheers of a large company of Norwegians who had assembled to see us depart. We arrived at the little island of Trono early in the morning of the 26th and took aboard 183 dogs, twenty-five of which were pups about five months old, and five little Siberian ponies looking the worse for their experience on the last expedition. We then steamed for the famous little town of Tromso on the northern coast of Norway in whose harbour many an expedition ship had anchored before. On our way there we crossed the Arctic Circle, and all members of the expedition who had not passed that parallel before, were seized by their comrades who had, and initiated as Polar explorers by being thrown overboard while the steamer was in motion, their safety first insured by a long line made fast around their waists. As they were hauled on deck spluttering and half drowned, Father Neptune, impersonated by one of the old tars aboard, scrubbed down the victims with a deck broom to the amusement of all. We stayed at Tromso only a day to take on some supplies, then hurried our steamer's bow northward through the beautiful fjords of Norway to the town of Vardo, a curious little place that betrays itself ere you see it if the wind blows your way. From Vardo we steamed down through the White Sea toward Archangel, the metropolis of northern Russia and Siberia, the White City on the White Sea. We arrived off Solombal, the port of Archangel, at 2 P. M. on July 2nd. On going ashore I was glad to find that the twenty-five ponies ordered from Alexander Trontheim, who purchased dogs for Nansen, Wellman, Baldwin, and the Duke of the Abruzzi, were all on hand and ready for embarkation. Several particularly tough looking specimens had been brought more than 800 miles overland fom Siberia. Stephan, one of the Russians who had been with the previous expedition, a splendid fellow, with tears in his eyes begged for the privilege of accompanying us. He said he did not wish any salary but would go for his clothing and food. But there was no room aboard for Stephan; we were crowded without adding to our number, so I regretfully denied his request.

At Solombal we coaled the bunkers which were quite empty after our long trip from Tromso. A lighter came alongside with twenty-five dogs and twenty-five of the most beautiful, lively Siberian ponies, intelligent and well conditioned. I succeeded in getting a moving picture as they were hauled aboard. About sixteen tons of oats and corn were taken on as provender and, almost like the proverbial "last straw," a boat came alongside with still another addition to the ship's load—our precious furs. Captain Coffin said to me rather grimly, "I think we will have to carry the furs in the main top." But they were finally placed safely under cover of the fore hatch.

In addition to the work of cleaning and loading the vessel we had visitors to entertain. Some very polite and intelligent officers from a Russian hydrographic expedition came aboard. I have to laugh when I think of it. I wore a pair of khaki trousers and a rough flannel shirt. Minus a hat, my hair tangled and artistic but not neat, I had been directing the arrangement of pony stalls and helping the men trim ship and was hardly in a presentable condition. But I escorted the officers around, all of them in resplendent uniforms covered with decorations and gold lace, some of them carrying jewelled short swords; one of them wearing the famous iron cross.

We left Archangel on our northward course just before midnight on Independence Day with the glowing orb of the sun cut on our northern horizon. As we steamed toward it the great, burning, red-and-golden luminary rose, flooding us with light and giving us a radiant pathway toward the Great White Sea. A number of Russians cheered us as, under the impetus of our fast revolving screw, we gained headway toward the river's mouth and passed the city of Solombal, the Russian flags politely dipping and the whistles of many steamers blowing us their God-speed. The Russian authorities had been most kind, remitting all harbour and pilot charges.

Our progress to Vardo, where we were to stop for a few hours to take on more coal before leaving civili-

sation for the ice, was delayed by a gale that sprang
up on the seventh of July and blew "great guns" for
about forty-eight hours.   It meant hard work for
those who were not seasick.   Neither Mr. Champ nor
I is subject to seasickness as a rule, but while the storm
lasted we could do little but lie in our bunks and poke
fun at each other when a respite from our distressed
condition permitted.   We made efforts—costly efforts!
I managed to crawl up over the cargo as far as the
ponies and dogs several times to satisfy myself as to
their condition.   Everything was attended to as well
as one could expect and none of the animals or cargo
was lost.

At Vardo we bade good-bye to Mr. Champ, who had
accompanied us thus far.   Before leaving I went
aboard his steamer, and in the privacy of his cabin we
talked over the affairs of the expedition and of the
Relief Ship that he was to bring up in the summer of
1904.   We agreed that Cape Flora, on Northbrook
Island, would be the place of rendezvous, as a large
store of provisions was there as well as houses and
boats.   I was to send a party to Cape Flora early in
the spring of 1904 with letters through which, should
the *America* not succeed in reaching Cape Flora
from her winter northing before the Relief Ship arrived there, Mr. Champ would learn of our whereabouts and of the success or failure of the expedition.
We discussed the probable ice conditions to be encountered and the personnel of the exploring party,
for I realised that the fate of the undertaking depended chiefly upon the moral fibre of the men.

I hoped to reach Crown Prince Rudolph Island with

the ship and winter in some safe harbour near there, or, the ice permitting, cast anchor at Coburg Island. From that point, in the spring of 1904, a march north with a large column of men, dogs, ponies, and sledges, would be made, the ponies to serve as dog food as the loads on their sledges were reduced.   The sledge party was to be composed of a number of supporting parties that were to be detached as the main column advanced and sent back to the base camp, the final advance party to consist of four or five men, who would strike for Cape Flora on their return should they be carried toward the west by the drift.

I told Mr. Champ that the *America* would start for Cape Flora just as soon as she could get free in the summer of 1904 and not to wait for the sledge parties should they still be in the field; that I would leave food along the British Channel on my advance north with the ship and, if necessary, on her return to Cape Flora where she would await the sledge parties and the Relief Ship.

Mr. Champ left at midnight.   The Norwegian steamer, upon whose deck he stood, passed close to the *America*, the steamers saluting each other by the dipping of flags and the shrieking of the steam sirens while the men of the expedition party cheered loudly.

The following day, Friday, the tenth of July, after fresh water and about fifty tons of coal had been taken aboard, we raised anchor and at six in the evening left the harbour with our bow pointed north. A fresh breeze was blowing from the southwest and, to save our precious coal, steam was shut off, and with all canvas set we sailed on our way in a spanking breeze.

CHAPTER IV

THE "AMERICA" FORCES HER WAY NORTH

ON THE afternoon of July 13th, we met the ice at Longitude 38° 37′ E. and Latitude 74° 51′ N., and there our progress north was barred by the close-packed, crystal fields. We steamed easterly in hope of finding an open water lead, but without success. On the 18th we sighted Nova Zembla and continued on our easterly and southerly course along the edge of the ice in an endeavour to find an opening near the land. But we were disappointed. Capt. Coffin suggested that it would be best to turn the ship around and return to Longitude 49° where the ice seemed loosest and then force our way north, to which suggestion I agreed as the only thing to do. So we steamed to where the ice appeared to make in to the north, and there we spoke a little Norwegian sealing schooner. Captain Coffin and I boarded her, taking with us an interpreter, our Norse carpenter, Tessem; we also carried a bag of mail, our last letters home. The sealers told it was a very bad year for ice, the worst they had ever experienced, and predicted that we could not reach Franz Josef Land, a prophecy which the cheerful spirit that prevailed then aboard the *America* would not endorse.

The ice in the Barentz Sea is on the approach of summer broken into fields by the action of winds and sea. A southerly wind is most effective as it brings with it the roll of the great open ocean southward, smashing the ice-fields. A northern wind then separates the floes and allows the swell of the sea to penetrate further. Thus before the end of summer the whole sea of ice is often broken into comparatively small floes between which it is usually possible to pick a way north to Franz Josef Land.

We seemed to have struck a late season. The ice was then about breaking, but the great lanes of water that should have given us a passage between the floes to our destination were not to be found. We steamed slowly along the edge of floe after floe of field ice, some of the floes from thirty to sixty miles long with never a break. Time and time again we were obliged to steam in great circles, miles out of our course, to work around the vast white mass. Under favourable conditions the voyage from Vardo, Norway, to Cape Flora, in the Franz Josef Archipelago, can be made in less than six days. But day after day passed without any appreciable progress north, and the impatient American spirit chafed under the delay, and many a young member of the expedition received his first lesson in Arctic exploration—the lesson of patience.

Possibly nowhere on earth was there just such a situation or quite such a community as existed aboard our ship. The *America* flew the burgee of the New York Yacht Club and had a commission as a pleasure yacht from the Treasury Department of the United States Government. But she was anything but a pleasure yacht. Crowded with thirty-nine men, 218 dogs, and

"WE SAILED ON OUR WAY IN A SPANKING BREEZE"

thirty ponies, and with every available deck space packed with cargo, she had more the appearance of an overloaded freighter or cattle steamer. Hard manual labour was the portion of all alike In addition to the regular work of the ship the animals had to be cared for, and with the crowded condition of the decks it was a difficult matter to fill the bunkers, and all hands, Field Department members as well as crew, were obliged to take part in the dirty work of passing coal.

We carried a heavy deck-load of cases, compressed hay, and coal. Amidships the ponies were stalled in a structure of timber. This rough stable was floored and roofed, and upon the roof, surrounded by a bulwark of thin boards, a number of the dogs were chained; the remainder of our pack were lodged on the forecastle head, where they passed the time away barking and howling in unison with their comrades on top of the pony stable, varying the monotony of their chained imprisonment by innumerable fights. Any dog within reach of another would improve the slightest opportunity for a quarrel, and with the savage snarling of the combatants the whole pack would yelp and bark encouragement, the result being general disorder. The noise generally brought Dr. Vaughn, who was in charge of the dogs, and Pierre LeRoyer, his assistant, who, with the aid of whips, speedily restored order Even the ponies seemed possessed of the spirit of combativeness and bit each others necks when they were not engaged in chewing up the lumber of which the stable was constructed.

· There was not room enough for all the ponies in the stable and five were tied up alongside the ship's rail. These had to be watched constantly as they endeavoured to eat all the rope within reach, besides chewing up the rail and eating out places in the deck made soft by the constant wash of the sea-water.

All of July passed with little distance to our credit. Again and again we were forced to tie up to the ice, the ship's yards and rigging glittering with ice, while a blanket of thick, damp, Arctic fog obscured the vision. At other times, the sky above our northern, eastern, and western horizons was white with the reflection of ice, the ominous "ice blink" that proved the absence of open water.

With the floes under pressure, we could do nothing but wait until a change in the wind caused the fields to separate. Then the *America*, though overloaded and weighted down at the head, under full steam, would squeeze her way between the floes, after charging the frozen masses, and hammer her way sturdily northward.

"Bucking" the ice requires skill and judgment and was always an exciting experience, particularly when viewed from the vantage-point of the crow's nest where the Captain, the Mate, and myself passed much of our time. The ship would be slowly backed in the narrow channel she had broken between the fields until there were about a thousand yards of water space. Then, from his position at the mast head, the Captain would send the signal for full speed ahead. With smoke pouring in great clouds from her funnel and mingling with hissing live steam, the engine throbbing and pounding under the strains of its supreme effort—Hartt, the engineer, was forcing his pet—men lining the rig-

"NORTHWARD HO!"

" WITH EVERY AVAILABLE DECKSPACE PACKED WITH CARGO "

Deck of the *America*, showing pony stable, with dog kennels overhead. The canvas cover was stretched to protect the dogs from falling ice fragments, shaken from the rigging by the wind

ging to mark the advance toward the coveted stretch of clear water, the *America* would crash into the heavy, glassy mass and under the impetus her great hulk would rise out of the sea and roll from side to side, as the ice broke and splintered under her armoured forefoot. Dogs barked and whined in terror; ponies stamped and stumbled as the impact of ship and floe threw them almost off their feet. Up in the crow's nest, where every motion was intensified, we hung on like cherries. Sometimes, it seemed that, with her heavy top load, the *America* must "turn turtle," but the ice always broke and, at last, on an even keel, we would gather steam to buck once more.

The ice had to be carefully watched and the course of every little water lead traced from the crow's nest before the ship's nose was pushed into it. In going south, toward the open sea, almost every lane of water can be trusted as leading toward safety, but, in forcing a way north it is like going toward the small end of a funnel, and, in a close season, many an opening, that from the limited view circle of deck and rigging seemed to stretch to the very edge of the earth, resolved itself into what is technically termed a "blind lead" ending in solid ice.

Captain Coffin, through the knowledge gained in many years of Arctic whaling, kept carefully out of these traps, which had caused the destruction of the *Jeannette*, the *Tegethoff*, and many another Arctic going ship, and we did very little useless steaming. Under the influence of the winds and currents the ice fields were either closing and under pressure, or separating and relaxing. At the times of pressure it was useless to attempt to force a way, and we could only stand by and wait. Every halt of the ship was accepted with impatience by some of the company who, though it was their first experience on a Polar sea, freely gave their opinions as to how the ship should be managed in the ice. The Captain at first thought it amusing, and often asked me to look down over the edge of the crow's nest to see his "ice pilots," strung in the rigging and on the forecastle head with their eyes glued to the ice.

On July 30th we had stopped the ship in a little open hole of water from which two blind leads extended, one threading its narrow way in a northwest, the other, in a northeasterly direction. Captain Coffin and I, in the crow's nest, anxiously examined both through our binoculars and with the long ship's telescope but could find no other evidence of water, and the horizon was white with the "ice blink." The Captain said to me, "We can enter either lead, but it would be foolish for we can only steam about three miles in one, or about four miles in the other. If we wait here, the chances are, that one of the leads will open and the other close; we will then be in a position to take the one that is open and push on." I saw the wisdom of his judgment at once and agreed that waiting was the only thing to do. On my way down from the crow's nest, I could see, from the lower level, one of the leads showing water almost to the horizon and could understand the critical comments made by some of my comrades at the seemingly unnecessary delay.

So much in life depends upon the View Point, and the higher our elevation above the earth level, and the

"THE PONIES ENDEAVOURED TO EAT UP ALL THE ROPE WITHIN REACH, BESIDES CHEWING THE RAIL AND EATING OUT PLACES IN THE DECK"

THE PONY "CIRCUS" JUST BEFORE HIS EXECUTION

Pierre LeRoyer

VIEW, TAKEN FROM THE "AMERICA'S" BRIDGE, OF THE DOG KENNELS ON TOP OF THE PONY STABLE

wider our horizon, the less hypercritical and the more just we are apt to be.

The following day, under the influence of a twenty-five-mile-an-hour wind, one of the leads closed into a small pressure ridge; the other opened and through it we eventually escaped from our pool.

The early days of August were the most discouraging of all. Our latitude was fully one hundred miles south of Cape Flora and the great expanse of ice gave little promise of opening up Gloom settled over the company and here and there an impatient or thoughtless one gave vent to his dissatisfaction in regrettable terms. The animals showed the effect of their long imprisonment, the dogs, craving sympathy, howled dolefully and held up their wet cold paws. The ponies relieved the tedium of the situation by biting each other and doing as much damage as possible to their stable. We were obliged to renew the wood-work of their stalls and the flooring, that had been eaten through in many places

The monotony of inaction was varied by visits from Polar bears which usually paid the price of their curiosity with their lives. They were shot and skinned on the ice, their pelts and carcasses being dragged to the ship where the meat served as fresh food for men and dogs. Thrice in the week after the evening meal, Mr. Peters conducted a class in nautical astronomy and, assisted by Mr. Porter and Mr Tafel, made observations on the floating ice for magnetic declination. Our weather observer, Sergt. Francis Long of the U. S. Weather Bureau, was the Arctic veteran of the party. He had been a member of the famous Greely Ex-

pedition and it was his fortunate shooting of a bear
which saved the remnant of that company from
starvation. Sergt. Long mounted his instrument shelter—the "chicken coop" as it was jocularly termed
by the members of the party—on the deck over the
America's upper cabin, and his anemometer on the
bridge, and began his weather observations. He was
generally known among the explorers as "Obs," from
the signature he attached to his memorandum slips.
All sorts of jokes were cracked at his expense, but
he kept serenely and good-naturedly at his work, setting many a younger man an example of diligence and
faithfulness in the performance of duty.

Gloom and disappointment gave way to joy on the
evening of August the fifth when a flood of sunshine
took the place of dull gray clouds and we discovered
a great open hole of water through which we steamed
with a fair sky and friendly winds until the following
evening, when, once again, the ice appeared and with
it the depressing fog which threw its chill, wet blanket
over everything and caused a rapid drop in the spirits
of my companions. I climbed up to the crow's nest
on the morning of August the seventh, and while there,
through a clearing in the fog, caught a glimpse of land
not far off looking very much like Cape Flora. I called
out the cheering news, but the ice was fast and under
pressure so we could do nothing but wait. It was
very tantalising to drift around in sight of land without
the power of approaching it. On the morning of the
eighth our Veterinarian, Dr. Newcomb, reported to
me that "Circus," one of the ponies that had been
sick, was infected with glanders and I was obliged to

HAULING THE CARCASS OF A POLAR BEAR ABOARD THE SHIP

"THE REMAINDER OF OUR PACK WERE LOADED ABOARD AS A DECK LOAD"

THE "AMERICA" ENTERING THE ICE

order his destruction, for the disease is communicable
and deadly to man and beast.   The poor little animal
was shot and thrown overboard with all his belongings
—halter, blanket, chain, and feed-bag.

We finally escaped from the pack at a point where
two enormous ice fields had crashed together.   These
had parted a little, leaving a long narrow channel
choked with heavy cakes.   We dislodged and shat-
tered the cakes with charges of guncotton, the crew
pushing the fragments out of the way with long poles.
Then we forced our way through, steaming between
two enormous blocks of ice, and escaping just in time, as
the fields crashed together with tremendous force
behind us.

On the afternoon of August 12th we arrived at Cape
Flora, the historic place where Jackson spent three
years with his party and where his dramatic meeting
with Dr. Nansen took place; where Leigh Smith lived
with his crew when his vessel was crushed by the ice,
and where the Duke of the Abruzzi cached a great
store of provisions against a time of need.   But our
destination was further north, and we left Cape Flora
with its relics of former expeditions in an attempt to
make a higher northern base for winter quarters.
We passed Cape Barentz, the southeast extremity
of Northbrook Island, steaming so close that we could
hear the chatter of thousands upon thousands of gulls,
guillemots, little Auks, and Loons, which make
their summer home in the crevices of the great basaltic
rock that guards the entrance to DeBruyne Sound.

The Sound was free of ice, but the British Channel,
through which the Duke of the Abruzzi's ship, the *Po-*

laris, had steamed so easily, was now one unbroken line of solid ice from shore to shore. We steamed east toward Cape Dillon to ascertain if there was an opportunity of going north through the interchannel route by way of Camp Ziegler, where Baldwin wintered in 1901–1902, or to the east of the Archipelago.

We could not make Cape Dillon in spite of effort. From the crow's nest, there was naught to be seen but ice—north, east, and south, showing that we were simply in a water hole off Northbrook and Hooker islands. We then turned west over the course we had come only to find farther advance in that direction blocked by heavy ice off Cape Grant. I then decided to return to the British Channel and fight our way north by that route if it took the rest of the season.

CHAPTER V

THE FIGHT UP THE BRITISH CHANNEL

THE heavy ice in the British Channel gave me reason to believe that we would be late in reaching our base and I found it necessary to order the men to begin to fit harness for the ponies and dogs, to put together the sledges, and to start sewing fur garments. Our passage up the British Channel occupied many days, days of anxiety for the leader. The ponies and dogs had been on the ship for almost two months and the long wait in cramped quarters was telling on them. Veterinarian Newcomb and Sergt. Moulton, who had the welfare of the ponies in mind, gave the tough creatures exercise by moving them from stall to stall, changing their places daily. A fortunate drift of the ice northward carried us through the channel past Cape Murray, and then we slowly steamed and worked our way north being obliged at times to explode heavy mines of guncotton to assist our advance.

On the night of August 29th, we were tied up to the ice in a bay near a little uncharted island north of Cape Hugh Mill on Jackson Island. My diary for the 30th reads:

"Had been up all night and climbed the hill on the island near us several times in anxious watch of the belt of ice that separated us from the navigable water north. I turned in about one A.M. and asked Mr.

Peters and Mr. Porter to watch the ice as they were taking a set of angles from the top of the hill. Tired out from many sleepless nights I fell immediately to sleep but was awakened in half an hour by Mr. Porter who informed me that the ice had opened. First Officer Haven was just climbing over the side of the ship for the purpose of going to the top of the hill and we three went together to have our eyes gladdened by the sight of an open lane through the ice. On return, I climbed the hill with Captain Coffin who gave one look then hurried back to the ship as fast as he could go and together we climbed to the crow's nest. On leaving the bay in which we had found refuge we steamed north toward Charles Alexander Island, the beautiful clear, atmosphere and glorious sunshine revealing the fact that Leigh Smith Island did not exist, but that what was supposed to be that island was really the northeast end of Jackson Island, and that instead of the channel marked as De Long Fjord, there was really a deep bay. At Cape Helland we could go no farther, a wide strip of ice preventing farther progress north. We tied up to the ice to await further developments. Second officer Nichols, Surgeon Shorkley, Seaman Burns, and I took the dingy and sounded in the bay north of Cape Helland, hoping to find a lane of separation between the ground ice and the floe, but to no avail. We then climbed the glacier and, from about 800 feet elevation, beheld the welcome sight of open sea as far as Crown Prince Rudolph Island. Returned to the ship convinced that when we did escape it would not be through the bay but farther out in the channel. Felt very tired on return to ship for want of sleep. About ten o'clock in the morning, I turned in and slept soundly until 4.30. After supper, I climbed to the crow's nest and noticed that the ice had opened a little. Reported it to Capt. Coffin, and in a few minutes we were under way. The

bugle then sounded the time of Sunday service and while we were engaged in a devotional meeting, the shaking and pounding of the ship denoted our entrance into the ice At the close of the service, we went on deck to find the *America* slowly forcing her way through heavy ice Before long we had passed our last barrier and were steaming in the open sea. Captain Coffin reported that when he started the chances were slim but as the ship advanced, the ice seemed to slacken and open What heavy masses of ice they were! Great, solid, green, shimmering, tons upon tons, extending from twenty to thirty feet under water! We steamed past Charles Alexander Island and toward midnight passed Cape Auk, the southwestern end of Rudolph Island, where we could see the cache left by the Baldwin-Ziegler Party in 1902. Teplitz Bay was passed in the sunlight, the skeleton-like remains of the framework of the tent where in the past had lived the brave Abruzzi and his companions standing out in plain view Open water extending farther north, we steamed on toward the midnight sun. On passing Teplitz Bay, Captain Coffin told me the good news that as far as he could see Teplitz Bay would be safe as winter quarters for the ship "

Early in the morning of August 31st, we made our highest north, the open Victoria Sea allowing us to pass beyond the 82nd degree of latitude. We returned to Teplitz Bay by six o'clock in the morning of a beautiful sunlit day, a female bear and her cub paying us a visit as we made fast alongside the heavy bay ice. Several of the men opened fire from the deck of the *America*, but I was glad to see the mother and her cub escape unhurt.

The tent where the Duke of the Abruzzi, Captain Cagni, and their companions had wintered in 1899 and 1900, and from which they started on their record breaking trip, had been destroyed by the storms and all that remained were the heavy spars of the framework sunk deep in the snow and the tops of the interior tents.

A large cache of food stores was found in good condition piled on a high rocky point where the winds would keep it free of drifting snow, and, down near the tide crack, a great heap of coal was imbedded in the ice. Between the coal pile and the cache on the rocks, numerous cases filled with food stores protruded through the snow, a veritable bonanza to the Arctic explorer. Not far from the coal pile was a great case containing a ruined balloon and near it a large military gas generator, and cases of sulphuric acid and barrels of iron filings were scattered around. Best of all was the discovery of two large steel tanks sunk to their tops in the snow containing a quantity of petroleum. Everything denoted a hurried departure. With all this great store of food we found heaps of glass bottles and many casks, but, though diligent search was made, we never found a bottle containing anything stronger than olive oil or vinegar or a cask with anything more exhilarating than molasses. Out on the bay ice we found the half buried stump of a tree on which the Duke and his companions had probably practised target shooting, and its unchanged position was an evidence to us that the ice of Teplitz Bay had not moved since 1900.

Our voyage was now over, and I gave instructions

"OBSERVATIONS WERE MADE ON THE FLOATING ICE FOR LONGITUDE AND FOR
MAGNETIC DECLINATION"

" THE WATERS ARE HID AS WITH A STONE AND THE FACE OF THE DEEP IS FROZEN"—Job xxviii: 30

to disembark the animals, unload the cargo, and prepare the ship for winter quarters.

ZIEGLER POLAR EXPEDITION
S. Y. AMERICA
ANTHONY FIALA, *Commanding Officer*

Date Sept 6, 1903.

GENERAL ORDERS NO 15

TEPLITZ BAY

1 Teplitz Bay is to be our winter headquarters, and in honour of the courageous men of Italy and their famous leader who occupied this site before us, we shall name our winter quarters camp "Abruzzi"

2. We have reached this northern point after many difficulties and trials in a particularly bad season of much ice—and great credit is due to Captain Coffin and Officers and crew of the *America* for the record she now holds

3 Our field work is practically in its very beginning and from the lateness of the season we shall be obliged to toil long and suffer some before we can be comfortably arranged in Winter Quarters.

4 The unfortunate stampeding of the ponies on landing caused us considerable labour and worry But now we have our forces together and our united efforts will soon effect permanent results, and hope of victory by earning it should lead us on, with the glorious example of the men who occupied the ground of camp "Abruzzi" before us, as an incentive.

Signed, ANTHONY FIALA,
Commanding Ziegler Polar Expedition

Sept 6, 1903

GENERAL ORDERS NO 16

CAMP "ABRUZZI"

1 Members of Field Department are to report daily after breakfast to Mr Peters my executive officer for orders

2 Heads of Departments are expected to carefully attend to stores in their charge to prevent loss by drifting snow or other causes

3. It is necessary to impress on the minds of all members of the ex-

pedition party, that all tools and small articles should be kept under cover before leaving camp at night, and even in working hours no article of use should be left on the snow to be covered by the drift and lost.

4. We are in a situation where habits of carefulness in all respects may mean the difference between success and failure.

5. Obedience to orders and cheerful compliance to required duty with a hopeful happy uncritical spirit will leave a record for each man to be proud of.

ANTHONY FIALA.

"THE GREAT EXPANSE OF ICE GAVE LITTLE PROMISE OF OPENING UP"

A TABULAR ICEBERG NEAR CAPE FLORA

Icebergs of the above type are numerous in the waters of the Franz Josef Archipelago

CHAPTER VI

CAMP ABRUZZI

A GANGWAY was now constructed from ship to ice and the sea-weary animals, wild for liberty, were disembarked. The poor beasts had been prisoners for two months, some of them longer. The ponies celebrated their new found freedom by rolling in the snow and kicking each other and the open air in pure delight, while the dogs, unchained and allowed to run free, with tails up and grinning jaws, found relief from the long strain in mischief and enjoyable fights. Our camp was established on a level tract of protruding rocks, the outcropping of a small terminal moraine, on the edge of which, in the snow, a picket line was stretched for the ponies. While the ponies were being lead across the rough bay ice to the shore, a number of them, in a wild desire for freedom, broke loose and stampeded, jumping hummocks and rocks like kangaroos and finally disappearing out of sight across the high glacier. Search parties were sent after them and all were brought back except five. Of this number four were found lodged in crevasses so badly injured that they had to be shot, but of the remaining one no trace was ever discovered. Sergt. Moulton, Assistant Scientist Tafel, and Dr. Vaughn distinguished themselves in the search. The anxiety caused by the stampede of the ponies was allayed, but we were assailed by a new trouble—the rising of the wind which broke off the ice around the ship. Every one had to work day and night to move the cargo to land. Quite an amount of equipment and stores, lumber, sledges, boats, etc., had been placed on the ice near the ship, and quick work was necessary to save them from being lost on the fast disappearing ice. The ponies did valiant service in dragging loads varying from 800 to 1,200 pounds over the hummocks and up the long hill to the camp. One little fellow, a survivor of the Baldwin-Ziegler expedition and not so strong as the others, died from exhaustion due to overwork.

After constant exertion we succeeded in getting all the new lumber, stores, and equipment ashore, but we lost the ship's dingy, some old lumber from the stable, and eleven dogs that floated away on broken ice in the gale. Thereafter I ordered the sledges loaded directly from the ship and nothing was allowed to be placed on the ice edge.

The violence of the wind and the breaking of the heavy bay ice indicated to Captain Coffin the possibility that Teplitz Bay would be an unsafe harbour for the ship. He told me on September 3d that he would be obliged to take the *America* away and look for other winter quarters, and that he would not be responsible for her safety if she was allowed to remain in Teplitz Bay. To send the *America* away with her crew, I would have been obliged to equip the entire ship's company with sleeping bags, dogs, and sledges—for there was the possibility of the ship's loss no matter where she might be taken in the Archipelago. Then there were the added disadvantages

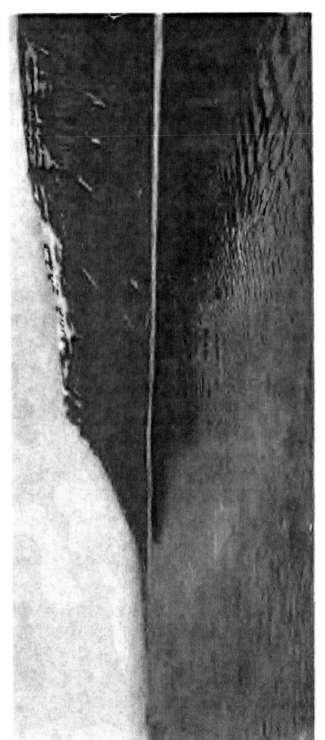

CAPE FLORA—August 12, 1903

"HEAVY ICE PREVENTED FARTHER PROGRESS NORTH"

of a divided party, the loss to the expedition of the services of the crew, and also the sacrifice of such facilities as were afforded by the work-shop aboard the *America*. There was only one other thing to do, and that was to add the shore party to the crew, take everything—ponies, dogs, large tents, lumber, food, equipment, and stores, and look for other winter quarters.

But the season was far advanced, and by going farther south we would have lost the decided advantage of a high base for the sledge party. After considering both sides of the question I explained to the members of the Field Department the nature of the risk we assumed by remaining in Teplitz Bay, and then gave orders to Captain Coffin to winter the ship in that neighbourhood.

A large tent twenty feet wide and eighty-eight feet long was erected, and, in it the ponies and dogs were stabled. In another large tent room was made for storage of food and forage for the animals. A house was built of lumber brought from Norway on the rocky ridge to the west of the stock tent; our company labouring late in the gathering twilight and numerous storms to complete this winter shelter.

On September 10th the greater part of the large cache of pemmican which had been stored by the Baldwin-Ziegler Expedition at Cape Auk four miles away was brought north by steamer to our present camp site.* The cache consisted of about 40,000 pounds of pemmican besides a small quantity of bacon, lard, and

*The moving of the Cape Auk cache to Camp Ziegler proved to be its salvation During the summer of 1904 an avalanche of water and rocks descended from the high face of Cape Auk and washed what remained of the cache into the sea, burying the site under a mass of rocks.

sausages. Having been one of the party detailed to make this cache in 1902, I recalled vividly the two months of hard sledging necessary to its accomplishment, and it was with a feeling of much satisfaction that I viewed the cargo of familiar tins on the deck of the *America* and realised that our labour had not been in vain. This new cargo was added to our supplies at Teplitz Bay, and then preparations were made to make the *America* snug for the winter. I had given Captain Coffin a little over half our entire store of provisions for use aboard ship as he had the larger party. The other half, together with the entire store of sledge provisions, had been moved by the united efforts of expedition members and crew to the vicinity of the camp; this work necessitating hard hauling in all kinds of weather. The sledges we had put together while coming up the channel stood the heavy loads and hummocky ice very well, and the ponies proved invaluable in sledging the stores over the mile of rough ice that intervened between ship and shore. In fact the ponies were less troublesome and more powerful than the dogs, the industrious little equines dragging loads that astonished us all.

On a ridge of rocks overlooking the bay, not far from our camp and near the cache of food left by the Abruzzi party, our busy scientists erected an astronomical observatory, inside of which the large vertical circle loaned by the Christiana Observatory was set up. Near the shore line, about two hundred yards below the stable tent, Mr. Peters and his assistants built the little hut that was to serve as a magnetic observatory. On September 24th the house intended

THE STAMPEDE OF THE PONIES

"While the ponies were being led across the rough bay ice to the shore, a number of them, in a wild desire for freedom, broke loose and stampeded"

for the home of the shore party was completed and the fifteen members of the Field Department and the ship's steward, who had volunteered for shore duty, moved their belongings into it. The interior of the house had been divided into one large living room and a number of small rooms just large enough for two or four bunks. A little kitchen was partitioned off for the steward. In the living room a long table was erected over which was hung an arc light connected by wire with the ship more than six thousand feet away, the *America's* dynamo supplying the current for lights aship and ashore.

Toward the end of September the days grew stormy and dark, the sun's visits became daily shorter until on October 15th our luminary dipped below the horizon in a blaze of scarlet fire, not to rise again until March of the following year, and a thick gloom settled over the ice of land and sea   By that time the camp had assumed quite a business-like aspect, with a regular routine of duties for all the members. The ponies were stored in the stable tent, half the space of which was shared by the dogs. The dogs were allowed to come and go at will, none being chained except those that were found to be incorrigible fighters   But woe to the canines which strayed on the pony side of the tent within reach of the heels!

A well tramped trail led over the ice of the bay between house and ship, and in the snow along the trail was imbedded the wire that conveyed the electric current   On this same wire Engineer Hartt and Electrician Vedoe had cut in three incandescent lights, mounting them on bamboo poles stuck in the snow about a thousand feet apart. Another electric light burned at the gangway of the ship. On windy days, when vision was obscured by flying drifts of snow, and at night these lights served as guides between ship and shore. The *America's* officers had been busy in the meantime, and the after part of the ship had been housed in with canvas and an extra door and partition placed before the entrance to the forecastle. The ship's store of provisions and her small boats were cached on the ice within easy reach. An electrically lighted workshop, with a stove to keep it warm, was arranged between decks. It was clean and comfortable and in it the work of putting sledges together and lashing the joints with raw-hide was carried on.

Wishing to test the dogs and equipment before the rapidly approaching season of darkness rendered the sledge journey impracticable, I left camp on October 15th, the last day of the sun's appearance above our horizon, accompanied by Dr. Vaughn and Pierre LeRoyer and two teams of dogs and sledges. We climbed the glacier north of the camp and then directed our way toward Cape Fligely. Old Pierre went ahead on snowshoes, and Dr. Vaughn and I followed, each with a team and a loaded sledge. We returned to camp on the morning of October 21st, having been delayed on our return from Cape Fligely by a bad storm in which we lost our bearings. After the storm, the twilight revealed to us that we were on the summit of the glacier. Over a thousand feet below us stretched the panorama of Teplitz Bay with the ship frozen in, a thin column of smoke rising from her funnel; the desolate shore enlivened by the houses and tents of the

COURSE OF THE S. Y. "AMERICA" FROM VARDO, NORWAY, TO TEPLITZ BAY, RUDOLF ISLAND, FRANZ JOSEF ARCHIPELAGO

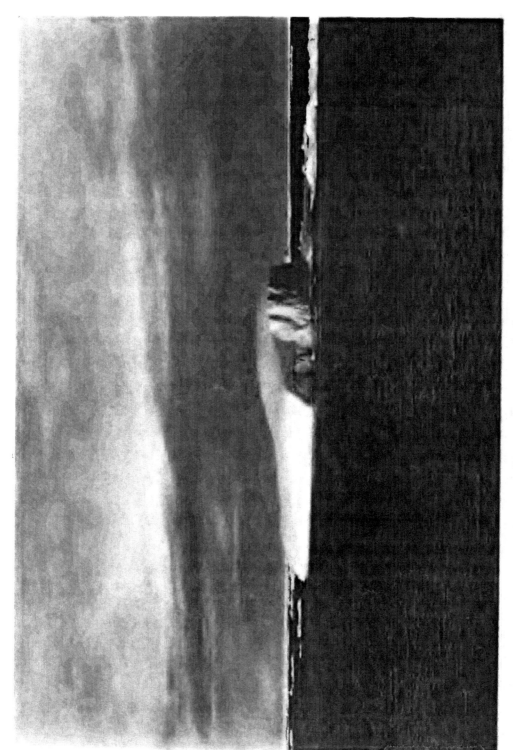

AN OVERTURNED ICEBERG NEAR CAPE DILLON

camp. The little black specks of life moving around we knew to be our comrades. The descent into camp from the snowy slope did not take long. We rough-locked the runners of our sledges with ropes but even then the speed was so swift that we had to turn a number of our dogs loose. We received a noisy welcome from the canines at camp, a great number of them advancing like skirmishers on our approach. The trip was a valuable experience, proving the sledges and equipment satisfactory and strengthening my reliance on them for future use.

CHAPTER VII

ADRIFT IN THE DARKNESS

TEPLITZ BAY was a place of many storms. On October 22d a gale sprang up from the southeast shaking the house all night with its fearful blast, the velocity of the wind increasing until it reached a maximum of seventy-two miles an hour. At half past nine at night the arc-light suddenly went out and we knew that our connection with the ship was broken. We feared that something was wrong aboard the *America*, but were helpless to assist, for in the storm it would have been impossible to find the ship or to return to the house again. All sense of direction is lost in an Arctic storm. The flying snow and drift are like a sand blast and blind anyone exposed to their fury. During the evening of the 23d, there was a lull in the gale and Mr. Peters and I carrying lighted lanterns ran over the wind-swept bay ice in the darkness toward the place where the *America* had been moored. We saw no guiding light from the ship's gangway, and, when we reached the place where the ship had been, to our horror, we found but a wild back sea. We ran up and down flashing our lanterns, but our ship with over half of the expedition company had disappeared! Fierce puffs of whistling wind warned us of the storm's return and we hurried back to camp fearing that our comrades aboard the ship were lost, reaching the protection of the house just as the wind started up again in increased violence. We flashed a number of signal lights and, to our joy, at last detected a faint glow through the driving drift which indicated an answering signal. However, a sudden increase in the wind made further communication impossible. For three long days the storm raged. On the fourth day our eyes were gladdened in the twilight of noon by the sight of our good ship steaming in from the north, her hull shining with ice, and slowly forcing her way through the thick slush back to her old mooring place. On going aboard we learned that the *America* had broken loose during the first night of the storm and had been drifting and steaming ever since without anyone on board having any knowledge of her whereabouts. The mooring lines became entangled in the blades of the propellor when she went adrift and men had to be lowered into the propellor well during the gale in order to cut the tangled mass from the wheel. It was a long and difficult operation. The temperature was low, and the men had to be relieved frequently. The heavy port anchor with seventy fathoms of chain first dragged bottom, then hung vertically and, as it could not be raised with frozen machinery, had to be sacrificed to save the ship. It was an awful experience, and I heard wild stories of the drift in the darkness and wind. The gale kept the water agitated and prevented its freezing, and thus allowed the *America* to steam back to Teplitz Bay. She had hardly been made fast to her old berth before the water's surface turned into ice, and in the calm after the storm young

ice commenced to form, solidifying the floating fields
and mushy sea into a cold, still dead-looking waste.

I had been living in the house on shore as it was
more convenient for me in the work of preparation
for the sledge trip. But, after the experience of the
last storm, with the drifting away of the ship, and
the uncertain feeling of safety aboard, I felt it my
duty to take up my abode there, and moved my little
store of personal belongings to my old cabin on the
America. After all the stores were cached there was
little for the ponies to do but draw ice which was to be
melted for fresh water. For the purpose of giving
them exercise, on afternoons when the weather permitted we mounted the tough little beasts and trotted
and galloped down the hill and over the trail toward
the ship and back. We had no saddles and several
of the party caused considerable merriment by using
their mittens to soften their seats on the ponies' backs.
Sergt. Moulton of the 2d U. S. Cavalry, who had been
detailed by the War Department to accompany the
expedition, acted as Guidon Sergeant of my little troop.
Some of the men rode quite well having gained their
firm seats through experience as cavalrymen or artil-
lerymen. Old Pierre had served in the Canadian Northwest Mounted Police, Sergt, Long in the 2d U. S. Cavalry through several Indian campaigns, and Commissary
Truden in the U. S. Artillery. Nearly all the dogs
in the pack accompanied us on our wild rides, barking
and running as if mad with excitement. We were
sorry when the days grew so dark that we could ride
no more. All we could do then to exercise the ponies
was to take them out of their stable for an hour each

"WE PASSED CAPE BARENTZ, THE SOUTHEAST EXTREMITY OF NORTHBROOK ISLAND"

THE "AMERICA" FIGHTING HER WAY UP THE BRITISH CHANNEL

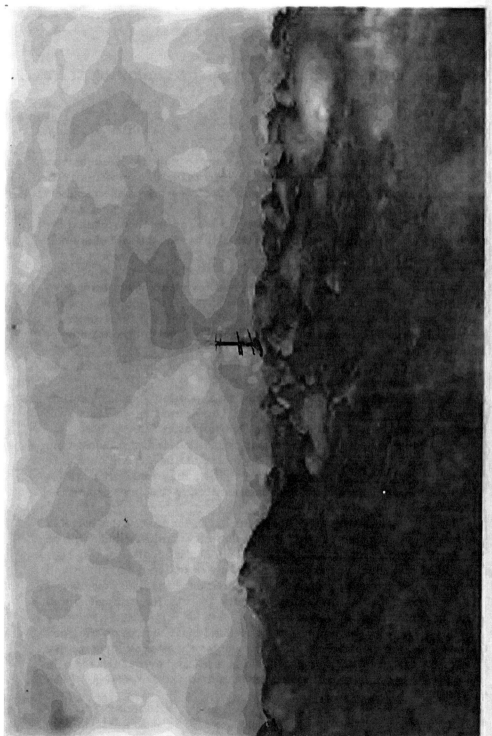

"WE MADE FAST ALONGSIDE THE HEAVY ICE OF TEPLITZ BAY"—AUGUST 31, 1903

day and tie them to a long picket line, allowing them to kick and roll in the snow.

Oct 29, 1903.

GENERAL ORDERS NO 26

1 The Commanding Officer finds it necessary to make his Headquarters aboard the *S Y America* from this date and takes this opportunity to express his appreciation of the loyal and effective work of the members of the Field Department since the arrival of the *America* in Teplitz Bay

2 The period of darkness is upon us and we can be thankful that we are housed so comfortably with such good facilities for the care of animals and opportunities for preparatory work for the Spring campaign

3 We individually represent the American Nation in this attempt North and the high personal privilege and responsibility of being representative before the world is an incentive to the development of the best in us—a spur to continued labour, so that when the time comes for heroic indifference to hardship we shall be ready for it by the training of the winter's work

4. Executive Officer Wm J Peters is in charge of Camp Abruzzi, and will keep record of events ashore

5 Assistant Surgeon Chas L Seitz is appointed Acting Quartermaster at Camp Abruzzi and Assistant Quartermaster J Vedoe will assist him in the care of equipment and Quartermaster Stores ashore

6 The house ashore as to its sanitary condition and cleanliness is in charge of Surgeon G Shorkley and members of the expedition are to cheerfully comply with any suggestions that he may make that are for health and cleanliness and to give him assistance daily in keeping the water barrel filled with clean ice

7 The cutting and sledging of ice for melter in tent and water barrel in house and the clearing of snow drifts from alley and vestibule will be part of the regular work of the Dog and Pony Departments.

8. Great care should be exercised in the use of material and stores and equipment and accounting made for every article used   Every member of the expedition should consider it his duty to care for equipment and keep everything in place and in order

9 As the plan of the Spring work depends for its success on the good condition of ponies and dogs at that time, every possible opportunity to exercise and train the animals should be used and every member help toward that end, giving all needed assistance to those in charge of the animals.

ANTHONY FIALA.

CHAPTER VIII

THE "AMERICA" WRECKED BY THE ICE FIELDS

NOVEMBER opened clear and cold, the temperature gradually falling. The minimum thermometer registered 47 degrees (Fahrenheit) below zero on the morning of the 11th. The ship froze in and seemed safe, every one was hopeful, and work for the coming spring sledge journey went on rapidly. There was a very faint twilight at noon with a low glow in the southern sky on clear days. Thereafter, it grew darker each day until there was little difference between noon and midnight.

On the morning of November 12th I was awakened about four o'clock by the shaking and trembling of the ship. I lay for some minutes listening to the groaning and moaning of the timbers under pressure of the ice, and then "Moses," the Captain's dog, pushed his way into my cabin and put his paws on me, looking into my face with his great black eyes as if beseeching me to rise. I learned later that after coming into my room he went below into the Captain's cabin and awoke him. I got up and putting on a heavy coat went out on deck. It was so dark that I could not see very far, but I could distinguish in the distance the ghostly form of the ice in a jumble of confusion, and could see the pressure ridges approaching the bow and stern of the ship and the enormous folds in the ice off to starboard. It felt rather cold, though the temperature had risen to 22 degrees below zero. I returned to the cabin to dress   While I was putting on my clothing, Captain Coffin knocked at my door and told me that he had ordered all hands to be ready to leave the ship.   I agreed with him that the order was necessary and went out on deck.   The *America* was shaking as if with the ague, while the ice was piling up ahead and slowly and fearfully nearing us.   Engineer Hartt coupled his engine and was ready to steam in half an hour   The sledges and stock of lumber were dragged out between decks and placed on the main hatch and, as the shocks increased and the *America* listed to starboard, I had the stuff lowered down on the ice   It was a scene of wild activity with a nerve-racking accompaniment of shrieks and groans from the protesting and resisting ship.   About six o'clock the Engineer reported to me that the water was above the fire-room plates and that he had started to pump the ship.   After all the sledges and material had been placed on the ice, I returned to my cabin to save some furs and records, which I placed in bags and gave to two sailors who passed them over the side to their shipmates on the ice.   Mr. Porter came aboard at that time.   He had been working in the magnetic observatory, and, noticing the light at so early an hour walked over to the ship to investigate.   I told him to tell Mr. Peters that should the arc light in the house go out he was to take it as a signal for assistance, and come at once to the ship with the members of the Field party and ponies and sledges.

About eight o'clock we received our worst squeeze.

The ship was thrown over to starboard and her bow raised up on the ice. The signal was sent and, flashing lanterns through the darkness, the men from camp came to our aid. The bags and equipment piled on the ice alongside the ship were first moved away to a place of safety. Later, the Engineer reported that the pump was gaining on the water and later still that the bilges were dry. The flood was probably caused by the bilge water running astern as the bow of the ship was lifted up on the ice.

With the last severe pressure the ice fields became quiet and we had an opportunity to inspect the ship. In the darkness, carrying a lighted lantern, accompanied by the ship's officers I crawled over the walls of ice blocks, tumbled in massive confusion around the *America's* stern, and looked for the rudder and wheel. But we could see nothing but a wilderness of ice, tons piled upon tons. The highest pressure ridges were about twenty-five yards forward of the ship's bow and about the same distance astern. Had the *America* been in either place she would have been destroyed. The edge of the heavy bay ice had been cracked in many places, and one of the ridges nearly reached the cache of ship's provisions. This valuable cache, which had been separated from the shore-ice by a great crack, was in a precarious position, so, sending ashore for more ponies and sledges, all hands worked at moving it to the shore side of the crack. All of the coffee and some of the other stores were sledged to the cache on land.

The ship in her new cradle of ice blocks seemed to be safer than before and the reassured crew carried

"THE SHIP WAS IN HER DEATH AGONY"

their blankets back to the warm and cozy quarters aboard. Days of storm and varying temperature followed the crush of November 12th and the nights were made unpleasant by the grating of the ice in motion and the groaning and shaking of the ship under pressure

Early in the morning of Saturday, December 21st, I was awakened by the old grinding and crunching of the ice and the trembling of the ship. As I was hurriedly dressing, the *America* began to shake as if on the wave of a mighty earthquake, she shrieked like a living thing in pain; every timber seemed to be under a frightful pressure to the very limit of resistance The First Officer and then the Captain and Chief Engineer came to my room where I was busy collecting records and valuables, and told me it was best to be ready to leave as the ice was bearing down on the ship.

I went on deck in the darkness only to realise that the *America* was in her death agony. The whole sea of ice to starboard was in motion, sweeping down in great lines and billows or breaking blocks that rose and tumbled over each other like an army of giants determined to destroy us Huge boulders of ice came over the starboard rail, crushing it like paper, and frightful sounds were heard from below as if the ship were breaking in half. The Engineer reported that the water was coming in fast and that the pump had been injured by the crush. However, he succeeded in getting it to work and soon its uneven thumping, that sounded like the painful motion of some wounded creature, resounded through the ship.

With the thunder of the ice fields in our ears, all hands worked sending equipment, clothing, bedding, and everything of value down to the fast bay ice. A sailor was sent ashore to the men at camp and they came over with the little ponies and sledges to help move our equipment to a place of safety on land.

About 7:30 Engineer Hartt came to me and, with tears in his eyes, said that the water was entering the ash-pits and that he could not keep up steam. Later he announced that the water had reached the grate bars, that the fires were out, and that he had sent his men ashore. The water steadily rose as the ice pressure ceased. With the failing steam, the electric lights slowly faded until they merely glowed red and dull. The donkey pump was quiet and a silence like death crept over the darkened ship. It was the passing of the ship's soul. By the light of a candle I was busily engaged placing small articles of value in bags and had just filled the last one, and had given it to a sailor to take over the side, telling him that he need not return, when a shout rose from the men on the outside, "The ice is opening!" The Engineer reappeared to tell me that he and I were alone on the ship and to say that I had better go if I did not want a bath. A view from the ship's deserted deck convinced me that if the ice fields relaxed their pressure but a moment, her water-logged hull would go to the bottom and that to remain aboard longer would be both unnecessary and foolhardy, and together we passed by the Jacob's ladder from the forecastle down to the ice.

But fate postponed the complete destruction of the

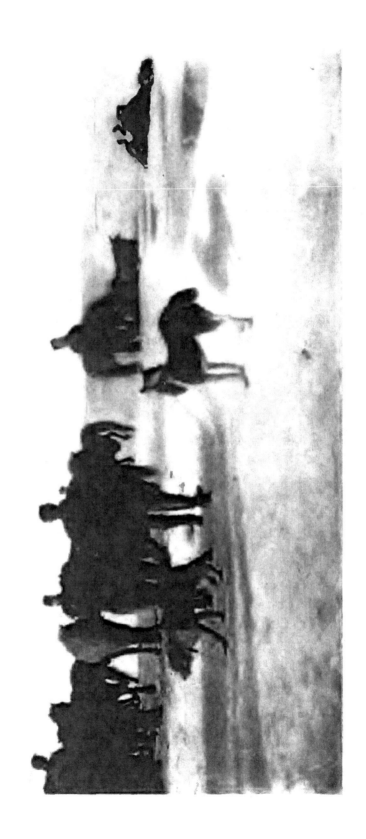

ALL THAT REMAINED IN 1903 OF THE WINTER QUARTERS OCCUPIED BY THE DUKE OF
THE ABRUZZI AND HIS COMPANIONS IN 1899-1900

THE DUKE'S STEEL GAS GENERATOR

THE SHELTER USED BY THE ITALIANS FOR THEIR
WEATHER INSTRUMENTS

America. Another pressure raised her high in the ice crib and in that position she froze, the storms drifting her in until she seemed immovable—a black, giant skeleton marooned in the icy waste of Teplitz Bay. Subsequent inspection revealed that the ship had been forced some distance northwest, dragging with her a 1,400 pound mooring anchor, which had torn its way through the ice. The *America* was terribly wrenched and strained. The timbers on the port side were crushed from the coal bunkers to a point thirty feet forward and about five feet below the lower deck, tremendous ice splinters still sticking through in places. Most of the upright stanchioning between the main-mast and the fore-hatch were displaced, some of it falling into the hold. The mainmast sagged to port, and the starboard rigging was loose and ragged. The ship was virtually a wreck and it brought a lump into my throat, as we clambered over the coal heaps in the hold or picked our way across the disordered decks, to view the devastation wrought in that one awful night. A lake of water in the engine room had begun to freeze and the desolation of the scene was accentuated by the incessant moaning of the wind.

The night of disaster was tinged with some flashes of humour, stories of which reached me later. While the crew were passing the bags over the side of the ship, the cook, who was of an excitable nature, suddenly appeared at the rail with a large bag which he heaved over with all his strength. It struck the ice below with a resounding crash; causing several of the sailors to exclaim, "Hello, Cook, what was that?" "Oh that's all right," he answered; "it's *lamp chimneys and flatirons!*"

But it was hardly all right, for during the winter we were obliged to cut the bottoms out of pickle bottles and use them in lieu of chimneys that had been broken.

With the disablement of the ship arose the necessity of sledging ashore all the coal possible and of dismantling the interior for the wood work that would be invaluable for enlarging our house, and all that afternoon, in a wind registering forty-eight miles an hour, men and ponies laboured, moving coal and stores from the ship to camp. The galley range was hoisted out with its 1,500 pounds or more of steel, placed on a sledge and hauled to the house on shore, where a little kitchen was built. The darkness and wind added to the distress of that memorable afternoon and evening—and at nightfall, when twenty-four homeless men had to be given a place to sleep, the cheapest, meanest Bowery lodging house would have seemed a palace compared to our little hut. Men slept on tables and underneath them, on benches, on piles of wet baggage.

In the few intervals of calm that followed the great storm, we made sledge journeys in the darkness over the mile of bay ice between the *America* and camp. Over two hundred bags of coal were thus sledged ashore as well as all the interior woodwork, sails, light spars, machine tools, dynamos, a lathe, and a small engine. A machine shop was built by our Commissary and Carpenter, under the shelter of which a boiler was constructed by the Engineer and his men, from an old gas generating tank left by the Duke of the Abruzzi. The boiler and engine were to serve with the dynamos

SLEDGING THE CARGO ASHORE BY HELP OF THE PONIES OVER THE ROUGH
ICE OF TEPLITZ BAY

WE START TO BUILD OUR WINTER QUARTERS

"A LARGE TENT WAS ERECTED, AND IN IT THE PONIES AND DOGS WERE SHELTERED"

INTERIOR OF PONY AND DOG TENT

Photograph was taken in the summer of 1904 during the absence of the ponies on the retreat south. At no
other time was there light enough in the tent for photography.

in the production of electric light at camp, a steam launch to be improvised from one of the whaleboats in the summer by use of this same machinery. The store house in which we kept some of our food supplies was cleared out, and in it bunks were erected and a stove was set up. It was banked in by a snow drift and this proved warm and comfortable. It was occupied by the crew of the lost ship, and was called "the forecastle." The work of enlarging the house to accomodate the entire company of thirty-nine men began at once but it was far into December before we were free from the noise of nailing and hammering. Preparations for the advance north were not neglected and on Thanksgiving Day, after divine service, I gave to the assembled members of the expedition the following provisional plan for the spring sledge trip;

An outline of the *Provisional Plan* for the Spring Sledge Trip North is presented herewith to the members of the Expedition. All wishing to take part in the march North should apply to the Commanding Officer before the end of November, 1903, and receive their allotment of skins for clothing, with the understanding that after preparation—should a member be unable to go on the Sledge Trip—his furs are to be turned over to O. O. for use on the trail.

ORGANIZATION OF THE SLEDGE PARTY

24 Men	20 Pony Sledges	12 Dog Sledges

Sledge Party to be divided into three Divisions as follows:

No. 1.	No. 2.	No. 3.
First Support	*Second Support*	*Final Advance*

First Support. Five Pony Sledges—One Dog Sledge—Carrying Seven Days' Rations for entire column, and Ten Days' Rations for the return of Ten Men. Return Transport—One Pony Sledge—Two Dog Sledges—Five Dogs to Team—Four Ponies to be used for dog food.

Second Support. Ten Pony Sledges—Five Dog Sledges—Carrying Rations for entire column for Twenty-seven Days' advance after the return of the First Support, and forty-nine Days' Rations for return of Eight Men. Return Transport—One Pony Sledge—Five Dog Sledges—Nine Ponies to be used for Dog food when sledge loads are consumed and Nine Sledges to be abandoned in the advance by Second Support.

Final Advance. Six Men—Five Pony Sledges—Six Dog Sledges—Rations for Six Men for ninety-two days.—The Five Ponies to be used for Dog food when Sledge loads are consumed and Sledges abandoned and Dogs to be killed off as Sledge loads become lighter. Transportation facilities provided for One hundred and Twenty-five days from Camp. Dogs to be killed not figured in calculation as Rations, but will serve as an extra food allowance.

In the choice of men for the different detachments the Commanding Officer reserves decision until in the field and all members of Field, Deck, Engine, and Steward Departments taking part in the Sledge Trip may feel that they have a chance for the highest honours, and that the choice will only be made after experience has proved each member of the Sledge Party.

The evident fact that only the few can go on the Final Advance, will necessitate the return of many possibly well qualified to continue to the end. As the success of the Sledge Trip will depend upon the successful work of the Supports, and on the efficiency, endurance, and loyalty of those forming the Supports as well as in the Final Advance—every man who takes part in the Sledge work should be prepared to take his place in any detachment, heroically accepting anything that may be expected of him that may help toward the ultimate attainment of the object of the Expedition.

Equipment should be completed and sledges loaded by February First, 1904.

Preliminary training in practice marches of entire column to start with the return of light, and sledge party to be under marching orders February 8th, 1904, every Man and Team ready to start at one hour's notice on the march North.

Each man will be provided with one sleeping bag, a pair of sleeping socks and will be allowed to carry in the sleeping bag one blanket not to weigh over seven pounds.

Each man will be allowed about twenty-five pounds of baggage to consist of spare clothing, the clothing in each case to be on the list and weight finally decided upon, and exactly the same for each member of the party. No extra weights to be allowed.

Each two men to be provided with a silk pyramid tent that is to contain the two sleeping bags and an allowance of hay as bedding, the weight of hay to be decided later and to be the same for each tent.

ANTHONY FIALA.

BUILDING A HOUSE AT CAMP ABRUZZI

LAYING THE FLOOR

Rear view, showing warehouse

"ON SEPT. 24TH, THE HOUSE WAS COMPLETED"

Front of our new home with view of the storage and stable tent. The two were connected later by a long covered passage.

CHAPTER IX

THE NIGHT OF PREPARATION

DECEMBER was a dark month, there being no difference between day and night. We missed the cheerful illumination of the electric arc and under the light of numerous little oil lamps we laboured making harness and sewing our fur clothing for the sledge trip. Because of our limited space I found it necessary to divide the workers into a day and a night force. In the carpenter shop, improvised from part of our storehouse, Quartermaster Rilliet, who had the assembling of the sledges in charge, toiled with the members of the crew. A light sectional boat was constructed and over a thousand rations weighed and packed for the trip north. In addition to the hard task of providing food for so large a party, Steward Spencer baked over six hundred pounds of pork and bean biscuit for use on the trail. It proved to be one of our most valued foods and was preferred on the trail to anything else.

The Christmas and the New Year holidays passed happily. We celebrated them with banquets, to which our hard working steward contributed many delicacies. A Christmas edition of the *Arctic Eagle* our camp newspaper, was printed, Assistant Commissary Stewart making up the forms and running the press, and Seaman Montrose, who had once been

61

a printer, acting as compositor. Nearly all the members of the party contributed to its columns and much amusement at its quips and personals was the result.*

Storms were frequent and drifts fierce, and it became quite a problem how to preserve the large number of sledges intended for the advance north from being buried under the snow. I finally had a large store house dug in the deep drift near the house and covered it with spars of the ship and old topsails, and under its grateful shelter the twenty-nine sledges were loaded as fast as the rations and stores were weighed out.

I had planned to shelter the party when in the field in little two- and three-man tents of pongee silk with a floor of khaki or light canvas upon which to place a layer of hay; each man to have a separate sleeping bag, the hay to act as a non-conducting mattress, to prevent the absorbtion of heat from the sleeper by the cold surface of the ice or snow, when out on the floating Polar pack. The hay was also to serve as food for the ponies, while fresh hay was to be had on the trail from the bales carried as forage. The hay proved very useful as camp bedding and the second year, when there were no ponies in the column, I had some of the sleeping bags covered with a bag of pongee

---

*On Sunday evenings the men were called together for a short devotional service, and a chapter or two read from the Scriptures out of an old Bible that had been the property of the Captain of the yacht *America* during her victorious cruise in the International races of 1851. Little packages of sweet milk chocolate were distributed every Sunday, and after the meeting a number of the men would gather around the long table in the living room and play poker for the little disks of chocolate!

OUR WEATHER INSTRUMENT SHELTER

The Astronomical Observatory is seen on the brow of the hill to the right centre of the view

THE ASTRONOMICAL OBSERVATORY

EXERCISING THE PONIES AT CAMP ABRUZZI

"WE MOUNTED THE TOUGH LITTLE EQUINES"

THE PONIES PROVED INVALUABLE IN SLEDGING THE STORES FROM
THE SHIP TO OUR CAMP SITE

Photographed in the waning light of the sun only a few degrees above the horizon

silk and senne grass or hay stuffed in between bag and cover, thus keeping the hay or grass clean.

Storms were many and the members of the Scientific Staff, in their walks to and from the observatories, often had to face winds of high velocity with driving snow and low temperature. Observer Long was often obliged to crawl on his hands and knees through the drifted passage from the hut, and in the whirling blast of frigid, wind-driven snow particles find his way to the " chicken coop" where he kept his thermometers. No matter how bad the storm, every evening he brought me the little slip of paper signed "Obs.," containing the weather instrument reading for the day

In going to the Magnetic Observatory it was generally necessary for an observer to carry a shovel and dig his way into the hut so as to free the man he relieved on watch.

At midnight of December 11th Mr. Peters and John Vedoe went down to the magnetic hut together in a 52-mile-an-hour wind to dig out Mr Tafel who was on observation duty. They were forced to walk backward the entire distance, guided by the electric wire. At half-past one I became worried about them and was getting ready to go out and show a light to guide them back, when they came in covered with snow and ice I helped Mr. Peters out of his frozen garments while others assisted Tafel and Vedoe. The snow had penetrated through their boots to their stockings and through their jackets and sweaters, which were worn under heavy wind coats

A full moon on the evening of January 2d, without a wind, gave me a long wished for opportunity to photograph the wreck of the *America*, and with camera, tripod, and lantern, I made my way over the wind furrowed surface of the frozen bay. Winds of high velocity had cut the snowy surface into ridges that looked as if a giant harrow had been dragged across them. The edges of the furrows were turned over where the eddies had tunnelled underneath, and they snapped under foot in the low temperature of 30 degrees below zero with a sharp tinkle like breaking glass.

The great pressure ridge which had caused the loss of the ship was drifted over with a concealing mask of snow and the winds had eddied around the *America's* massive hulk leaving a deep hole—down to the original level—on the port side toward the direction of the prevailing winds. After setting up the camera and opening the lens I went back to camp, returning to the ship again in about an hour and a half to end the exposure. On my way over I witnessed one of the most beautiful auroras of the year. It started in a bank of clouds on the southern horizon with a faint golden glow. Then the cirrus clouds that were floating in the sky seemed to become electrified and stretched in long parallel rays across the zenith from the cloud bank in the south to the north where the brilliant star Arcturus was shining. A corona of swift moving lacy folds, highly coloured in pinks and greens, actively scintillated directly overhead, and from it shot a long snake-like ribbon of auroral fire terminating in a hook in the clear western sky. The stars gleamed bright through the luminous veil, but the moon, at full, was shining at the time and with its own light obscured some of the glory of the radiant northern fire. Later the clouds moved slowly toward the zenith, spreading out and crossing the moon, the aurora changing in form and playing across the grating of light filaments at right angles, forming curves within curves from the corona to the west, and then moving in rapid darts toward the east, a subsidiary smaller band forming parallel further north   The display was over at nine P M., on my return to the hut, so I did not get an opportunity of recording it permanently by means of sketches.

I made many attempts to photograph the aurora on the Baldwin-Ziegler Expedition, but always failed. By long exposure, I could get some small effect of the light with that of the stars on the sensitive plate, valueless however as a matter of record, for the swift moving aurora, to be correctly depicted, would have to be photographed instantaneously, and, for that purpose, it does not give enough light.

In connection with Mr. Peters's work in the Magnetic Observatory I made a number of sketches of the auroras using for that purpose a board upon which was a compass for orienting, and a number of black sheets of paper upon the surface of which I had drawn a circle representing the horizon. The sheets were so placed together, and pinned at the corners, that they could be torn off as the sketches were completed. A pin at the centre represented the zenith point   Opportunities were few for its use on account of the prevalent bad weather, and sketching in the open air when the temperature was from 30 to 40 degrees below zero was anything but pleasant   However, some interesting sketches were secured.

January was a wild month, noted for its variable and high temperature. The maximum thermometer registered 31 degrees above zero on the 21st, during a storm in which the wind reached a hurricane velocity. This storm continued until the morning of the 23d, when we found that the bay ice had been broken up. The great frozen mass, the accumulation of years which we thought nothing could move had been crushed and blown away, and we could see where monster waves had washed on the shore almost to the rocks of the ridge on which our house was built. We thought at first of a tidal wave, but in the dim glow of noon-time—for the sun was on its return to us—we discovered that the glacier had calved for miles along its face. In the bay near us we could see the ghostly forms of the icebergs that had been born during the wild hurricane. At our feet lapped the inky waters of the bay in which floated a number of small ice fields. We could not see far enough, on account of the darkness, to know whether the ship was in the bay or not. Several of the party explored the questionable harbour by jumping from cake to cake, but no sign of the ship or the provision cache could be found, not even a case, barrel, or spar. The *America* had disappeared in the darkness of the Arctic night, and shrouded her doom in mystery! Whether she went to the bottom under the blast of that awful gale or whether she was blown toward the northern axis of the earth, where now she floats in unheralded victory, no man knows.

By January 23d our little lighting plant was complete and our Engineer ready to illuminate the camp with electricity, but with the disappearance of the

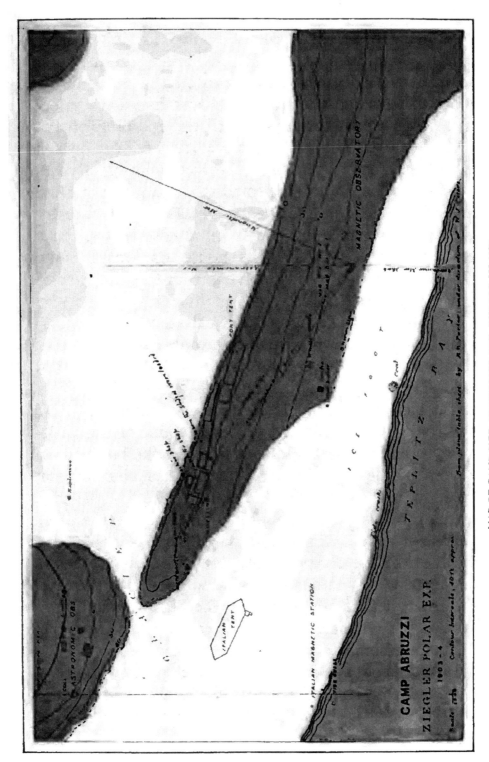

MAP OF CAMP SITE AT TEPLITZ BAY, RUDOLF ISLAND

"A THICK GLOOM SETTLED OVER THE ICE OF LAND AND SEA"

" WE CLIMBED THE GLACIER NORTH OF THE CAMP"

America vanished the large store of coal in her hold, and we could not afford to keep up steam by using the coal pile ashore. So we economically continued our work under the light of oil lamps and candles.

January was a busy month. Rations for men, ponies, and dogs were weighed and packed and preparations made for an early start; but the month of February, with its dimly lighted and very short days, was a period of storms and our departure was delayed. The returning light revealed a vast body of open sea to the west and northwest of the island, which made it imperative for me to plan to leave from the northeast, at Cape Fligely.

ZIEGLER POLAR EXPEDITION
CAMP "ABRUZZI"

G O. NO. 32.   Thursday, Jan. 14, 1904

1 The consolidation of the entire Expedition party ashore since the twenty-first of November, 1903, consequent upon the loss of ship, resulted in considerable extra labour for the members of the Expedition, in the necessary hauling, sledging, excavating, and constructing to provide larger quarters

2. Since the *America* experienced the crush in the ice, a brief summary of work accomplished is as follows ·—

3 Cache of ship's provisions moved from line of ice pressure to place of safety

4. Ship dismantled for lumber, and storehouse at camp converted into sleeping quarters for crew, kitchen built, galley stove brought from ship and set up, and house enlarged

5 New storehouse for Quartermaster stores excavated and constructed

6 New storehouse for Commissary stores excavated and constructed

7 Sledges brought ashore and completed in workshop improvised from part of storehouse

8 Two hundred and twenty-two bags of coal filled aboard ship and sledged to camp, and ship's boats sledged ashore.

9 Magnetometer completed.

10. New magnetic hut erected

11 Silk tents completed for sledge trip

12. Machine shop constructed, and dynamo engine and generators with machine stores brought ashore.   Lathe set up and machine work started.

13. Seal boots completed for sledge party.

14. Pony blankets completed for sledge party.

15. Forage for ponies weighed out and packed ready for trail.

16. Storehouse for sledges 65 x 15 excavated and constructed from sails and spars.

17. Dogs arranged in teams and teams assigned.

18. First section of sectional boat framed.

19. Over 600 lbs. of pork and bean biscuit baked for sledge trip.

20. Fur clothing nearing completion.

21. Weighing and packing of dog rations now in progress.

22. We have not forgotten to celebrate the festivals of Christmas and New Year with enjoyable banquets and perpetuated the memory of the time by the publication of a six page newspaper.

23. The Commanding Officer takes this opportunity to compliment officers and men of all departments, on the splendid results achieved thus far under the difficult conditions of darkness and cold, in an Arctic night of unprecedented record for high and continued wind storms.

24. The contemplated training of dogs and ponies during the past period of moonlight has been unavoidably delayed. Those who have their dogs can be prepared for the next opportunity by daily practice with their teams, two men taking a team at a time. This is very important. The dogs require considerable training and members must become acquainted with them.

25. Members of expedition who are to remain at camp should render assistance at every opportunity to their comrades intending to go north, remembering that the success of the expedition depends upon the triumph of the sledge trip.

26. The storehouse is now in use as a place to pack sledge rations. Loose dogs must be kept out.   Doors are to be kept closed.

27. Clothing bags issued for trail use should be filled with the following articles of clothing:—combination suit, Jaegersuit, sweater, guernsey, knitted drawers, three pairs Jaeger socks, two pairs long stockings, three pairs woolen mittens, one pair seal mittens, silk overalls, one pair seal boots, one pair moccasins, one pair fur boots (to be issued later), Jaeger camel's hair cap covered with silk.   Icelander can replace sweater if desired.

28. Instructions in detail for sledge party will be issued later.

29. Camp routine until further orders:—

Reveille	7.30 A.M.	Luncheon	1 P.M.
First call for breakfast	7.50	First call for dinner	5.50
Breakfast	8	Dinner	6
First call for luncheon	12.50 P. M.	Call to quarters	10

Taps 10.30 P. M.

IN THE ASTRONOMICAL OBSERVATORY AT CAMP ABRUZZI

Assistant Scientist Porter taking a time sight with the vertical circle on the North Star

THE "AMERICA" IN WINTER QUARTERS IN TEPLITZ BAY EARLY IN NOVEMBER, 1903
Photographed by moonlight

THIS PHOTOGRAPH WAS TAKEN BY MOONLIGHT AFTER THE "AMERICA'S" DISAPPEARANCE
IN JANUARY, 1904. IT IS THE SAME SPOT AS PHOTOGRAPHED IN THE UPPER PICTURE

Coffee served at 11 A. M. and at 3 P. M.   Chocolate at 10 P. M.   Coffee for night force at 6 A. M.

30. Members of the Expedition not on night duty are expected to be in their quarters after taps.

31. As work is proceeding day and night, a consideration for those who are obliged to sleep while others are awake, will tend to prevent unnecessary noise.

32. The sun is on its way toward us and soon darkness will give place to light.   Let us salute the return of the sun with a spirit of enthusiastic activity, ready for the task that is before us, rejoicing in the opportunity to attempt the discovery of that which has been sought for centuries.

Anthony Fiala,
Commanding Expedition.

CHAPTER X

PRELIMINARY SLEDGE WORK

BY EARLY February the preparations for the sledge trip were complete, and twenty-five sledges, loaded with rations all carefully weighed, were ready under the shelter of the great snow storehouse. With the return of the twilight the men started to train their dog teams and ponies—running a trail from the camp over the glacier to Cape Saulen and back. The ponies had their advocates and the dogs had theirs. Old Pierre contended that since the dogs could eat the ponies and the ponies could not eat the dogs, the dogs were naturally the key to the situation. I planned for a party of twenty-six men, sixteen ponies and sledges, and nine dog teams and sledges. The column was to be divided into three supporting parties and one advance. Each supporting party was to carry provisions for the support and advance march of the whole column for a certain number of days, and food for its own return to Camp Abruzzi. The sledges were all numbered and coloured according to the detachment in which they belonged, as were also the rations. The choice of the men to be made in the field, the weaker ones to be placed in the supports first to be detached and sent back to land. The First Support of four men, one pony sledge, and one dog sledge, was to carry two days' rations for the ad-

"A BLACK, GIANT SKELETON MAROONED IN THE ICY WASTE OF TEPLITZ BAY"

"PRINTING THE CHRISTMAS EDITION OF THE 'ARCTIC EAGLE'"

vance march of the entire column of men, dogs, and ponies, and, five days' rations for their own return to the land.

A Second Support of eight men, four pony sledges, and one dog sledge, carried food for the advance of the column six days more, and rations for ten days' return march of the support to Rudolph Island. Two of the ponies of this support were to be used on the outward march as food for the dogs. The Third Support, consisting of eight men, six pony sledges and five dog sledges, was to continue on the march north sixteen days longer and provide food for the entire column from the time the Second Support left on its return march. The six ponies were to be considered as dog food on the advance. This supporting detachment was provided with twenty-six days' rations, packed on their five dog sledges, for their return to Camp Abruzzi.

On the departure of the Third Support the final party (the "Advance") of six men was to continue on the march provided with eighty-two days' rations on six dog sledges and five pony sledges. The dogs were not considered as food in the calculations, and would have (in the latter part of the journey) meant so many extra rations.

With the transportation facilities of the column, there was ample food to allow the Advance party to stay in the field 135 days—and if about seven miles a day could be averaged, the pole could be reached and the party brought safely back. It was expected that the supporting parties would return at least part of the way back to camp over a made trail, but there were the possibilities of delay from storms and bad ice, and to insure a sufficient food supply, and as an allowance for delay, each detachment was provided with several days' extra rations.

During the winter and spring we found the prevailing winds to be from the southeast and east. They broke up the ice and caused a great hole of water to extend off the western and northwestern shores of Rudolph Island, sometimes stretching so far north that from the top of the glacier, which commanded a view of about thirty miles, we could see nothing but open sea. When the wind ceased, the water would freeze over and sometimes stay smooth for several days. Then a pressure would come in from the west, and what had been a fairly smooth road—became an impassable mass of ridges of young, thin ice, mixed with great cakes that came in from the west, and numerous water holes. It was on such smooth ice lanes that Captain Cagni made his best marches north, and it explains his rapid run from the island, so rapid that, before the first detachment was sent back, they had reached something like forty miles from land.

To me the loss of the first detachment seems due to their inability to find any of these smooth lanes on their return. While they were marching north, the pressure must have come in from the west and destroyed them all, the men starving to death, struggling over impossible ice. The safe return of the second detachment was helped by the southeast winds which in early summer clear out all that broken ice, the heavy ice then coming in from the north thus helping the second detachment on their homeward march.

Sigurd Myhre, who died May 16, 1904

Christmas Dinner 1903
Camp Atrepi:

OUR CHRISTMAS BANQUET

When they reached the edge of the pack they were close in to the island, and could send a man ashore in a kayak to communicate with their comrades on land.

Winds and storms! Only three hours of calm were recorded on the self-registering instrument during the month of February. On the twelfth we had the first let up from wind and Mr. Peters utilised the few hours of light that day by going over the glacier to Cape Auk where he erected a signal pole to serve as a meridian mark for the astronomical observatory at camp. He was accompanied by Assistant Engineer Vedoe and Assistant Surgeon Seitz, with two dog sledges and camping outfit. We communicated with him with prearranged signals of red and white lights and the marking of the meridian by the firing of a rocket. A storm raged all of the 13th and the 14th, the party not returning to camp until the afternoon of the 15th. Mr. Peters reported a very cold experience, the temperature falling so low that the cooking oil froze to the consistency of cream and became full of clots. The temperature at Camp Abruzzi went down to 44 degrees below zero and it must have been lower still on the glacier at the elevation where, exposed to the violence of the storm, the party was encamped. The prevailing southeasterly winds kept an open channel of water off the western and northwestern coast and I early realised that our descent to the sea ice would have to be made from Cape Fligely, the northeastern extremity of the island, to accomplish which, we would be obliged to cross the high wind-swept glacier.

For the purpose of marking a safe trail, on February 25th, I sent Dr. Vaughn in charge of an advance party with dogs and sledges to cross the glacier. He was provided with signal flags on bamboo poles to mark a trail free from crevasses on which the column was to follow later. He was also to cache some food at Cape Fligely. The party returned two days later, Dr. Vaughn reporting that they could not reach their destination on account of bad weather. Three flags had been placed and the provisions and forage cached on the glacier at the third flag, which was about half the distance to the Cape.

On return of this unsuccessful party Mr. Peters volunteered to make the journey. On the morning of March 2d, accompanied by Steward Spencer with his dog team and sledge, he left camp. I was anxious to leave soon on the poleward quest and before Mr. Peters left I gave him instructions not to remain away from camp longer than three days, but to return should storms delay his progress. On the morning of the day after their start Mr. Peters and Spencer returned, having reached a point on the glacier near the third flag planted by the previous party. A storm had arisen and Peters had returned in obedience to his instructions.

The continuance of the bad weather gave me the impression that most of it was local and that if we could get away from the influence of the ice-capped islands and open bodies of water we would be comparatively free from storms and squalls.

At noon on March 3d our eyes were gladdened by the first appearance of His Majesty the Sun breaking through a bank of clouds to the south, bringing new life in his shining rays. On the morning of the 5th of

"A LIGHT SECTIONAL BOAT WAS CONSTRUCTED"

BY JANUARY 23D, OUR LITTLE LIGHTING PLANT WAS COMPLETE AND OUR ENGINEER
WAS READY TO ILLUMINATE THE CAMP WITH ELECTRICITY

Electrician and Asst. Eng. A. Vedoe   Engineer H. P. Hartt
Asst. Eng. C. Hudgins   Fireman Hovlick   Seaman Perry

A STEAM BOILER WAS CONSTRUCTED OUT OF THE STEEL OF THE DUKE'S GAS GENERA-
TORS BY OUR ENTERPRISING ENGINEER AND HIS ASSISTANTS

March I had all the loaded sledges dragged out of the storehouse and placed in line on the snow, and ordered the men to lash on the toploads of tents, sleeping bags, clothing bags, and extras. The interior of the hut that day presented a busy scene. The men getting ready for the sledge trip taking out their sets of dog harness, clothing, and ration bags, and packing their little silk tents with sleeping bags and hay. Ten pounds of hay were allowed each tent for bedding, and on this the sleeping bags were placed, the small space in the interior of the house not allowing more than one tent to be packed and lashed at a time. At last all was ready. But that moment, as if called forth by the Imp of the Perverse, a wind began to blow with great violence and we were obliged to unlash the top-loads as a protective measure against bears and dogs and place them under the shelter of the storehouse roof. The following day, Sunday, was still stormy but, dreading a further delay, I resolved to begin the march and gave my last instructions to Commissary Truden whom I left in charge of Camp Abruzzi to await my return from the ice. I also gave instructions to Captain Coffin who, after the return of the supporting detachments from the field, was to conduct the party south to Cape Flora where the Relief Ship was expected in the coming summer. Three bears visited us that day, causing great excitement in camp, the men with guns in hand falling over each other in their anxiety to get out of the house through the long dark passage to the exterior. One bear was killed out on the bay ice and triumphantly dragged to camp. In the evening a bear chased the Steward and Cook up to the house. They had fired all their ammunition away, and on nearing the camp they called lustily for help. Assistant Commissary Stewart came to their rescue and made bruin retreat under heavy fire.

I wrote my last letters on the evening of the 6th. It was Sunday. After the usual divine service I gave instructions to the men in regard to the care of themselves and the animals when in the field, and told them that I and my party would begin the journey north the next day.

INSTRUCTIONS FOR SLEDGE PARTY NORTH

CAMP "ABRUZZI," FEB. 16, 1904.

1. Follow the trail, unless ordered to leave it.

2. You may think some other way an easier one but it is *your duty to follow the trail* and to train your teams to obey you in that particular.

3. Be careful and do not allow your team to run up on the sledge in front of you.

4. Do not fall behind; train your team to keep the required distance from team ahead.

5. Do not leave the last man too far behind, particularly in rough ice and thick weather. Pass word to front of column when some one is missing.

6. Keep snow out of interior of tent. Take off overalls when turning in and all damp clothing. You will be more comfortable by doing so.

7. To take care of the feet is of the utmost importance. Wear a pair of wool socks that can be changed when dirty and one or two pair of long Jaeger stockings over them. Take off the outside stocking and put it in the sleeping bag at night to dry and put your feet in sleeping socks. Sleeping socks should not be used to walk out in snow with. Feet should not be bound tightly; they should have room to move in shoe or boot.

8. Snow should be brushed from felt boots and the boots put under or in sleeping bag at night to dry out; one on each side of the head would be advised.

9. Hot utensils containing food should not be placed on sleeping bags; remember that water and moisture make the sleeping bag anything but comfortable. Wet spots tear easily, the hair falling out, and burned spots break off. Repair any holes at first opportunity.

10. When fur boots or moccasins are worn with senne grass, take the grass out at night, pulling it apart and spreading it to allow moisture to escape and solidify. The frost crystals can be shaken out in the morning.

EXCAVATING THE GREAT SNOW STOREHOUSE

LOADING THE SLEDGES IN THE SHELTER OF THE STOREHOUSE

Sergt. J. E. Moulton.

A TYPICAL SLEDGE PONY

11. There is no provision of spare articles of any description to allow for carelessness in the sledge column, so if you lose parts of your equipment you will be obliged to go without.

12. Take care of your team, being particular at camping to consider the comfort and well being of your ponies or dogs before turning into your sleeping bag.

13. Any part of harness broken should be repaired at night before turning in so that the column will not be delayed by one team's disability.

14. It is advised in the matter of clothing to wear just as little as possible while working, so that perspiration will not be induced; if too warm take off coat and simply travel in shirt and wind coat. A man cannot keep warm in damp clothing no matter how much he puts on, and skins are easily ruined when they become wet. Be particular and keep your skin coat dry to keep you warm at halts.

15. Should an accident occur and a sledge or pony break through the ice keep your place in line unless in position to assist and be sure your own team is not in danger.

16. Reveille will be sounded in the morning from the cook tent and breakfast will be served about ten minutes later. On the sounding of the assembly tents will be taken down, sledges loaded with camp equipage, and teams harnessed ready for the advance.

17. Each man before leaving Camp Abruzzi will receive 7 days tent rations of bread, butter, pemmican and sugar, and two weeks' rations of milk. No issue of tent rations will be made for seven days, so use accordingly.

18. Do not shout unauthorized orders to any member of party, but be helpful and considerate, ready to assist a comrade when in need.

19. No riding on sledges to be allowed without permission.

ANTHONY FIALA.

CHAPTER XI

THE FIRST ATTEMPT NORTH

IN a twenty-mile wind, on the morning of March 7th, we left Camp Abruzzi. The party comprised twenty-six men, sixteen pony sledges, and thirteen dog sledges. We reached the summit of the glacier the same afternoon, after a hard pull up the steep slope in the face of the drift and wind. Here we were obliged to camp since everything ahead was obscured by the flying drift. On the order to camp the ponies were unharnessed and blanketed and chained to the picket line out on the face of the cold wind-swept glacier. The dogs were also unharnessed and attached to the steel ropes that each man carried—ropes just long enough for the nine dogs of a single team. Tents were raised after the animals were attended to.

The camp was an interesting place, though the howling wind and flying drift brought discomfort in their train. There were eleven silk pyramid tents flapping in the wind, each one numbered in flaming red on all sides of its peak; the cook tent with its bold insignia, "Cook Tent No. 1," breathing the vapour of the evening's pemmican stew; the sixteen ponies huddled together in a line overlooking the impenetrable mist-enshrouded distance of glacier and sea. Meanwhile the dogs barked and fought as the men went about

ON THE MORNING OF MARCH 5, THE LOADED SLEDGES WERE DRAGGED OUT OF THE STOREHOUSE AND PLACED IN LINE ON THE SNOW

their duties in their white silk wind-coats, looking like so many Bedouins or Crusaders.

The cook tent was a great convenience. It was attached permanently to the sledge with cookers, food, and oil inside. On camping the tent had only to be set up and everything necessary was found within. Cooking in a low temperature is one of the troublesome features of Polar work. Moisture collects on everything under cover and forms a coating of thick hoar frost, which rapidly increases the weight of tent and clothing. Thus, by having a separate place in which to prepare food, the tents occupied by the men were kept comparatively free from moisture, and in consequence were lighter and warmer. My intention had been to have the men take daily turns in the cook tent, but I found that economy would result if two of the party only undertook the task. Accordingly Steward Spencer and myself did the cooking on all the sledge trips in which we took part.

The wind went down during the night and in the early morning we broke camp and marched for Cape Fligely.

We reached there the same afternoon in a drifting wind, one man disabled by a rupture from over exertion, another with a strained back, and three others not in condition to go forward. While getting supper two of the cookers gave out, and in the fierce gale it was a difficult and unpleasant task to provide for twenty-six men with a disabled apparatus. The wind increased in velocity the following day and the flapping tents made a sound like many machine guns of heavy calibre in close action, and to be heard by a companion in a tent it was necessary to shout. Our last cooking machine gave out just as we were preparing breakfast. I spent several hours in an attempt to solder the joints of the oil-tanks that had opened, but the grease and cold for a time precluded success. Ultimately they were made air and oil tight by the use of some cement I had taken along for the purpose of repairing kayaks, and with joy we completed the meal for the hungry party of storm-bound men.

The storm raged all of the ninth and the tenth, drifting over the sledges and partially burying the small tents. We were held prisoners with a temperature outside of 38 degrees below zero. The injured men suffered considerably, and their condition caused me much anxiety. The only comfortable ones were the dogs, they curled themselves into little fur balls, and, covering up their noses with their tails, were soon blanketed over with the snow, and slept through all the raging storm. But the poor ponies, with tails to the wind and heads down, shivered in the freezing blast. As long as the wind blew it was impossible to give them hay to eat and even the nose bags of oats were blown away unless closely watched.

The poor condition of five men, the leaky cookers, and the fact that one man had torn his sleeping bag and that two others complained that theirs were too small, decided me to return to camp, to refit and to reduce the number of men for another attempt North.

The wind subsided the morning of March 11th, and after digging our sledges and tents out of the snow drifts, with one man lashed in his sleeping bag on the top of a sledge, we tramped back over the glacier—reaching the camp at 4 P. M. the same day.

On the return to camp and after the cold experience on the glacier there was much disappointment expressed, some of the men criticising the dogs, the equipment, and the ponies, stating that the last named were not adapted for Polar work and would fail us when we reached rough ice. The enthusiasm which before the short journey had blazed so warm, dropped to the cold of an Arctic night.

The discussions were many, the men of the Field Department talking as they worked at night sitting around the stove in the large living room. Many a revelation of character was made during our sojourn in the land of ice. To really know a man you must live with him away from the distractions and conveniences of ·civilisation; live with him in a house where there are no other houses; have him for a neighbour where there are no other neighbours. And then if you obey the divine command and love him as yourself, and if the love is returned in the same spirit, your companionship is a happy, helpful one.

I entered into some of the discussions and will never forget a little talk with several of the members. Courage was the topic. In illustration, I told an incident of the Civil War of 1861–65. During the battle of Chancellorsville the 11th Corps, which had occupied the plank road in front of Hazel Grove was in full retreat, and General Jackson's Division was coming through the woods in pursuit. If something were not done, and at once, the Army of the Potomac was doomed. General Pleasonton, Chief of Artillery of

the Union Army, surveyed the scene of disaster, and
attempted to place a line of guns on the plank road to
stay the advance of the victorious host.   To do it he
must have fifteen minutes.   General Jackson's Division
must be stopped.   A squadron of cavalry was there
in the saddle which had not joined in with the rush to
the rear of the panic-stricken Eleventh Corps.   General
Pleasonton galloped up to Major Keenan, in command
of the squadron, and ordered him to charge the woods
with his handful of men, and engage the Confederate
army just long enough for him to get his guns in position.   It was a more perilous charge than that of the
Light Brigade at Balaclava.   But—to their glory—
they went.   They were, of course, routed, and many
saddles were emptied.—But the charge made Jackson
halt and form his line to receive cavalry, and that halt
saved the army of the Potomac.

I said to my men, "Would you not have done the
same?   Would you not have obeyed the order and
followed the flag, risking your lives for the ultimate
good, and for a principle?"   One of them answered—
"The h—l we would!   Self preservation is the first
law of nature.   As for me I would follow any old rag
as long as there was something in it for me!"   And I
realised that the spirit of "Graft" had penetrated even
to the regions of ice and snow.   Some of the men
though were anxious for another attempt to capture
the Pole and Assistant Scientist Porter made my
heart glad with his enthusiastic expressions of belief
in victory on our next march North.   The Chief
Engineer, though he could not accompany me, also
cheered me with his strong words of hope and belief

A HALT ON THE GLACIER

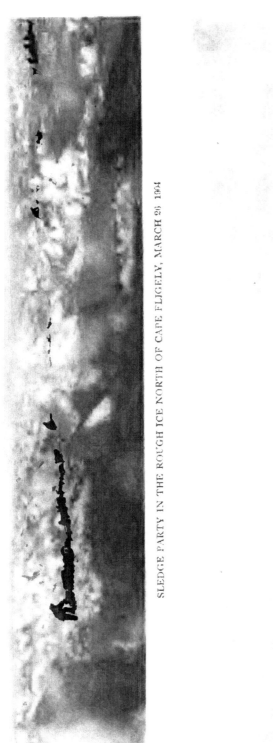

SLEDGE PARTY IN THE ROUGH ICE NORTH OF CAPE FLIGELY, MARCH 26, 1904

A HALT IN A SMOOTH OASIS IN THE DESERT OF ROUGH ICE

in success. A number of the men came to me wishing to be added to the next sledge force, the members of the crew evincing a strong desire to take part and do their best.

CHAPTER XII

THE SECOND EFFORT NORTH

THERE was much to do before we could start again.
The cookers, which through faulty workmanship
had failed us, were taken apart by our Engineer and his
assistants and thoroughly overhauled. Important
joints, which the manufacturer had carelessly neglected,
were brazed and the tanks were made tight.

With the necessary preparations and the revising
of, weights and equipment, with the reloading of
the sledges, and with the delay caused by storms,
it was not until March 25th that we could leave Camp
Abruzzi.

On the morning of that date we left, climbing the
glacier once again, a party of fourteen men, nine dog
sledges, and seven pony sledges. The weather was
cold and beautiful and we ascended the steep slope of
the glacier with little trouble. Cape Fligely was reached
the same evening and, after supper, Mr. Peters and I
descended to the sea ice for the purpose of picking out
a path for the sledge column down the slope. The sea
ice itself was in very bad condition, nothing but a
rubble of ice cakes in one confused mass, piled, ridge
upon ridge, as far as the eye could see from the highest
point of the Cape.

The following morning, after an early breakfast, the
sledge party descended the glacier and forced a way

"THE POOR PONIES, WITH TAILS TO THE WIND AND HEADS DOWN, SHIVERED IN THE FREEZING BLAST"

"THE PONIES WERE SURPRISING IN THEIR ABILITY TO CLIMB AND GET OVER ROUGH ICE"

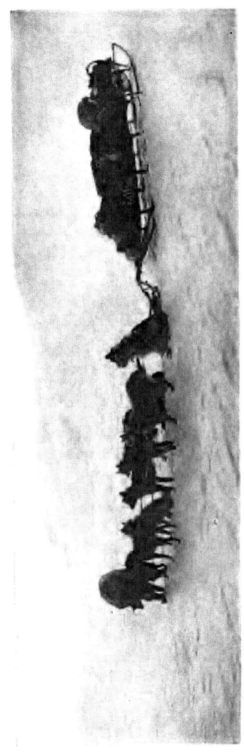

CAPE HABERMAN

"We found a place to descend on the east shore, between Capes Rath and Haberman"

"WE FORMED A HAPPY CAMP CIRCLE"

north about one and a half miles over very bad ice, until progress was barred by a partially frozen lead over which the ponies could not travel. The ice seemed to be of very recent formation and was in slight motion, a mass of jagged, broken pieces on end, covered with salt crystals and almost bare of snow. It was difficult to discover sufficient snow for a halting place where our numerous animals might find the means of quenching their thirst I was obliged to keep from six to eight men in the advance with picks and axes to clear a path for the party. The dogs were in splendid condition and the ponies were surprising in their ability to climb and get over rough ice. At no time was it necessary to extricate a pony from a hole in the ice There was a man to drive each dog team, and in get- . ting over the worst places two, three, and, sometimes four men were necessary to one sledge Four men took care of the seven pony sledges, the ponies exerting their strength when most needed. The greatest difficulty was caused by the continual capsizing of the unattended sledges, the ponies dragging them (in their frantic efforts to keep up with the column) until the sledges were solidly wedged in ice, requiring the united efforts of their drivers and others to extricate them.

That day's experience convinced me that the ponies were valuable auxiliaries to Arctic work, but that the sledges would have to be built with five or more runners around a central load, with swivel bar in front, the loads to be placed inside the sledges from the rear. The ponies would then hardly require attendance. They did not need urging like the dogs, on the contrary, they exerted their utmost to keep up with the column.

As the sun was sinking and the temperature falling I decided to halt at the lead until the semi-frozen mass should become solid. Should it not be possible to advance the ponies I resolved to continue the march with the dogs, the sledge loads having been arranged to provide for that contingency. On inspection of the column during the halt I found that the sledges were in a deplorable condition. Bows were smashed, top-rails broken, and the front curves of the runners splintered and divided in two. Practically, all the injuries were in the forward ends of the sledges for, unfortunately, they had been loaded too heavily in the forward ends.

With the sad realisation that there was not even the possibility of breaking the record under the conditions, and wishing to save the equipment, for another assault I gave orders to return. It was too late to think of making another march north that year. I could only plan for another winter in the Arctic and another sledge journey toward the Pole in the spring of 1905. I would have abundant opportunity to strengthen the dog sledges and to build new pony sledges after a model described before.

To my men the set-back should prove a valuable experience—a help in future work. It was the test through which all who had the real fibre of the explorer would pass triumphant to belief in and effort toward ultimate success. I felt that the true American spirit would answer the check with the words of John Paul Jones—"*I have not begun to fight yet!*"

Previous to beginning the second march north I had arranged for Mr. Porter to conduct one of the sup-

Asst. Eng. A. Vedoe   Steward Spencer   Asst. Scientist Porter

"WE REACHED CAPE AUK AT MIDNIGHT"—APRIL 24, 1904

Rounding the cape on the fast ice and approaching Teplitz Bay

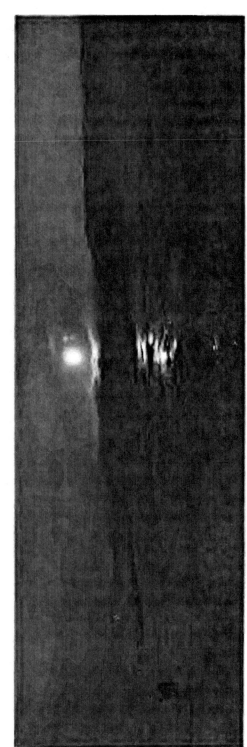

THE EVENING SUN OVER THE RUDOLF ISLAND GLACIER

THE RETREAT OF 1904

"TEPLITZ BAY WAS FROZEN OVER WITH A NEW SHEET OF THIN SALT ICE"

Sledge column leaving Camp Abruzzi, April 30, 1904

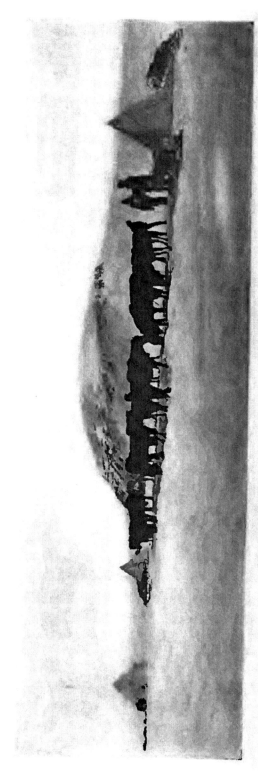

OUR FIRST CAMP ON THE RETREAT OF 1904

porting parties back to camp and on his return to Camp Abruzzi to head a small party south on an exploring and mapping expedition in the direction of Cape Flora. Before our return to Cape Fligely, from which point we had but lately made our second attempt north, he had asked leave to attempt a passage toward White Land in company with Assistant Engineer Anton Vedoe. I was pleased at his request and gave him the required permission but told him if the ice did not improve to go south toward Kane Lodge, to visit the boat cache at the southern entrance of Collinson's channel, and, if time allowed, to return by the way of Cape Hugh Mill examining ice conditions toward the British Channel and bringing a full report of what he discovered. This I thought would be of value to me in preparing for the retreat of a party to Cape Flora. I said I would expect him at Camp Abruzzi by April 20th, or at the latest by April 30th, 1904. Porter's sledge was one of the few that had escaped injury, and as it was already loaded with supplies for two men for thirty days and one dog team for twenty-five days it was only necessary to provide dog food for Vedoe's team from the sledges in the column

We said "auf wiedersehen" to the adventurers out on the ice and struck tents for the march back to Cape Fligely. We returned to land over our outward bound trail climbing the glacier slope and camping on the summit of the cape. The slope was steep and it was midnight before the last sledge reached the top. On the following morning the sledge loads were rearranged and one loaded sledge with broken runners was left at Cape Fligely to be sent for later. Camp Abruzzi, the home site, was reached at six P. M. March the 27th, from which place but two days before we had begun a march which I hoped would advance America's prestige in the field of exploration.

The returning column travelled against a cold, drifting wind that increased in violence through the afternoon and made the trip one to be remembered. It soon destroyed the trail we had made on our outward journey, but we could see the sun, a very indistinct disk, shining at times through a shower of cold snow particles that cut our faces like a sand blast, and it served as a guiding light. The red signal flags that had been placed on the glacier to mark the trail were spots of joy that afternoon, for they indicated to us that we were travelling in the right direction. Before evening we arrived at Camp Abruzzi filled with the pain of a second failure, the only balm the thought of the future and the hope that through the bitter lesson just experienced Victory might yet be wrested from Defeat.

After the failure of the second sledge journey many of the men lost interest in the northern campaign and openly expressed their deep felt desire to go home. I called for volunteers to stay with me for another attempt in 1905. Quite a large party offered at first, but as the time of leaving drew near a number weakened and the little band of true explorers grew smaller and smaller.

I now set about preparations for a sledge journey to Cape Flora where the Relief Ship was expected to arrive in July or August of that year—1904.

There were two routes by which Cape Flora might be reached. The shorter one led across the glacier to

THE RETREAT OF 1884

The sledge column leaving Cape McClintock

"WE CAMPED NEAR CAPE FISHER, THE BOLDEST HEADLAND ON THE COAST." CAPE FISHER TO THE NORTH

THE HALT AT CAPE FISHER—APPROACHING CAPE FISHER FROM THE NORTH—3 A. M. MAY 6, 1904

the east of Cape Brorak, where I believed a descent could be made to channel ice, thence down between Alexander and Rainer islands through the channel to the east of Jackson Island and around Cape McClintock to the British Channel, down which we might make our way to Cape Flora. The other route was by way of Kane Lodge, Collinson's Fjord, and Camp Ziegler, through Young Sound or along the ice foot to the south of Hooker Island to Cape Barentz and then west to Cape Flora. This route was considerably longer and the first was to be preferred if the British Channel was closed. I was daily expecting Porter and Vedoe with information of the condition of the channel.

On April 19th I placed Dr. Vaughn in charge of a party with instructions to go to Coburg Island, upon which food had been cached by the Baldwin-Ziegler Expedition in 1902, and to place there a cache of pony forage for the use of the party going south Signal poles were furnished and he was instructed to mark a safe trail across the glacier and to bring me information about the condition of ice south of Rudolph Island and also to look for signs of Porter and Vedoe

The party returned three days later, Dr Vaughn reporting that they had been to the summit of Cape Auk but, having found a descent from the glacier impossible, had abandoned further progress toward Coburg Island. The Doctor added that while they were encamped on the glacier a storm arose and the corner of their tent was ripped by the violence of the wind.

And so they came back.

Disappointed at the failure of the party and anxious for news of Porter and Vedoe, confronted also with the

necessity of finding a safe route across the glacier
for the party soon to retreat south, early next morning, I sent Quartermaster Rilliet with John Vedoe (a
brother to Porter's companion) and Seaman Duffy
with two dog sledges and a boat, with instructions to
go to Cape Fligely and look for signs of the absent
ones, camping there if sea was open to render assistance with the boat.   At the same time I left camp
with a dog team and sledge accompanied by Steward
Spencer, who had been one of Dr. Vaughn's party,
and who expressed himself as very anxious to go with
me.

We climbed the glacier to its summit, finding a
place to descend on the east shore between capes Rath
and Habermann, and then set our faces down the
Newmeyer Channel toward Coburg Island.   The channel ice was fairly smooth and we hurried on only stopping for an hour at the western end of Hohenlohe Island
(the place where Payer, discoverer of the archipelago,
probably camped in 1876) for the refreshment of a
cup of tea.   We reached Coburg Islet (the most northern of the Coburg islands) at 10.15 P. M., and there we
put up our tent.   After a meal we turned into our sleeping bags, tired after a thirteen-hour march.   The loud
barking of the dogs awakened us at five o'clock next
morning.   Under the impression that a bear must be
approaching, I hastily reached for my rifle and started
to crawl out of my sleeping bag—when Mr. Porter
put his face through the flap of our tent and wished us
good morning!   Mr. Vedoe appeared a few minutes
later. It was a very happy reunion and to me one of
the most pleasant experiences of the expedition.   There

was no more sleep for us that morning We formed a happy camp circle breakfasting together, while Porter and Vedoe recited the incidents of their travels since they had parted from us out on the Polar Ocean north of Rudolph Island. They had found the frozen sea very rough while attempting to go toward White Land. It would have taken longer than their supplies would allow, so they went south, as I had directed, toward Kane Lodge on Greely Island, returning by the way of Cape Hugh Mill and Coburg Island. They had camped the night before at Houen Island and were marching to Rudolph Island when they spied our little tent. Mr Porter gave an interesting report of condition of caches and ice in the channels While we were talking together the sharp angry bark of our dogs denoted the approach of a bear. Pulling out their stake chains, Vedoe's team made off over the ice after the bear, while the other dogs tugged and pulled, and whined and howled in their desire to join in the fun. The bear started to retreat as soon as he saw his pursuers. But they soon caught up with him and engaged him at close range. The dogs, chained together, were at a disadvantage. Fearing for their safety Vedoe dispatched the bear. As it was, one of the best of the team came back from the fight with a piece of skin hanging from a cut in his side, where it had been ripped by the bear's claws It called for a surgical operation on the part of his owner, and Vedoe sewed the raw flesh together disregarding the yelps of pain, stating, when it was finished, that his dog was " as good as new."

Latitude sights were taken at noon. Afterward,

remembering that it was the Lord's Day, I read to my
comrades the 107th Psalm.   At one P. M. we folded
our tents and directed our way toward Rudolph Island,
reaching Cape Auk at midnight.   We rounded Cape
Brorak by cutting our way through the rough pressure
ice piled on the southwestern coast of Rudolph Island
as far as Cape Auk.   We came that way as I was anxious to ascertain if it was possible to reach Camp Abruzzi by the way of Cape Auk.   We approached to
within sight of the camp, but could not ascend the
west slope of the glacier at the Cape as the snow had
melted off and it was a shining surface of slippery glare
ice.   We ascended several hundred feet with the assistance of our ice axes, and, from that point, Teplitz
Bay beneath us seemed black with the dark waters of
an iceless sea.   It was necessary to return to the southern slope where we ascended to a point of rocks and
encamped at 1.30 A. M., April 25th.   It was stormy
all of the 25th, but at midnight the wind lost some of
its force and we broke camp and climbed the southern
slope of the glacier to the summit of Cape Auk, reaching the top a little after 4 o'clock in the morning, the
steepness of the ascent making it necessary to hitch
two teams of dogs at a time to a sledge.   The wind
calmed as we mounted the summit, over a thousand
feet high, and in a mist which rendered sight ahead
difficult we crossed the glacier and descended toward
Camp Abruzzi, reaching that point at 6.10 A. M.

CHAPTER XIII

HOME LONGINGS

I FOUND, on my arrival at camp, that the Cape Fligely party had returned in safety and that in my absence Teplitz Bay had frozen over sufficiently to bear the weight of men, animals, and sledges, and so the high glacier need not be crossed when the retreating party went south. The time was now drawing near when the homeseekers were to start for Cape Flora to meet the long desired Relief Ship. The zest with which they packed their kits and discussed the prospect of mingling in the great world once more, had its enticing effect upon the weak and undecided. The politicians in the retreating body used their influence and persuasiveness to enlarge their own party— until those to whom "Northward!" had become a shibboleth, became, like Gideon's band, fewer and fewer.

Unfortunately, I was obliged to lead the retreating party to Cape Flora in person, returning to Camp Abruzzi before winter; a plan that had the effect of increasing the number of those who were anxious to march south, and leave the field of exploration. I did not wish any one to remain on Rudolph Island to await my return—and march north with me the following year—unless he was anxious to stay, and I gave orders for all who wished to go to Cape Flora and await the Relief Ship for home to prepare for the march south.

Each member of the retreating party was allowed forty-two pounds of personal baggage, the same to consist of thirty-five pounds of clothing and a pair of sea boots weighing seven pounds, sufficient clothing to provide for a stay at Cape Flora should the Relief Ship be unsuccessful in reaching the station. Each man was also allowed a sleeping bag and blanket, the limit of weight being twenty-five pounds for both, and members of the Field Department and Officers of the ship's company were furnished either a rifle or shot gun and ammunition. Nine silk tents were taken for the accomodation of the party. Food for thirty-eight days on the march was provided for men and beasts, and was to be hauled on sixteen pony sledges, the ponies to be used as dog food as their loads disappeared. Two months' food for use of the party at Cape Flora in addition to the thirty-eight days' rations was carried on eight dog sledges with the camping equipment and personal baggage of the party. In addition to full rations for three and a third months for the men, an extra load of 240 pounds of pemmican was distributed on the sledges in the column. When packed, the loads on the pony sledges averaged from 620 to 700 pounds, those on the dog sledges from 546 to 628 pounds including the weights of the sledges. In addition to seven dog teams that were chained up awaiting my return to Camp Abruzzi I wished to reserve some of the best ponies for use on the sledge trip north in 1905. Dr. Newcomb, the Veterinarian, had reported glanders among the ponies from time to time and had been obliged to shoot five of them. On the eve of departure, he notified me that it would be best to send all the ponies south as there were indications of the spread of the disease, which might menace the lives of the men So I was obliged to order all the ponies hitched up to drag the sledges south, and all I could depend upon for success in 1905 were the few dog teams reserved to remain behind. It is true that there was the alternative of keeping all the dog teams at Camp Abruzzi, the men who were leaving hauling extra loads, but there was the possibility of the non-arrival of the Relief Ship and the need of clothing and equipment for a winter at Cape Flora—which necessitated loads too heavy for the men to haul.

After arriving at Cape Flora I intended to return with a few men in the fall to my Northern Station, Relief Ship or no Relief Ship. But it would be almost impossible for that large party to make the return trip to Camp Abruzzi after the good sledging of early spring was over. So when the men left Teplitz Bay it was for good and meant the loss of service to the expedition of nearly all of them, and they could not be considered in any other light than as a care and source of anxiety to the leader until they were aboard the Relief Ship.

ZIEGLER POLAR EXPEDITION
CAMP "ABRUZZI," TEPLITZ BAY, O P. R I.

April 30th, 1904.

TO THE MEMBERS OF THE ZIEGLER POLAR EXPEDITION

During my absence from Camp "Abruzzi" Mr Wm J Peters, representing me as Commanding Officer, will be in command of Expedition party and in charge of all Expedition property at this point

Members of the Expedition at Camp "Abruzzi" will observe any rules Mr. Peters may make for the government of party.

Let no question of who shall be this or that distract your attention. Remember that he that serves most is he that deserves most, and that the poorer man he is and the further removed from a gentlemen the more he expects—the louder his expressed self-conceit.

I appreciate the spirit of loyalty that prompts you to stay and I realise that you know the hard work that will be necessary before we can go home with honour.

Be particular in regard to care of the dogs and in moving stock, sledges, boats, etc. No boat of any character is to be taken from camp without permission of Mr. Peters or the man he may appoint to command should he leave before my return, and no one is to leave camp without permission.

Members of the Expedition advance post! You are to help the cause of the Expedition in the future by habits of carefulness in the present, and a gentlemanly, considerate conduct toward each other that will make your stay at this northern latitude a happy and successful one.

Necessity takes me south, but my thoughts will be up here and at the first possible opportunity I intend to return. As the party is a small one each member is particularly valuable and sickness of one or two would be extra work for the others, so be particularly careful in regard to health and take no unnecessary risks.

Ammunition should not be wasted and bears should not be shot away from camp.

Should Mr. Peters leave camp before my return, the member that he will place in command will be responsible to me for conduct of affairs at camp and members will recognise him as representing the Commanding Officer in his absence.

With deep felt desire that a good Providence will bring a new reign of peace and prosperity over the affairs of the Expedition, I am

Yours truly,

ANTHONY FIALA,
Commanding.

ZIEGLER POLAR EXPEDITION
CAMP "ABRUZZI" CROWN PRINCE RUDOLF ISLAND

April 30, 1904.

MR. WM. J. PETERS, Chief Scientist.

Dear Sir:

In leaving camp, you as my representative will be in complete charge of party and equipment at Camp "Abruzzi," and I will leave to your judgment the management of affairs. Mr. R. W. Porter, Mr. Chas. E. Rilliet, and Mr. Anton Vedoe are to leave in about ten days on an exploring and surveying trip and before their departure Mr. Rilliet will assist you in taking care of equipment and rearranging quarters, matters that we have discussed together. As understood you are to leave Camp "Abruzzi" with Mr. R. R. Tafel, Mr. J. Vedoe, and Steward Spencer for Cape Flora toward the end of July, 1904 with the Indian canoe, tent, and two sledges and teams. There is a small sledge at Cape Auk, and another could be constructed so that the whole party could occupy the Indian canoe if necessary to cross open water. Mr. Porter will give you a list of caches on the way down.

Before leaving you will place the man who in your judgment is most able and loyal in charge of camp, giving him written instructions.

Should Relief Ship appear early I shall attempt to return before you leave.

I am anxious that the men should not leave camp without your permission and that they should take particular care of their health.

One Mannlicher rifle is to be kept in rack for general use and a Henry or Remington, and men are to be cautioned about use of ammunition. No one must be allowed to take boat from camp without your permission or to cross ice crack after bears.

Allow me to express to you before leaving my deep feeling of appreciation of your valued assistance and loyal help through the trying times of the last ten months.

Yours respectfully,

ANTHONY FIALA,
Commanding.

ZIEGLER POLAR EXPEDITION
CAMP "ABRUZZI," CROWN PRINCE RUDOLF ISLAND
April 30, 1904.

MR. RUSSELL W. PORTER, Artist and Asst. Scientist.

Dear Sir:—

In approval of your report on sledge journey from which you and Mr. A. Vedoe have just returned it gives me much pleasure to compliment you on the excellent work done and on the conscientious and able manner in which you have carried out my instructions, and the good condition in which the entire equipment returned to Camp Abruzzi. I am pleased to know of the good work done by your companion Mr. A. Vedoe.

As already discussed between us, you are to leave in a week or ten days on a sledge trip for the purpose of exploration and survey, to report at Cape Flora by July 15th, 1904.

You will be accompanied by Quartermaster Chas. E. Rilliet and Mr. A. Vedoe, and be equipped with two sledges, two kayaks, and two teams of dogs, with camp equipment and provisions as already provided for. The details of the work we have already talked over several times and you know of my desire for more definite knowledge of Graham Bell Land, and of the unexplored country in Zichy Land.

In compliance with an expressed wish of Mr. William Ziegler you will simply letter or number newly discovered islands or lands.

Wishing you Godspeed, I am

Respectfully yours,

ANTHONY FIALA,
Commanding.

CHAPTER XIV

THE RETREAT SOUTH TO CAPE FLORA

ON THE evening of April 30th, after the column was formed on the snow in front of our quarters, I called together the little band who were to stay at the Northern Station, and told them that I would return in the summer or fall, and that I would bring with me letters from home expected on the Relief Ship that year—and possibly new men and dogs. We shook hands all around, and then I gave the signal to start our backward march. At 7.45 P. M. we left, a party of twenty-five men, sixteen pony sledges, and eight dog teams and sledges. Teplitz Bay was frozen over with a new sheet of thin salt ice upon which the sledge runners dragged hard. We found the ice around Cape Auk piled up in confused masses of great blocks and we had considerable difficulty in helping the ponies and dogs up a steep slope of ice on to the rough surface of the heavy floe. Little "Rabbit," a pony veteran of the Baldwin trip, created laughter and surprise by hauling his heavy load up the steep grade and walking over all sorts of obstacles alone and seemingly without much effort, leaving his driver some distance behind. From Cape Auk to Cape Brorak we found the ice in ridges and broken floes through which we forced our way all night only halting for an hour at 1.30 in the morning when the cook

99

and myself prepared tea for the troop of thirsty men.
The ice grew better as we neared Cape Brorak where
the rough surface was drifted over with hard packed
snow.   I had hoped to make Coburg Island the first
march, but the hard work of rounding Cape Auk told on
some of the men, and about 5.30 A. M., on the smooth
channel ice, near a berg from which we could get ice
for fresh water, I ordered the column to halt and camp.
The sun was shining brilliantly, and the assemblage
of tents backed by the high, towering, basaltic slope
of Brorak made a very effective picture.   The long
picket line was stretched in the snow by Sergeant Moulton and two of the sailors, and then the little ponies
were taken out of their harness and picketed in a row
to the line and given a feed of hay.   In the meantime
the dog drivers unharnessed their noisy charges, and
made them secure for the hours of rest, the dogs
promptly starting to dig holes in the snow with their
paws, from which occupation they did not desist
until the odour of pemmican filled the air.   When the
yelps and fights which accompanied the evening meal
were over, and when even the most vigilant eye in the
pack could find not a morsel more, they crawled into
their holes and were soon asleep.

I chose the night to travel in for our course was
toward the south, and there was less possibility of
snow-blindness with the sun at our backs.   Though
the season was too far advanced for very cold weather,
and the thermometer in May very seldom dropped
lower than 20 degrees below zero, still the warmer rays
of the sun shining on our tents at the time of its greatest altitude conduced to sleep, and our numerous

animals luxuriated in the sunshine. A further advantage was in the fact that the surface of the snow was harder and afforded better going, when our luminary was low and in the north, during the time we arbitrarily termed night.

Little Jimmy, our English cabin boy, who could blow the bugle, and who sounded the "reveille" every morning, was often obliged to shake the ice out of his instrument, and warm the mouthpiece before placing it to his lips. As on our marches north, we found the cook tent to be a great convenience, and it meant besides economy in fuel, food, and weight. The tent was held up by a single pole and the walls stretched out by guy ropes made fast to pins pushed into the hard snow or tied to other sledges if the surface was too soft or too hard. On entering our canvas domicile, Cook Thwing and I took down our sleeping bags from where they had been placed on top of cookers and food and stowed them in a corner of the tent, and then, while Thwing went to some convenient berg or glacier face for ice, I lighted the cookers. They contained large Khotal burners, an American improvement on the Primus burner used by Doctor Nansen and the Duke of the Abruzzi. They worked very well—giving a large hot flame on a small expenditure of oil—but had a tendency to get easily out of order, through poor construction of valves and oil containers. This necessitated careful manipulation and a supply of tools always within convenient reach. In very low temperatures the Primus is undoubtedly the best form of burner as it is the simplest and so light in weight that several can be carried against the possibility of one's

giving out.   For a large party the four and a half inch
Khotal burners were very effective, and many times
I halted the column after a four or five hours' march
and prepared hot coffee, and in one hour from halting
we were on the march again, each one of the twenty-
five men having received two cups of the steaming
beverage and all the water he wished to drink; quick
time when it is considered that all the water had to be
melted from ice at the temperature of the air.   The
regular meals of the day, of course, required more
time.   Daily, each man received a bread ration of one
pound of army bread and three pork and bean biscuits.
Once in seven days the Commissary distributed to
each man the weekly ration of a pound can of condensed milk, twenty-one ounces of sugar, and one
pound of butter.   Sweet chocolate was also furnished,
about three ounces a day per man.   The ration used
was the same as that put up for the sledge march
north, and the packages prepared during the winter
for use on the floating ice fields served excellently in
the retreat south.   About fourteen ounces of meat
a day were allowed each man.   Pemmican constituted
the larger proportion of our meat allowance, but
corned beef, Mortedello sausage, beef tongue, smoked
beef, and Vienna sausage helped to add variety to
the menu.   A daily allowance of three and a half
ounces of either the U. S. Army Emergency Ration of
cracked wheat and beef, or Erbswurst (peameal)—
to be alternated with the Blue and Red Bovril Rations
of beef and potatoes and peameal—was carried, besides
cornmeal and oatmeal.   Two meals were cooked each
day in addition to the coffee prepared at the mid-

night halts. One was distributed to the men immediately after the sounding of the "reveille" before the
march, the other after the tents were pitched for the
hours of rest. The menu consisted of coffee or tea,
bread, butter, cold meats, and a stew. It was upon
this stew that the Cook and I bent our energies in the
hope of producing something appetising and new each
day. The Erbswurst stew seemed to be a favourite
with the party, and when filled with little pieces of
Vienna sausage and seasoned with onions it was a
pleasure to hear the comments of approbation wafted
through our canvas walls from the other tents.
Bovril beef and potatoes was also liked, and several
times we took the pork and bean biscuits, baked by
our industrious Steward during the winter, and made
a stew from them. Mixed with a little Erbswurst it
was thought to be delicious. The pemmican stew
that was so relished in all our sledge journeys in very
low temperatures was not in favour on the retreat,
particularly when the summer drew on and the temperature gradually rose toward the zero point. Besides the cook tent there were eight small pyramidal
tents of pongee silk. When a meal was ready one
man from each tent came to the Cook with a mess tin
for the share of food allowed his tent, his comrades
meanwhile turning into their sleeping bags. On his
return, sitting in the pleasant warmth of the bag of
deerskin, they partook of the hot food, and smoked
their pipes of peace. Nothing so delights a sailor's
heart, as a smoke after a warm meal, and a chance to
swap stories with his mates before he falls off at last
into restful sleep.

From Cape Brorak we marched toward the eastern end of Alexander Island, stopping at Coburg Island for a hot drink. The cache of pemmican left there by Baldwin in 1902 was found to be in good condition, though there were indications that Polar bears had visited the place. I wished to add some pemmican and sugar to the loads at this point, but could not find a man in the column whose sledge load seemed light enough to justify it. At our second camp near the glacier face of Alexander Island, we killed our first pony for dog food. "Rabbit," who had done so much hard work in 1902, had swollen legs and was condemned to be shot. From the second camp our course was changed to southwest and we made our way through a fog travelling in this new country by compass.

When the sun broke through the clouds we found that our course was correct and before long we entered the Italian Channel. a short cut to Cecil Rhodes Fjord.

In this march to Cape Flora over the frozen channels of the Archipelago, a distance of about 160 miles, we were favoured with good weather generally, and many long stretches of smooth ice and hard packed snow where the men had only to walk beside their sledges. I was quite pleased with the progress we made as the days went by, though our rate of marching was of necessity slow, being always determined by the speed of the slowest man in the column, There were many places where the ponies could have been put to a trot, but some of the men would then have been obliged to ride on the sledges and that was never permitted save in cases of sickness or emergency, for the loads were

heavy enough without adding the weight of a man
We arrived at Cape McClintock, the northwest extremity of Salisbury Island, just before midnight of
May 5th.   There had been some complaint in regard
to the weight of the loads, and to lighten the sledges
I cached 240 pounds of pemmican at the Cape, near
a great needle of basalt that would always stand out
as a prominent landmark, the cache to serve as a depot
in future sledge operations.

We were glad to find the British Channel solidly
frozen, with a comparatively smooth ice, and no dark
clouds on the horizon indicative of water holes.   In
the channel we were assailed at times by rather cold
winds of which I was always glad, as the column would
then travel much faster. On those days the halts were
few in number, and the distance covered greater.   We
camped at Cape Fisher, the boldest headland on the
coast, and then pitched our tents at Cape Richtofen,
from where, on the 8th of May, we reached Point
Arthur, the northern end of Koettlitz Island, where
we camped   And then our troubles began! Our
progress was obstructed by rough ice jammed in between Cape Murray and Prince George Island and
Koettlitz Island. We had been favoured with comparatively smooth road up to that point   The wider
part of the channel, opening at its northern end into
the Victoria Sea, had undoubtedly, been cleared of its
broken ice in the fall by the many southeast winds
and then frozen over evenly during the winter   The
same winds that opened the upper waters forced the ice
in the lower channel, in a great jam of broken cakes,
into the narrow space we were about to enter   After

supper on May 8th I climbed the cliff of Koettlitz
Island and walked down toward its southern end,
reaching the place of its greatest height. It had been
foggy but just as I reached the elevation the sun broke
through the clouds and illuminated the channel, showing me the ice in inconceivable roughness piled against
the western shore of Koettlitz Island, with just a
short streak (about a mile) of smooth ice inshore in a
little bay. It was fortunate I could see the great
towering ridges that closed the southern end of the bay
and surrrounded it to the west—a veritable "cul de
sac"—for it saved me from leading the column into
a place from which there was no escape, except by
retracing our steps.

Farther out toward the centre of the channel the
ice was in smaller cakes. There were no high pressure ridges, but instead a confusion of rough ice,
mingled with thin smooth streaks. A large tabular
iceberg, that bore W. S. W. by compass, marked a
seemingly smooth course to the south, a swathe that
it had probably cut in its drift north, and I resolved
that our next march would be to the south of that iceberg. Just as I got its bearing the fog descended and
nothing was visible but the smooth streak inshore
and the circle of rough ice to the west through which
we would have to force our way toward the channel's
centre.

I went on my long walk back to the camp, and as
I reached the overshadowing bluff, I stopped to gaze
at the picturesque grouping of tents containing my
sleeping comrades, the little black spots—each spot a
sleeping dog—and the long line of ponies their heads

dropped in slumber. I met the Captain and Mate who had just climbed the hill, and were looking anxiously toward the channel whose broken fields of ice were so rapidly disappearing under a thick veil of fog that hardly anything remained visible but the deceptive streak of bay ice inshore.

The following day I led the party toward the channel centre. Though rough going it was considerably better ice than I expected. We camped south of the berg I had sighted the day before. Some of the wise ones in the column wondered in grieved tones why we did not take the smooth strip that they had seen from the camp before we started, while others, troubled by the roughness of the ice, became critical of the route chosen. I had come to realise that much of the criticism emanated from fatigue and empty stomachs. Judgments were more just after a rest and a good meal. Contrary to the generally accepted theory regarding a sailor on foot, the members of the crew of the lost *America* proved particularly good travellers, and were cheerful and helpful during the entire march. Seaman Montrose accompanied me in the lead through the rough ice, and with an axe helped me clear a track for the caravan. Sergt. Moulton, who had the leading pony sledge, was also always ready with his axe to clear a way. I found that the ice was broken in somewhat regular lines extending from the southeast to the northwest, and that cutting through the ridges directly at right angles to the breaking line, was the shortest way of crossing these rough places.

We usually were able to go quite a distance southeast down the line of lifted ice cakes between ridges until we would run into a V formed by a junction with another ridge, which necessitated another cut at right angles. So our trail took the form of the teeth of a gigantic saw, but led us on slowly but surely toward our destination. Fog added its depressing influence and delayed us some, and, inopportunely, just before we entered the worst ice, one of our ponies died from exhaustion, and his load had to be distributed among the other sledges. The dogs were not in immediate need of a meal, having been fed the evening before, and we could not afford to drag the extra weight. So we left his carcass behind us as food for the Polar bears that once in a while we sighted in our rear. The bears, however, came into camp when we reached Cape Flora later on, and we killed and ate them, and so our faithful pony undoubtedly returned to us.

THE CAMP AT CAPE ROOSEVELT—MAY 4, 1904

"ONE OF OUR PONIES DIED FROM EXHAUSTION AND HIS LOAD HAD TO BE DISTRIBUTED
AMONG THE OTHER SLEDGES"

CAPE FLORA

The arrival at Cape Flora, May 16, 1904—Putting up the tents and unharnessing ponies and dogs

THE LAST OF OUR FAITHFUL PONIES

CHAPTER XV

CAMP JACKSON

AT NINE o'clock on the morning of May 16th, sixteen days after leaving Teplitz Bay, we rounded
the sea front of Cape Flora, and ascended the height
of land upon which were situated the houses of the
Jackson-Harmsworth Expedition of 1894–97. As we
reached the top of the raised beach all eyes were turned
south in hope of beholding an open ocean. But disappointment was ours. A vast sheet of glistening
white, the Barentz Sea, from horizon to horizon, lay
silent and dead in the grasp of the Ice King. The
column reached its destination in splendid condition,
men and animals and stores. The twenty-five members of the party were in excellent health, and the dogs
and ponies vied with each other in hauling the sledges
up the slope to the camp site we were to occupy.
Three of the ponies had been shot for dog food on the
march and one died from exhaustion, leaving twelve
in harness. There were sixty-four dogs in the eight
teams, and twenty sledges with their loads.

Our tents were raised on the historic snow-covered
rocks of Cape Flora where Jackson spent three years
with his comrades, and where his dramatic meeting
with Doctor Nansen took place; where Leigh Smith
and twenty-five men passed a winter existing on walruses
and Polar bears, and where the Duke of the Abruzzi

109

had stored eight months' provisions for twenty men—stores of incalculable value to us, as was proved later.

Our arrival at Cape Flora was marked by an event, which to me was one of the saddest of the two years. The ponies which had served us so faithfully for many months and, as their last hard task, had dragged down from Teplitz Bay the heavily loaded sledges, were reported to be infected with glanders and condemned to be shot.

In my plans for the future I had arranged to embark all the dogs and about six of the best ponies on the Relief Ship, when she arrived, and, with a few of the old party and some volunteers from the newcomers, have Mr. Champ, whom I expected to be in charge of the Relief, land us at Camp Ziegler, from where, just as soon as the channels froze over, we would make a rapid march to Camp Abruzzi. I thought it more than probable that the ship could make the trip, for Cape Flora was isolated from the rest of the Archipelago by water ways that often remained open all fall and winter and according to observations made by Jackson in the spring as well. The Relief Ship could then return to Cape Flora, take on the large party there, and steam home.

When I asked Veterinarian Newcomb to choose out four of the ponies in best condition, he told me that all were infected with glanders and farcy except two, one a balking, badly broken pony we had named "Happy Hooligan"; the other, the slowest moving animal in the column. This equine had been dubbed "Windy" in honour of one of the doctors of the party, who had received that sobriquet because of his ever ready and overflowing fountain of speech. After the Veterinarian's verdict, all the ponies save the two just mentioned were led off to the slaughter. "Happy" and "Windy" throve and grew sleek and fat on the vegetation found underneath the snow and on the wind swept flats at Cape Flora. The dead ponies served as food for our hungry dogs.

The Relief Ship was expected to arrive in July or early August, a long wait, to provide for which, we had on our sledges over two months' food supply for the twenty-five men, in addition to about four hundred pounds of sledge rations and several hundred pounds of pemmican that had been brought along as dog food, but which would serve admirably for the men in case of need. In addition to the supplies we had brought with us, were the great cache placed there by the Duke of the Abruzzi and the food supplies left by Jackson and the Andrée Relief Expedition.

As there is nothing certain above the ice line in the Arctic, it was necessary to extend our preparations at once to provide for a stay through the winter should the Relief Ship not arrive. The officers and crew of the lost *America* therefore laboured industriously to remove from their icy envelopes the barrels and cases of food deposited by other explorers. The larger proportion of the food thus obtained was secured from the cache of the Italian Duke. A quantity of good bread, meat, coffee, tea, etc., was found which had been left by Jackson while the smaller cache of food of the Andrée Relief Expedition provided us with sugar, coffee, butter, medicines, and clothing. The Duke's stores were found packed in a ten-sided portable house. This place was cleared of its stores and the eight members of the Field Department were quartered there.

An abandoned cooking range was found out in the snow and repaired, Fireman Hovlick manufacturing a stove pipe from old petroleum tanks, doing this work on an anvil improvised from a packing case and an iron grate bar. After the food stores had all been tallied they were placed in the building that was originally the stable used by Jackson for his ponies.

"Elmwood," Jackson's house, which he had thought crowded with his party of eight, was cleared of its accumulations of years and in it bunks were built to accomodate seventeen men.

By May 24th, the entire party was housed and the tents were taken down and stored away.

In the early days of June, thousands of gulls, loons, and guillemots came in from the south and the high rocks of the cape resounded with ceaseless chatter of innumerable birds. The sun circled above our horizon day and night, melting the great snow drifts and exposing the rocks. Beautiful little Arctic poppies lifted their white and gold cups to the King of the Sky, and green mosses and coloured lichens gave relief to the eye after the constant glare of snow and ice.

Next to the absorbing occupation of scanning the horizon for signs of the Relief Ship—was the anxious watch for Polar bears which constituted the major part of our supply of fresh meat. Hunting these creatures was the most exciting sport at Cape Flora, or "Camp Jackson," as it was named. The sailors in "Elmwood" vied with the Field Department in the roundhouse (Little Italy, they named it) in the hunt for Ursus Polaris. The man who first sighted the bear was privileged to track the game assisted by his comrades, and this rule was generally observed Sometimes a bear was sighted on the ice off shore by the men of both houses at the same time and this usually resulted in a race, a hunting party from each house setting out. The one to first cross the tide crack below camp, and set foot on the sea ice had the honour of chasing the bear. From that moment the hunt was a question of legs, for the Polar bear is an arrant coward and generally makes off at the least indication of danger. Exceeding in intensity the hunting fever displayed by the men was the wild excitement among the dogs on the advent of a bear. Their sense of vision was not keen enough to sight game that was as far as a mile off shore, but they seemed to read the actions of the men, and when a party left the camp with guns every individual canine would appear yelping with delight and running as if mad in the thirst for blood. Out on the ice they would spread, like a battalion of skirmishers in advance of the hunters. The height of the ice blocks and the dogs' low stature prevented them from seeing their prey at a distance, and they would extend their line in every direction in an aimless search for the bear. At last one would sight him from the top of an ice cake, and with a sharp bark, and like a projectile from a gun, he would fly on the track of the retreating beast, every dog in the pack within hearing of that signal, running and leaping with new vigour over the rough ice, several of the wise ones making flank movements to get around in front of the enemy. Before long the pack surrounded him, their united yelps indicating the place and progress of the fight, the bear answering the cry of the pack with low heavy growls of anger and moans of fear. What must the Monarch of the Ice have thought of these strange creatures, who showed no fear of him, who evaded his sharp claws and teeth so easily, and had the temerity to attack his sacred person! While he chased five dogs, ten of them would crowd his rear and draw blood. With a frightful roar he would wheel to crush them, but presto! they had jumped back, and he faced a circle of open jaws. At last, in desperation, with powerful leaps, he would make for the open sea and safety. But these new enemies— they were neither seal nor walrus, they could outrun him, and sink their wicked fangs into his muscles and make him stop to fight for his life. Just as he was exhausted after his long effort, and at bay within the ever narrowing circle of his pursuers, a new enemy draws near, the sight of whom is Fear itself, and Death. With one supreme effort he frees himself from the imprisoning teeth and makes a dash for liberty. A flash and a roar—a torturing pain—a world gone red! Of what avail his long, hard fight? Victory is on the side of the heaviest artillery!

During the summer our party secured seventeen bears, and we luxuriated in bear steaks fried in butter. Most of the men enjoyed the meat which was not unlike beef when carefully prepared by cutting away all fat before frying. The fat gave the meat a rancid taste.

In the nesting time of the gulls and loons, several

of the sailors went up the talus daily dragging with them a long ladder that they had constructed and, at the risk of their lives, clambered up the precipitous side of the great rock and robbed the nests. Many of the eggs were fresh and when fried with the ham we had found in the Duke's cache gave us a breakfast not to be despised.

Eight brant and several hundred loons were shot and added to our larder, and sixteen great walruses and about the same number of seals. Walrus liver was considered a delicacy but the meat proper was rather tough and made one think he was dining on automobile tires.

Two men who had elected to remain at Camp Abruzzi, surprised us by their arrival at Cape Flora, on the evening of July 5th. They made no secret of the fact that they had grown discouraged with the outlook. Annexing themselves to Mr. Porter's exploring party they accompanied it as far as the northern extremity of Northbrook Island. When Porter stopped there to make observations, they proceeded to "Elmwood." Porter and his party joined us two days later. He had run a traverse and mapped the islands from Camp Abruzzi down to Cape Flora by the way of Kane Lodge and Camp Ziegler, and, in compliance with my instructions, had attempted to enter the unknown country named by Payer, Zichy Land, but in this he was unsuccessful.

He reported the fact that his party had shot a number of ptarmigan, interesting as the first recorded appearance of these birds in the Archipelago.

CHAPTER XVI

THE VAIN WAIT FOR THE RELIEF SHIP

THE days of waiting palled. It was now mid-summer and as yet there was no sign of the vessel that was to carry the homesick sojourners back to their native land. The men spent many anxious hours straining their eyes to glimpse a sail and often we were called out of our huts by a cry—"the ship! the ship!" But it was invariably a false alarm and the "ship" proved to be a distant iceberg with its shadow side turned toward us, or a column of vapour rising out of a water hole near the horizon giving the appearance of a steamer's smoke.

As late as the end of July, a closed sea stretched to meet the sky—a sullen sheet of rugged ice.

Thinking that there might be an open sea to the east beyond our view circle in which a ship could reach the land, and feeling the necessity for action, I made a sledge trip to Cape Barentz accompanied by Seaman Duffy. We carried a canoe lashed to our sledge in which we placed our tent and equipment. The high and numerous pressure ridges piled up against the glacier face of Northbrook Island obliged us to trend several miles seaward. The going there was better but we were troubled with open holes and moving ice cakes—and although, as the crow flies, Cape Barentz was barely twenty miles from Cape Flora, we did not

CAPE FLORA

"Elmwood" in early July, 1904.—No water visible seaward

THE COAL MINE AT CAPE FLORA, 300 FEET ABOVE THE LEVEL OF THE SEA

SIXTEEN WALRUSES WERE CAPTURED AT CAPE FLORA DURING THE SUMMER OF 1904

reach the former rocky promontory for two days. When we gained the summit of the cape we were disappointed to find nothing but ice off to the horizon, the only open water, the hole over which we had paddled our canoe to reach the shore. We erected a signal pole on the highest point and cached a message at its foot in a cairn of rocks. We turned our faces in the direction of Cape Flora with very little hope in our hearts that relief would reach us that year. The ice bound condition of the sea at that late date precluding the possibility of a ship's arrival.

When we were not engaged together in hauling the sledge out of a water hole or in helping the dogs drag it across a high ridge, I ran ahead to pick out a way and Duffy followed with the dogs and sledge often singing some popular song. His favourite was "My Sweetheart Lives in Tennessee." Near Cape Barentz we found a number of loons swimming in a water hole and with four shots from my Mannlicher carbine I knocked over nine of the birds, Duffy launching the canoe and picking them up, killing the wounded ones with his paddle. In attempting to cross a water lane, I leaped for what I took to be a cake of ice floating in its centre, intending to jump from that on to the solid ice beyond. It promptly let me through as it was only a mass of snow. The dogs, close behind, seeing my plight, jumped for what looked like a solid cake off to my right, and the whole team went in. The ice on each side of the lane was high and rounded off on the edges by the action of sun and water and I could not grasp its slippery surface. The dogs incumbered by their harness floundered around in danger of drowning.

Duffy made a flying leap and succeeded in getting upon solid ice. He helped me out and together we got the team on to the floe. Poor dogs! They had been in the water so much on the trip that we could not blame them for refusing to cross when we reached the next water hole, and we were obliged to drag them through the freezing sea. I will never forget how they trembled with fear, when we embarked on a small cake of ice—Duffy, myself, the sledge, and the team of dogs. It was a heavy load on a cranky craft with the sea awash, but we ferried across the lead in safety.

The dog food gave out on our return. Two bears crossed our path several days before, but we did not need the meat then, and our load was heavy enough for our little team.

Two dogs had followed us from camp running loose. It was one of these free rovers, Monkey by name, who came to our help in this hour of need. His keen eye sighted a bear and he immediately gave chase. One wee dog seemed but a good mouthful and bruin stopped to make a meal. But by this time Monkey had reinforcements—his late comrade and a man with a gun. When I came up Ursus Polaris was circling about in a water hole growling and hissing at the two dogs which prevented his getting out on the ice. He would draw himself half way out and drive at the dogs with his claws only to be forced back into the pool. A bullet from the Mannlicher ended the contest. A cold drizzle was falling and I felt for Duffy holding the team and waiting for me somewhere out on the ice. It was sometime later that together we trudged beside an empty sledge to where the dead bear lay. The team knew what was in store for them and pulled like mad. If the road had been smooth we could have sat upon the sledge and have enjoyed a ride. The bear was heavy and it was all we could do to haul him to the tent. While we were removing the pelt and cutting up the carcass two bears approached to within twenty yards of us and watched proceedings. Fortunately the team was chained or there would have been a chase pell mell over water holes and ridges.

I succeeded at last in driving the beasts away without harming them. Believing in the preservation of game, especially in a barren land where little food is I had early instructed the members of the expedition that, except in defence, no bear must be killed unless needed for food.

The temperature on the trip varied between twenty-six and 41 degrees Fahrenheit. Our clothing was soaked at times by rains, and we did not enjoy the luxury of a dry pair of stockings until our return to "Elmwood."

Pressure ridges were high, the pools of water many and treacherous, the snow deep and troublesome, but, notwithstanding, the trip was to me a sort of pleasure excursion. After the toil of the day we raised the tent and prepared our simple meal of pemmican stew and tea. While the pot was steaming we sat on our sleeping bags, Duffy contentedly puffing his pipe and telling me sailor yarns in a rich brogue. He always enjoyed his meals and complimented the cook. He was good company and I was sorry when our week's outing came to an end.

On my return to camp, Assistant Engineer Vedoe

showed me samples of coal that he had found in a vein about 600 feet up the talus not far from " Elmwood." The coal burned freely and its discovery relieved us from much anxiety, as the failure of the Relief Ship to appear indicated that the larger part of the party would have to remain for the winter at Cape Flora. Only a small amount of coal remained from the supply left by Jackson and the Duke of the Abruzzi but over twenty tons of it were mined out of the frozen clay and carried down the steep talus on the backs of the men. Thus the problem of keeping warm during the winter of 1904–05 was solved for the Cape Flora party.

Chief Scientist Peters joined us on the last day of August, accompanied by Assistant Scientist Tafel and John Vedoe. The party had left Camp Abruzzi July 8th, in a canoe, and arrived at Eaton Island August 4th after a trying passage down the British Channel by water and ice. Scientific instruments and records weighing about 200 pounds were brought down to Eaton Island where they were cached. Mr. Peters's party found DeBruyne Sound filled with broken field ice in motion, and they waited at Eaton Island for the sound to clear, subsisting on a cache of food that I had placed there in 1903. The ice remaining fast, and the sound showing no signs of clearing, Mr. Peters and his companions pushed their loaded canoe over the rough surface to Camp Point, the passage occupying five days. There the canoe and camp outfit were cached and they proceeded in a fog over the glacier of Northbrook Island to our camp.

Mr. Peters brought the sad news that the Nor-

wegian Fireman, Sigurd Myhre, had died at Camp
Abruzzi on May 16th, after an illness of several weeks.
He had been laid to rest in a frozen grave on the summit of the rocky plateau toward Cape Saulen, the most
northern tomb, I believe, in the world.

The birds left us in the latter part of August and we
missed their cheerful chatter. As the sun sank lower
the temperature fell and cold freezing winds and driving flurries of snow assailed us.

Our brief summer was over all too soon and the
darkness and frigidity of another winter drew on apace.

Duffy, said to me, "Shure this is a great counthry!
The summer commences on the 26th day of July at
noon, and, begob, at half pasht one of the same day,
we are in the middle of winter!"

In the early days of September fierce winds and
storms broke the solid sea ice into huge blocks and we
saw open water southward for the first time.

With the failure of the Relief Ship to arrive by
September 10th, I made preparations to winter the
large party remaining there and to return myself to
the men at Teplitz Bay, to engage once again in the
work of the expedition at its Northern Station.

I could no longer depend upon the Relief Ship to
assist me in my march north or lift from my shoulders
the care of the body of men at Cape Flora whose stay
would mean a tax on our resources.

Autumn is the worst time of the year in which to
travel. The channels freeze over in thin sheets of
salt ice that hold the sledge runners like glue, and which
without warning, break up under influence of the winds
into impassable currents of churning water and broken

ice. The sun disappears below the horizon, and land and sea' are wrapped in the blackness of Arctic Night.

Under the hard conditions of sledge work in the fall I could only hope to take a small party of chosen men with me, and about twenty-five men would be obliged to remain at Cape Flora for the winter.

Thanks to the large caches of the Duke of the Abruzzi and Jackson, in addition to our own supplies and the game, there was sufficient food at Cape Flora for the party remaining there during the winter.

The two ponies left over from the slaughter of spring, were shot for food, and thousands of pounds of walrus meat were hauled to the camp from the caches that had been made along the shore and placed out of reach of the dogs, to augment the winter supply of meat and blubber.

During the summer the party had secured seventeen bears, sixteen walruses, eight brant, about 250 birds' eggs, and about sixteen seals. The large supply of fresh meat placed the men in splendid condition physically and also prevented the exhaustive use of the canned provisions in the caches. I had hopes from the experience of Jackson that the party would be able to secure bears during the winter. I instructed the party, as soon as the sun should reappear in February, to send men and sledges to Camp Ziegler on Alger Island, eighty miles distant, to where a large supply of provisions had been cached in 1902.

The distance from camp Abruzzi (from which place I was to make the third start north) to Camp Ziegler was about 140 miles, or nearly twice the distance intervening between Camp Ziegler and Cape Flora where the men were awaiting the Relief Ship. Notwithstanding this fact I promised that just as soon as my supporting parties should return from accompanying me part of the way north they should carry supplies from Camp Abruzzi to Camp Ziegler, and keep at it (in the field) all summer until the dissolution of the ice rendered sledge work impossible.

In the meantime the Cape Flora party could work continuously at hauling supplies from the Camp Ziegler cache to their camp at the Cape. Thus an abundance of food was assured. To assist the Cape Flora party in the work of hauling supplies I gave them about twenty-five dogs.

Northbrook Island is isolated from the rest of the group by DeBruyne Sound, and as long as that waterway remained open, it offered a serious obstacle to the advance north. The temperature was too changeable in early September for me to think of leaving Cape Flora.

The canoe and kayaks that I would be obliged to take along to insure the safety of my party formed such a large part of the total weight we were able to carry that not more than twenty days' rations could be taken on the sledges for men and dogs, and a delay at any point on the march might prove serious. On the other hand, there was the fast approaching season of darkness and the danger of its overtaking us on the way if we delayed our departure too long. The men I had chosen to accompany me north could hardly wait for a cold snap to lock up the waters, and wished for an early start.

Mr. Peters was anxious for an early return to his scientific work at Camp Abruzzi, and so I instructed him to prepare to leave as soon as he thought practicable. I gave him two good men, Assistant Engineer Vedoe and Seaman Mackiernan, and two fine teams of dogs with sledges, a tent, and twenty days' rations. For a boat, on his arrival at Camp Point, he intended to pick up the canoe he had cached there in August. There was a cold snap on the night of the 18th and on the morning of the following day Peters and his party left for Camp Abruzzi. Those days of September were troublesome ones for me. The spirit of the men who were to remain at the Cape bent under the disappointment. None of the anticipations of success of the first winter had been realised; there was no word from home; no hope of escape until the cold, six months' night had passed—no relief from the deadening monotony of camp life. All these things had combined to discourage them and hard words were often used to bewail their sad lot. Almost every assembly of men has its Epicureans and its Stoics. There were representatives of each class at Cape Flora.

I learned in those days the saddening truth that a large proportion of humanity is governed by fear and selfishness and that many a man's actions are inspired by the thought of self-aggrandisement rather than by the sense of principle or the love of his neighbour.

The unlettered and uncultured man is coarse in his selfishness, while the man of education has learned to conceal his baser instincts under a mask of seeming modesty and virtue; but in the end it is a toss up as to which is the worse.

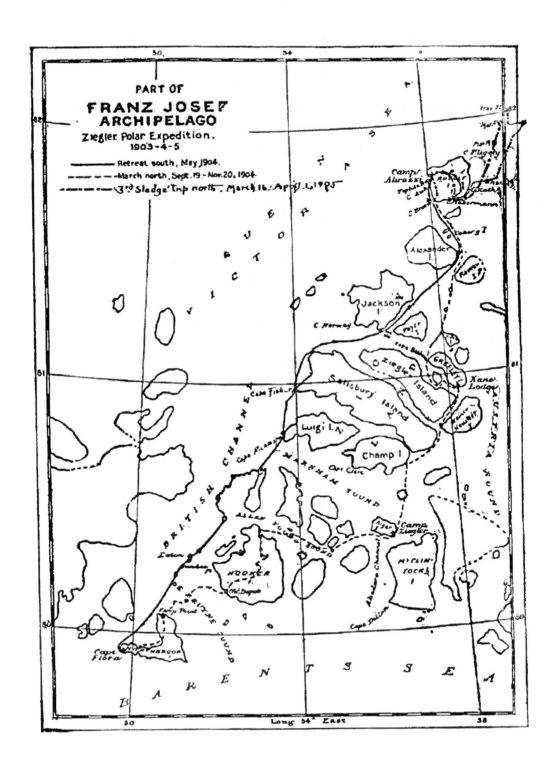

PART OF
FRANZ JOSEF
ARCHIPELAGO
Ziegler Polar Expedition.
1903-4-5

Retreat south, May 1904.
March north, Sept.19.-Nov.20, 1904.
3rd Sledge Trip north, March 16.-April 6 1905

On one of those days of reflection and sadness I wrote in my diary:

"Sometimes, I think I would like to write just as I feel, but the thought comes to me that in the changing atmosphere of Time there is much that would be put down in unchanging black and white for which some one would suffer later on, whose spirit by that time had passed through trials and become chastened and humble. So much I could write at times in bitterness of spirit, but I know all shall be well and that Time shall be the great proofreader and correct the careless work and thoughtless haste, and bring harmony out of this orchestra at last, though there seem to be a few who play as if they had no soul for music."

CHAPTER XVII

THE START FOR CAMP ABRUZZI

EIGHT days after the departure of Peters and his companions for the north I bade good-bye to the men at Cape Flora. Before leaving I placed good, faithful Francis Long in charge of the party in the Roundhouse and all expedition property, and Captain Coffin in charge of the ship's company in "Elmwood." I turned over to each house one of the two whaleboats for use the following summer in the securing of game, and also assigned a team of dogs to each party to be employed when the light returned in 1905 in the hauling of food from Camp Ziegler.

On the morning of September 27th, accompanied by Assistant Scientist Porter, Assistant Surgeon Seitz, Steward Spencer, Quartermaster Rilliet, Seaman Duffy, and Cabin Boy Dean, I left Camp Jackson on the march north to Camp Abruzzi

We carried our camping equipment and seventeen days' food for men and dogs on four sledges drawn by thirty-two dogs A canoe was also carried and two canvas kayaks. We arrived at Camp Point, the northern extremity of Northbrook Island, the same evening and camped in the darkness. A heavy storm from the southwest arose at night and continued through the following day. The wind was so violent that we were obliged to take the pole out of the tent and tie

126

the collapsed fabric together in a great knot to prevent its being torn to pieces. We spent an uncomfortable time in the restricted space in our sleeping bags, the drifting snow walling us in.

At Camp Point a message was found from Mr. Peters stating that he had been delayed by the impassable condition of the channel, but that he had left to cross DeBruyne Sound the morning of the 27th, the day we arrived at the Point. The storm gave me reason to be anxious for his safety. DeBruyne Sound had been opened in a number of places by the high wind of the 28th On the morning of the 29th, we attempted to cross the sound but were forced to return to land by a wide stream of broken ice and mush in a rapid current—impassable either by boats or sledges.

Two other attempts were made to cross the sound, one on September 30th, the other on October 11th, but we were obliged to return both times to Camp Point Each attempt to cross was followed by a rise in temperature and high southerly winds, accompanied by the breaking up of the ice and the opening of the Sound

As the days passed by our food stores dwindled, and the poor dogs chained out in the snow. gave vent to their craving for food in long drawn howls.

We built two little igloos of snow blocks in the side of the glacier. They were connected by a passage and for a time all of us lived together in the "Tombs," as the igloos were called, but later the Steward and I preferred to live in the tent, considering our chances to be better there in an outlook for game On Sunday, October 9th, we held a service in the "Tombs" where

I read from the Sixth Chapter of Matthew the words which at the time seemed to be particularly suited to us: "Take no thought of the morrow, of what ye shall eat or drink."

The Steward and I had just returned to our tent when, sitting together in the cold, I expressed the wish for a bear, as it would mean food and fuel. At that moment a quick, short bark sounded outside, followed by a chorus of savage, frantic yelps from all our chained canines. Looking through the flap of the tent, the Steward exclaimed, "A bear! A bear!" We both ran out to behold a bear making up the glacier. Our best bear dog, Little Wyckoff, was loose and worried Bruin by biting his heels, so delaying the beast that I was enabled to get within about 150 yards. With an anxiety that cannot be expressed, I fired, bringing down the animal. He was sledged in triumph to the "Tombs," and that day, and many days after, we had the luxury of fried bear steak. Our hungry dogs, too, got a full meal of fresh meat. As the bear was very fat, all the blubber was carefully cut and preserved for cooking fuel.

To wait often takes more courage, more effort of soul, than to perform. As the days went by and the period of light shortened some of my good comrades became restless. The active, little Steward would look over toward Hooker Island and wistfully say, "If we were only there! All our troubles would be over, for then we could proceed easily over the frozen channels to Camp Ziegler and from there to Teplitz Bay. This awful channel! This horrible island!"

As I looked at the dark water clouds hanging over

the glacier on that island which indicated to me that the channels beyond were open, I was filled with anxiety for the safety of Mr. Peters and his party and for our own escape.

The sun was rapidly sinking. After considering the rough and treacherous character of the ice in De-Bruyne Sound, I realised the impossibility of crossing the wide channel in one march, and saw that at least one of the long October nights would have to be spent on the ice in the sound. With every storm, the ice would break up and drift, and as storms came often and without warning we would have to be prepared to take to the boats in an emergency. The frail kayaks could not be depended upon in the current of the channel when it was filled with grinding ice fragments. The canoe alone was deemed reliable. But as the canoe was not large enough to hold the entire party, I determined to send two members back to Cape Flora with one sledge to obtain a supply of provisions sufficient for us to reach Camp Ziegler where we could replenish. The poor dogs had been living on quarter and half rations, but for them I could ask no food, their salvation depending upon our reaching Camp Ziegler in time, for I did not intend to return to Cape Flora no matter what came.

On the 17th Mr. Porter expressed his willingness to return to Cape Flora with one man to stay there through the winter. On the return of the light in the following spring (1905) he would make a sledge trip to Camp Abruzzi to accompany me on my final march north.

So I gave him instructions to return to Cape Flora,

placing him as Third in Command of the expedition
and in charge of the party at Cape Flora and in command of the whole expedition should I and Mr. Peters,
my Second in Command, both be lost. I detailed
Jimmy Dean, our cabin boy, to accompany him.
Jimmy almost wept in his disappointment. He wanted
to stay with my party and share our adventures in the
march north. I gave Mr. Porter five of our best dogs,
a sledge, and a kayak and he and Jimmy set out for
Cape Flora. They were accompanied by Steward
Spencer and Seaman Duffy, with a dog team and
sledge, who were to return to me with a small supply
of food.

On the 17th the temperature was 31 degrees F.
above zero, five degrees above the freezing point of
sea water. The Sound was filled with an impassable
mass of ice fragments grinding their way in a rapid
current out to sea. The roofs of our igloos had been
dripping during the long siege of abnormally high
temperature and we were obliged to prop them up to
prevent their caving in. Our sleeping bags were
soaked with water. It looked as if the cold weather
would never come, and as if we would be imprisoned
by darkness without an opportunity to cross the
eighteen miles that separated us from Hooker Island.
But after Porter's departure the column of the thermometer slowly dropped until on the night of the
21st it reached one degree below zero.

Spencer and Duffy returned on the 21st, and on the
22d, the day the sun disappeared for the winter, we
made our fourth attempt to cross the channel.

The party comprised Asst. Surgeon Seitz, Quartermaster Rilliet, Steward Spencer, and Seaman Duffy with three dog teams of nine dogs each and three sledges, a canoe, and a two-man kayak

We left land at nine o'clock in the morning in a very dim twilight and made our way over much rough ice. I directed the path of the column toward the north as I noted that there was a pressure on the ice fields from that direction and reasoned that the ice would jam in the narrow part of the sound between Old Depot on Hooker Island and Camp Point on Northbrook Island, but would open into lanes and drift seaward south of these two points   So instead of directing our way in as nearly straight a line as we could, across the Sound to Old Depot (our objective), our trail curved up the channel, above the danger zone of opening leads, and fast moving fields   We crossed one open lead by means of canoe and kayak at the cost of an hour and one dog   While picking a path through moving ice cakes, I climbed to the top of a small pressure ridge which suddenly gave way beneath me. I was in the water some minutes surrounded by a muddle of small ice fragments which prevented my reaching the heavy floe before my absence was noted.   Then I had the rather unpleasant experience of disrobing on an ice cake to put on a complete change of dry clothing. Fortunately the temperature was not low—only 4 degrees below zero!

After crossing much broken ice, mixed with rubble and thin sheets, we reached a large old cake that seemed to be fixed.   As it was difficult to see ahead in the gathering darkness, and being uncertain of reaching another large cake before night, I gave orders to encamp. The following day we reached Old Depot on Hooker Island, crossing rough places and wide stretches of young salt ice just thick enough to bear the men and sledges, the moving caravan causing the thin stratum to roll in waves and move under the feet like jelly, one sledge—the one bearing the heavy canoe— breaking partially through. We helped the dogs drag the heavy sledges up the slope of the glacier on Hooker Island to a level spot near some protruding rocks, and then turned our eyes toward DeBruyne Sound. In the gloom we could see great black stretches of water in which floated dark looking masses of ice, and open lanes steaming in the cold air. The rising moon illuminated the scene and intensified the gloom of the shadowy Stygian expanse. Our hearts beat thankfully in the realisation that we had crossed just in time, and that after the long wait of twenty-six days we were able at last to proceed.

Storms and rolling clouds of the past were forgotten as, above the massed vapours of the waters, we happily raised our tents, a full moon giving us light, and revealing in glittering splendour the mountainous glacier above us, whose cold, high crest was to be our next battlefield.

Dr. Seitz, Rilliet, and Duffy occupied one tent and Steward Spencer and myself the other. While we cooked our evening meal above the hum of the blazing khotals in both tents, I could hear Duffy singing and catch snatches of the animated conversation of the others, denoting their happy condition. In our own little tepee Spencer fairly beamed with happiness, and talked enthusiastically of next year's opportunities north, expressing the hope that we would break the record. Camp Abruzzi seemed near to us that night and Camp Ziegler only a short way off.

The temperature dropped to 12 degrees below zero while we slept and, in the gloom of the returning twilight of another day, it was cold work harnessing dogs and breaking camp. But we were glad that the temperature was low for it meant as a rule good weather and a long march

Before leaving me at Camp Point, Porter had told me that on his spring trip he had been obliged to cross the Hooker Island glacier—that he had found a high glacier face on the north shore of the island and that there was only one little place where it was possible for a sledge to leave the island with safety. Rilliet had accompanied Porter on his trip and stated to me that he knew the trail across the ice-capped island and the place of descent mentioned by Porter where the glacier sloped down to the level of Young Sound.

So I asked Rilliet to act as guide while I helped Duffy with his heavily loaded sledge in our long haul up the slope. After surmounting the dome, over 1,400 feet high, we made a rapid descent down a steep declivity at the bottom of which our guide expected to find a short cut to the sea level. But distances are deceptive on a glacier and five hours were spent in a reconnoitre, which was made possible by moonlight. We were stormbound the following day. The temperature rose to 6 degrees above zero, dropping to 19 below on the morning of the 26th. This colder weather generally meant a respite from the howling winds. It calmed near noon and we lashed our icy tents and sleeping bags and stirred up the protesting dogs from the holes they had dug in the snow drifts, and put on their stiff harness. We could not afford to feed them the night before, but they seemed to have accepted the situation stoically. Poor things! they may have wondered but could not know what it meant ‚his continual hauling and suffering. Despite their snarling and fighting they were hard workers and faithful helpers, and I often thought we did not appreciate their worth as we should.

There was a haze in the air that obscured vision. Under foot, fortunately, the wind had packed the deep snow so that the sledges did not haul as badly as we expected. I did not like the looks of the glacier and suggested to Rilliet that we rope together and go ahead, thinking particularly of his safety as he was to be the guide. He told me the precaution was unnecessary as he had gone all over the place and did not believe there were any crevasses in it.

AN AUGUST DAY AT CAPE FLORA IN 1924

Fireman Hostick and his anvil and forge, Seaman Myers blowing the bellows

HOUSE-MOVING—PREPARING FOR WINTER AT CAPE FLORA

CAPE FLORA

"The men spent many anxious hours straining their eyes to glimpse a sail"

CHAPTER XVIII

"HE BROUGHT ME UP ALSO OUT OF AN HOR-
RIBLE PIT."—*Psalms*

WE HAD travelled on the glaciers so often that we had grown free of care in regard to the hidden danger of crevasses. These deep chasms were arched over by the drifting snows and levelled with the surrounding surface of the glacier, and it was impossible to detect them. On the Rudolph Island glacier I had broken through on three or four different occasions, but had always been successful in scrambling out, not having fallen deeper than to my armpits. Frequent halts delayed our progress. Because of the thick weather I often went ahead to assist Rilliet in picking out the shadowy nunatucks that guided us toward the slope where we wished to go from our present elevation to Young Sound.

It was at one of these halts that I walked out ahead of the sledges when the snow gave way beneath my feet and I hung over a deep crevasse. Steward Spencer ran from his sledge in an attempt to help me. He had but just touched my hand with his fingers when I began a frightful descent and knew no more In the semiconscious state which followed, came a chill of horror, for I thought I had been buried alive. But returning memory helped me to realise that I was entombed in ice. I found myself wedged between two curves in the

135

walls of the crevasse, the convex surfaces near enough together to hold me between my breast and back, my left arm bent over my breast and jamming having prevented me from falling through the neck of the funnel. Beneath me was a great black void in which I could move my legs without touching the walls, and to my right a cavern that made me think of the bottomless pit.

The darkness was intense. Away above me shone a luminous spot, a faint halo of blue iridescence which showed where I had broken through, and a few straight pencil-like rays of light penetrated the chasm exposing the black surface of the walls of ice and also revealing the fact that had I fallen but a little farther to the right I would have gone to depths beyond the reach of human aid.

I heard voices calling from above and I answered, asking for a rope, and requesting haste, as I thought I would slip through. Up to that time I was not aware that Spencer was in the chasm. While the rope was being lowered, I heard most awful groans beneath me in the crevasse. My first thought was that a team of dogs had fallen in with me. Soon the noise became articulate speech, and I realised with horror that another man was in that prison, and like myself was wedged in between walls of ice. It was the Steward who in trying to save me had fallen in too. I could not see him in that black pit, but thought that his voice, with its awful echoes came from somewhere beneath me. He called out, "Commander, are you in this place too?" He was lying on his side and felt the unspeakable torture of his position and begged me

"AT LAST I SAW ABOVE ME THE END OF A ROPE"

to save him. "What an awful place to die!" he said
again and again

I told him to trust in God and we would get out,
but I must confess, at that moment of shock and pain,
help seemed very far away.

To add to our discomfort, pieces of ice became
detached from above and thundered down the abyss,
the sound reaching us until it was annihilated by the
awful depth. It need not be told what would have
happened if either Spencer or myself had been in the
path of the falling fragments.

At last I saw above me the end of a rope which
gradually neared as I shouted directions to those out
of sight above who were lowering the line, our only
hope of escape

My right arm was free, and at last the precious line
was in my hand. I painfully made a bowline in the
end of the rope, the fingers of my left hand being fortunately free. Slipping the noose over my right foot,
I called to those above to haul away. Soon I was
swinging like a pendulum in free space. I called to
them to move the rope to the right and then lower me.
I swung around in the black chasm and felt the icy
walls but could not discover the Steward.

In desperation, as I felt myself growing weaker, I
called to him, "Look up and try to see me against the
light above!" He obeyed, saw my suspended form
and directed my movements. In answer to my shouts
the men above moved the rope along the edge of the
crevasse and lowered me to where I could reach the
Steward, though I could not rescue him on account of
a projection of ice that interfered. But I could pass

him a foot and a hand, and lift him from his prone
position, and help him to stand on the cake of ice that
had broken off when he fell and had jammed, saving
him from death. Unable to give the Steward further help,
I told him it would be best for the men to haul me up
and send the rope down for him. He agreed and I was
drawn to the surface—just in time, as I fainted on reaching the top. The Steward was hauled up next. A tent
was erected and within its shelter Doctor Seitz examined us. No bones were broken, but a cut in the Steward's
face required several stitches. We were helped into
our sleeping bags as the temperature had fallen to 27
degrees below zero.

On measuring the rope Seaman Duffy found we had
fallen into the crevasse to the depth of seventy feet.
It was a providential escape. If we had fallen but a
little to either side where the crevasse widened, we
would have descended beyond the reach of help.

While swinging in the dense darkness of that sheol
like abyss, a thin line only held me to life—a cotton
cord with braided covering, only three-eighths of an
inch in diameter! I thought of a place on that same
line where, only that morning, I had noticed, while
lashing a sledge load, that all the inner fibres had
parted.

It was a dangerous but concealed break, and at the
time I mentally resolved to have it cut out and the
line spliced at our next camp.

"Had the break been noticed!" The horror of the
question troubled me.

In a conversation with Duffy after the accident I
learned that he had gone over every inch of the rope,

and that the weak spot had been discovered—and the rope repaired.

The Steward suffered all night, and indeed there was little sleep for either of us. The other members of the party had worked hard to save us and despite our pains we were a happy party.

Camp was established near the crevasse, and the following morning the Steward, still in his sleeping bag, was lashed to his sledge. We then left the glacier descending to the level of the Sound. At every halt Spencer would call to me and ask if we were still on the glacier, and how long before we would reach the channel ice. Poor fellow! he had had enough of the glacier and preferred the known perils of the sea to the unknown dangers that lurked in the hidden depths of the mountain of ice.

On the last slope of the glacial ice, just before it joins the salt waters of the sound, we were electrified by the discovery of sledge tracks which made us hope for the safety of Peters and his party. The surface of the Sound, a chaotic mixture of ice boulders of all sizes, mixed brash, and thin salt ice just thick enough to bear our sledge runners, offered anything but good travelling. We broke through in places and were all troubled with water soaked footwear before the day's work was over.

Duffy was the strongest man in the party, so I gave him the Steward's sledge, knowing that the warmhearted sailor would save Spencer many a bump on the ice, and I took Duffy's sledge and his well trained team of dogs. I tried at first to lead the party through the bad ice but found that I was still suffering from the effects of the fall in the crevasse the day before, and had difficulty in seeing ahead, often falling over ice cakes, and deviating from the correct course. So I asked Rilliet, as he did not have a team or sledge, to act as guide again, while I took the rear of the column. I shall never forget that day's march! The sledge with its heavy load of canoe, tent, equipment, and stores was often overturned on the rough road and it took every ounce of strength I possessed to lift it back on to its runners, the chief strain coming on my chest which had been bruised by the jamming between the ice walls of the crevasse, giving me the impression that my ribs were broken.

Our course was toward Cape Beresford, about thirty miles away, which point we reached after two days of travel over a hard trail of rough ice and deep snow, alternating with stretches of young ice covered with a wet salty efflorescence that held our sledge runners fast. We were also troubled with fog and mist.

Early on the morning of the 29th (October) the air cleared with a temperature of 23 degrees below zero, and the waning moon lit up the towering glaciers and frozen channels. The pain in my chest kept me awake and I lay watching the curious effect of the moonlight shining on the silk of the tent, and talking to the Steward at times, for he too slept but little. At half-past three, I heard Duffy, always an early riser, outside discoursing on the beauty of the scene. I called out to the men to get ready to move. The order was obeyed with alacrity. Before long the khotals were singing merrily, melting the ice for our breakfast of tea and stew. With the moon for our only illuminant, we left the Cape and made good time over a comparatively smooth course, reaching the West Camp on Alger Island an hour after noon, the twilight allowing us to see our way when the moon left us. This place was the site of Baldwin's first station in 1901, and he had placed there coal and provisions.

We found traces of Peters's party in the sledge marks crossing the tide crack and saw their canoe carefully cached, and a fresh trail leading in the direction of Camp Ziegler. We hurriedly set up a tent into which the Steward was carried and while I made tea for the party the men dug out of the snow two barrels of coal and a case of emergency rations, and put them on a sledge in place of the canoe which we cached alongside the one we found there.

I knew that there were provisions in the two houses at Camp Ziegler, but was not sure that we would find coal there and so provided for that contingency. The canoe I did not expect to use in continuing my march north, for it was then the last of October and I trusted that the temperature would remain low and that the channels would be frozen between Alger Island and Teplitz Bay.

It was seven days since the sun dropped below the horizon for the winter, and the periods of twilight were daily growing shorter. At 3.15 P. M, when we left West Camp, the gloom of night was upon us, clouds helping to darken the air. But our dogs smelling the fresh tracks in the snow were all excitement and followed the trail at a rapid trot We passed over the six miles that separated us from Baldwin's old headquarters in less than an hour and a half reaching the huts in the darkness.   Our arrival was heralded by a number of dogs that came out in the gloom, and greeted us and our teams with joyful yelps. We could just distinguish a heap of snow out of which protruded the tops of the houses and a chimney from which a cheerful smoke was escaping. Through a hole in the snow, a dim light was shining and against it stood the form of Mr. Peters. We shook hands, and, after our sledges were arranged and the dogs set free from their harness, we went down into the warm interior where I was glad to see Vedoe and Mackiernan. Mr. Peters told me that he had been delayed on Hooker Island by open water in Young Sound and had arrived at Camp Ziegler only four days before.   He gave an account of a narrow escape from being carried to sea on the ice in DeBruyne Sound, drifting in the storm from near Eaton Island to a point near Old Depot, and escaping with his party and equipment by a rush over moving ice to Hooker Island.   He was preparing to winter at Camp Ziegler as Seaman Mackiernan had several toes on both feet frost bitten and could not travel.

That night the wind howled and for five days the storm kept us fast indoors. We utilised the time in thawing and drying out our sleeping bags and tents and clothing, and in preparing for the march to Camp Abruzzi. There was not any pemmican at Camp Ziegler that we could use for dog food, but we found some tallow which we melted and mixed while hot with emergency ration (U. S. Army ration of cracked wheat and beef). We poured the mass into pans and when it was cool, cut it into one pound blocks. The mixture made a very good ration and the dogs liked it. Dr.

"THE ABSENCE OF LIGHT MAKING OUR ADVANCE A MARCH OF FAITH"

Drawn by J. Knowles Hare

Seitz reporting to me that there was no danger to be apprehended in regard to Mackiernan's frost-bitten toes, though he would be unable to travel and needed rest, and Spencer having recovered from the effects of the fall into the crevasse sufficiently to march with us north, I requested Rilliet and Mackiernan to remain in Camp Ziegler for the winter—placing the former in charge of the station—and provided the two men with a team of five dogs, rifle, and a shotgun. Ammunition and food in plenty were stored at Camp Ziegler.

I told Rilliet to spend the winter in digging out all the provisions he could find, so that when the party came from Cape Flora in the early spring they could load their sledges without trouble, and also instructed him to clean out both houses and make them habitable. On the arrival of the men from Cape Flora he was to let them have one of the houses as a comfortable place in which to rest after their journey and in which to dry out their sleeping bags and clothing. But no unnecessary time was to be spent in the house during the good sledging season, for it would require continuous effort to transport the provisions required to Cape Flora

I instructed him to help Mr. Porter on his way north, when he arrived, in every way possible. I also told him that in the spring and summer I would send down provisions from the north, and that Camp Ziegler would be the station at which the members of the Camp Abruzzi party would await the Relief Ship in 1905.

CHAPTER XIX

WE WERE stormbound at Camp Ziegler until November 5th. It was the worst time of the year to travel and the trip was one that none of us who took part in it will ever forget. The party was composed of six men, Peters, Vedoe, Seitz, Spencer, Duffy, and myself. We had four dog teams and sledges and one kayak. The channels seemed at last to be firmly frozen and I left the two heavy canoes behind, as we would have to travel fast, for the periods of twilight were very short and each day there was less light.

We camped the first night at Cape Trieste and then directed our way toward Kane Lodge on Greely Island. It was almost midway between Camp Ziegler and our destination, and we looked forward to it as a sort of "half-way house" and a shelter from the dark, windy autumn days.

While nearing Weiner Neustadt Island, a little after noon on November 6th, we were treated to a diversion that we hardly expected. Grey, one of our dogs, who had got loose and was running far enough ahead to be out of catching distance, stirred up a bear. There was charge and counter charge between them, the bear chasing "Grey" to within a few feet of the leading team.

The harnessed canines were almost ungovernable

in their desire to participate in the fray and, indeed, several of the teams.did help in the chase which drove the bear to the top of a ridge. From that safe vantage point he tantalised the teams until it was next to impossible to hold them in a line. Every dog in the column undoubtedly believed that it would be considerably more fun to follow up the chase than to haul the heavy loads. But at last, to save the loads and prevent complete demoralisation, I fired a shot and frightened the bear away. We could not spare the time to kill and skin him and, as I have mentioned before, I objected to the unnecessary slaughter of game.

As we neared the entrance of Collinson Channel I anxiously watched ahead for the dark clouds that denoted the presence of water. In March and April of 1902, on the previous expedition, we had seen there a great open hole of water, the rapid current from Rhodes Channel joining with the great water of Austria Sound and keeping the place open in the coldest time of the year.

In May 1902 the water hole was so large that on account of it the sledge column was obliged to cross a steep spur of the glacier on Weiner Neustadt Island, and I had reason to fear trouble. On arriving there, as expected, we found the place open—a great steaming black void sending up columns of dark vapour in the cold air. We rounded its fearsome edge, like the entrance to Inferno, in an almost lightless night, our sled runners only a few yards from the water, and gained the solid ice of Collinson Channel, camping that night on land far from the uncertain crystal covering of the sea. On November 7th we reached the shelter of

Kane Lodge where we found some pemmican to augment our supply of dog food, and where the hearts of
my comrades were made glad by the discovery of a
bag of tobacco. On leaving Kane Lodge our troubles
increased on account of water holes, rough ice, and the
darkness. Among those islands the scenery was a
strange medley of uncertain shadows in a ghostly grouping. The high hills in their icy coats cut sharp enough
in dark purple relief against the dim yellow of the
southern sky; black water pools sent up columns of
slowly rising vapour that stratified into streaky still
clouds against the background of shadows, the whole
looking like a Doré conception of the regions of pur-
gatory. As the twilight passed into the gloom of
approaching night the scene took on the frightful
aspect of Dante's idea of the lowest circle of hell—a
hell of ice.

West of Kane Lodge our progress north was barred
by a large, open, inky lake whose farther shore was
lost in clouds of steam. Upon its bosom floated ghostly
icebergs whose crests were lost in the darkness and
mist. On one side the high face of the glacier on
Greely Island forbade advance; the other shore was
locked by a wall of precipitous rock. We retraced
our steps and rounded the southern end of an island
in the channel that we called "Coal Mine Island"
on account of the find Porter made there the previous
spring. We passed another large and dark body of
water on a narrow thin ice foot just wide enough for
our teams and sledge-runners, passing the point of the
island where the waters washed the steep shore on a rock-
ing bridge of ice that fortunately happened to be there.

On November 9th we camped at the northern extremity of Kuhn Island and the next day, after a short march, reached Stoliczka Island. From there to Rainer Island was a distance of about 18 miles, over a wide sound connecting with the Victoria Sea by Back Channel. There was danger of finding the Sound open, washed by the seas from the Channel. We could see only a few yards ahead for in addition to the darkness a mist covered the face of the ice—the vapour itself an indication of some nearby body of water. As it was nearly eleven o'clock in the morning we could expect only about two hours more of very poor twilight and under the best conditions of ice could not hope to reach Rainer Island that day. We would have to camp on young autumn ice that a storm might destroy.

I discussed the situation with the men and said if they were willing to take the risk of camping on the uncertain Sound we would go on; if not, we would camp on Stoliczka Island until the following day when a clearer air might allow us to choose a smooth trail. Doctor Seitz stated that they all wished to go ahead and take chances, Mr. Peters adding that if we met rough ice we could return.

We then took to the ice like so many shadows, feeling our way through a maze of pressure ridges, the absence of light making our advance a march of faith. Mr. Peters and I went ahead and a few feet behind us came the dog teams and their drivers in Indian file. Time and time again men and dogs would fall into crevices between the massive blocks, and sledges were overturned on obstructions that could not be seen.

The darkness was so impenetrable that we who were in the lead would stumble over monster blocks of ice and into holes and actually walk into icebergs without seeing them. We felt our way with long poles and travelled by compass. Sometimes we came to places where the floor loomed up black and forbidding, and the horror of the thought of the open sea troubled us, but on touching the surface with our poles we found it to be young ice but heavy enough to bear the caravan. We made good time over these recently frozen level openings though the men had hard hauling in assisting the dogs to drag the sleds over the sticky surface.

For three days we forced our way across that awful space. Peters went ahead to lay the course at times, and I followed with an ice axe at the head of the dog teams trying to avoid the worst places. Trying to lead the column away from the holes that Peters fell into I often tumbled into worse ones myself with a dog team to keep me company. We were like two blind men groping their way. We fell continually. The cursing of the dog drivers, the howling of the dogs, and the darkness—the awful darkness! made the journey like a passage through the regions of torment. Viewed through the lapse of time what was then a horrible reality seems like a wild, bad dream. On crossing two particularly high pressure ridges, that I had hoped marked the shores of Rainer Island, we struck better ice but then the wind which had not ceased to blow from the east increased its force and we were obliged to camp. During the night the east wind subsided and a light breeze came down from the north, and our weather indicator, the thermometer, prophesied fair weather by dropping to 22 degrees below zero Sunday, November 13th, dawned beautiful, the clear light from a starry sky revealing the fact that we were in the channel between Rainer and Alexander Islands.

We reached Houen Island that day and on the next camped on Hohenlohe Island where we were storm-bound five days with temperatures ranging from 23 above (7 A M Nov 15) to 26 degrees below zero (8 P. M. Nov. 19) and a driving wind that seemed to penetrate the fabric of our tents.

The condensation, the drifting snow, and the varying temperature had played havoc with our sleeping bags, clothing, and tents. Everything was either water soaked or frozen, the warmth of our bodies thawing pools of water in our sleeping bags which did not conduce to comfort as the temperature dropped. During a lull in the storm, while breakfast was being prepared and the hum of the cookers gave a certain sense of cheerfulness, we heard Duffy singing in the other tent, "Shure Oive found McCarty's whiskers in the stew!" It raised a laugh all around for at that moment we were engaged in removing from our coffee and stew the deer hairs from our worn sleeping bags

While the storm kept us prisoners in our sleeping bags the last glow of faint twilight at noon left us and we were in total darkness Our salvation depended upon the moon which appeared when the storm ceased on the evening of November 19th In her light we folded our tents and lashed the loads on our sledges, the dogs wagging their tails as anxious as we were to march again. During that November advance, as we were nearing Rudolph Island, we saw a light north of us, just above the level of the snow, burning in brilliant red, then flaming into yellow. It was Jupiter—the planet whose light I had watched year after year; the planet I thought I knew better than any of the glittering lights that move in the firmament.

We cut our way through great ridges of ice at Cape Brorak to Rudolph Island whose glacier we crossed in a misty moonlight, reaching the hut at Camp Abruzzi at 3.10 o'clock Sunday morning, November 20th, a ship's light that was kept burning on the roof of the house in hopes of our return guiding us down the steep descent from the glacier.

Our advent caused great excitement among the dogs at camp. Like ground scouts of an advancing cavalry attack, they came rushing up the side of the glacier, barking and yelping with joy, for they recognised their old comrades in harness, who seemed as wild with delight as themselves.

Seaman Meyer met me outside and then came Stewart and Tessem and Perry and lastly Engineer Hartt. We found the party all in good health but without Fireman Myhre of whose death I have already spoken.

THE TOMB ON SAULEN'S ROCKY HEIGHT

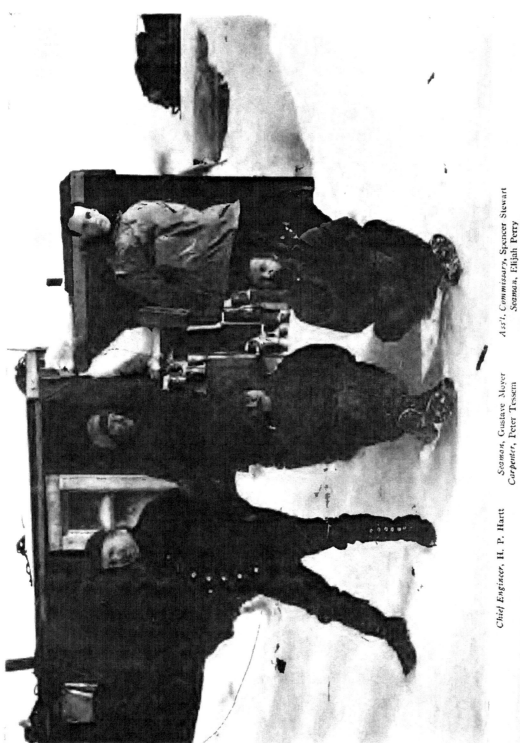

Chief Engineer, H. P. Hartt   *Ass't. Commissary*, Spencer Stewart

Seaman, Gustave Meyer

Carpenter, Peter Tessem   *Seaman*, Elijah Perry

THE MEN WHO STAYED AT CAMP ABRUZZI

OUR LAST BATTLES WITH THE POLAR ICE

1904—1905

Out of whose womb came the ice? And the hoary frost of heaven, who hath gendered it?

The waters are hid as with a stone, and the face of the deep is frozen.

JOB.

CHAPTER XX

THE POLAR NIGHT OF 1905

IT SEEMED very cozy in the hut after our fifty-four days on the trail   Carpenter Tessem prepared a breakfast of hot waffles and cornmeal mush with delicious coffee.   It was good to sit at the table with my united band of happy men and to hear the good news that there was an abundance of everything needful.

They told me that the past summer had been a wonderfully warm one at camp, and the whole of Teplitz Bay had cleared of ice.   The snow had melted off the rocks and around the Duke's tent, making it possible to find tools, etc., lost during the previous season, also uncovering a mass of coal left by the Italian.   The melting was accelerated by the industry of the small body of men who directed streams of water through the frozen caches, and cleared the camp site by hydraulic means

The coal and stores had been put under cover and thoughtful provision made for the winter.

While at the table we heard the story of the long wait of Meyer and Perry at Hohenlohe Island, of how they camped there and kept a lamp burning from October 5th to November 1st, watching for our arrival in the hope that they would be able to succor us, and also of their attempt to reach Kane Lodge from the north—futile because of an open sea south of Hohenloh Island.

Mr. Hartt recited his experiences while trying to reach Cape Flora where he hoped to be of assistance to me. On July 19th, accompanied by Seaman Perry, he set out in a steam launch he had constructed. While in the British Channel he almost lost the boat and had to throw the boiler overboard to save the launch. This accident necessitated their return, and on August 18th they reached the place from which they had started a month before.

Assistant Commissary Stewart, Carpenter Tessem, and Seaman Meyer were the last men at the post, and they laboured hard hauling the coal and supplies and preparing the house and shelters, including the great stock tent in which the bags of clothing and equipment were stored.

After our arrival at Camp Abruzzi the party was allowed about a week's rest. Then work was started for the contemplated sledge journey in the early spring of 1905.

November 24th we celebrated as Thanksgiving Day with a true feeling of gratefulness. Instead of the time-honoured turkey we were treated to a ptarmigan fricassee by our capable Steward. Four of these birds had been shot at camp during the previous summer and saved for this special occasion.

The smallness of my party, the lack of ponies, and the few dogs at my command, together with the necessity of providing a number of dogs to be used by my Camp Abruzzi party in transporting food supplies to Camp Ziegler, rendered it impossible for me to arrange

OUR CHRISTMAS DINNER AT CAMP ABRUZZI IN 1904

Bernard E. Spencer
Spencer Stewart
Peter L. Tessem
John Duffy
Henry P. Hartt

Wm. J. Peters   Chas. L. Seitz, M.D.
Anton Vedoe   Gustave Meyer
Elijah Perry

THE APPEARANCE OF THE HUT ON THE RETURN OF LIGHT IN 1905

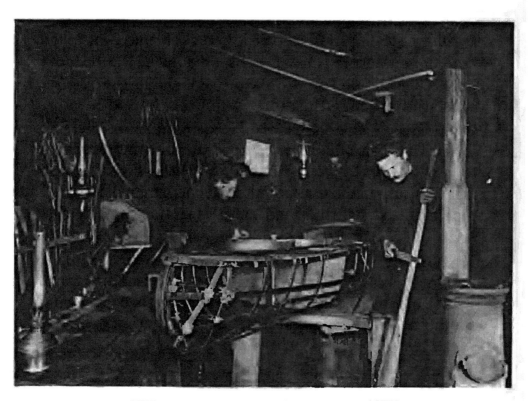

BUSY DAYS IN THE WORKSHOP AT CAMP ABRUZZI
Preparing for the last struggle to reach the pole

for supporting parties to accompany me except for a short distance from land.

After much thought I decided to leave early in March 1905, with one companion and three dog teams and sledges in an effort to reach the Pole, a supporting column of three small detachments to accompany me

The first support included two men and was to have a lightly loaded sledge drawn by such dogs as were left after the other teams were chosen, and was to go only one day forward

The Second Support of two men and one dog team and sledge was to return two days later, while the Third Support, comprising four men, two dog teams, and sledges, was to accompany me seven days' march north.

I made plans for a light canoe for two men to be constructed at camp. Six sledges needed strengthening—the lignum vitæ under-runners which caused us trouble in 1904 were taken off and hickory substituted. The dog harness required repairing, picket lines for dogs were manufactured from light steel rope, and tents were constructed on an improved model providing a low wall and an adjustable opening at the top to allow the exit of vapour generated by cooking

With such a small party it would be impracticable to carry the extra cook tent, so four little cookers were manufactured, one for each tent. The kayaks demanded repairing and painting and more pork and bean biscuit had to be baked. In addition, the men had their sleeping bags to repair and their personal equipment and clothing to make ready. The faithful and efficient work done by the small party at Camp Abruzzi during my absence in placing stores, coal, and supplies under cover and in putting the storage tent and warehouses in repair, relieved the party of much outdoor work during the winter of 1904–05 and allowed opportunity for recreation—as well as for preparation for the sledge trip.

The days of the winter were among the pleasantest experienced on the expedition. The party was congenial and the hut warm and comfortable. We were all very busy. It was pleasant to hear the whirl of the lathe and the sound of hammering in our little shop, interspersed at times with the singing of the men.

After the evening meal, in the periods of moonlight, in parties of twos and threes we would walk over toward Cape Saulen and view from its height the vast expanse of water or dark young ice to the west and northwest, the rapid changes in temperature and the numerous storms keeping the sea open. The dogs seemed anxious for human companionship and accompanied us on these walks—a noisy, romping, mischievous crew.

During the storms, which were many, and when the clouds obscured the feeble light of the stars and absolute darkness kept us imprisoned, the men made use of the excellent library after the hours of labour, and played chess or cards—usually listening at the same time to the strains of music from a Regina music box or a phonograph. After December 21st we were glad with the thought that the sun had turned in its journey away from us and that each day brought us nearer to the time when we should see his face again—when light would take the place of darkness and the winter of night would be over.

Double-page cartoon that appeared in the Christmas edition of the *Arctic Eagle*, published at Camp Abruzzi, Dec. 26, 1904.

Christmas time was celebrated as the year before by a banquet at which Polar bear steak was the "*pièce de résistance*" and a special edition of the *Arctic Eagle* was printed.

Before leaving Tromso in 1903 I had received a daily calendar from home upon the leaves of which friends had written greetings and thoughts, each leaf a message. The calendar ended in September 1904, but I had carefully preserved the leaves and it was doing service for another year. It had always been a source of much pleasure to me, but at this holiday time its pages were read with more than usual interest. In my diary, I wrote:

"I have been thinking in these days of holiday cheer of home and friends, and my heart is full, so full! I look over my calendar leaves with their expressions of friendship and love and think of those who have written them. Another year before the possibility of an opportunity to see once again the home land or the faces of those who make it a home land! And I think of one———What will be her experiences and what mine before we meet?"

From a maximum temperature of 13 degrees above zero, reached during a storm on December 13th, the temperature fell slowly until on Christmas night the minimum thermometer registered 53 degrees below zero. On the night of January 5th, our weather observer at Camp Abruzzi, Mr. Stewart, came into the hut from his regular evening observation and excitedly asked Mr. Peters and me to go out with him and witness the low temperature recorded on the minimum thermometer in the instrument shelter. Under the light of Stewart's lantern, we saw that the alcohol column with its little glass index had reached the low record of 60.2 degrees below zero. It was a beautiful, calm night with a faint aurora playing overhead. As it was the experience of cold was keen; with a wind, it would have been unbearable. We were glad to have a warm house to go into.

We were fortunate in the latter part of December and in early January in having a number of periods of starlight. Almost every clear cold night the fires of aurora played in the sky. A rapidly moving luminous veil often of many colours through which the stars gleamed bright generally started like a little cloud of light near the horizon, throwing long streamers toward the zenith, the streamers ending in a beautiful circle of light, the corona, which quivered directly overhead. Other long curves of fire shot over the sky toward that part of the horizon directly opposite to the side from which the aurora had started. The display usually ended in a dull yellow luminous vapour near the horizon.

On the afternoon of January 17th one of the members came to my room to tell me that he had seen what he believed to be a signal on Cape Auk to the south. We expected a party from Cape Flora in the early spring and we ran out to look, though we wondered how a signal could be placed there in the darkness. Surely it was a beautiful sight—a flaming red spot that changed colour and seemed to move—an effect of refraction. I knew it could not be a signal and instantly thought of Venus, whose coming denoted that before long the sun would light our southern sky. While

Drawn by J. Knowles Hare

"A WIND, FILLED WITH DRIFTING SNOW PARTICLES, STRIKING OUR FACES AND TURNING OUR CHEEKS AND NOSES WHITE"

we watched the light left the side of the mountain, gradually rising and moving eastward Daily she arose becoming more beautiful to the eye, shining with dazzling brilliancy.

In addition to being objects of beauty the stars were our dependence for time when the sun was not visible, and many long cold hours were spent by Mr. Peters at the transit in the astronomical observatory on the hill. When the temperature dropped lower than 30 degrees below zero observing was a trying occupation. The small tangent screws could not be managed with the fingers in mittens, and to expose the hand to the frigid air for only a few seconds was painful While looking through the eye-piece of a transit or a theodolite the observer could not breathe with freedom for every exhalation had to be directed away from the instrument or the lenses, divisions, and the verniers would become coated with ice ,While preparing for the spring sledge work I spent much time in the open air with a small theodolite and had reason to understand the troubles of an observer.

Cold weather during the Christmas holidays and in the early part of January gave me reason to hope for a colder spring than that of 1904. During a period of moonlight we observed a sheet of smooth young ice which gave promise of a good road north. But the southeast wind—that ever present wind—destroyed all visions of an easy path. By January 18th the temperature had risen to 10 degrees above zero and the howling gales had blown the ice from the land and opened the sea On January 24, 1905, I wrote:

"The wind is howling without as if pandemonium were let loose and the house is shaking under the blast. Darkness covers this part of the earth, for the sun is still below the horizon. It is near noon, but our only illumination is a number of oil lamps that burn day and night in a feeble attempt to apologise for the absence of His Majesty the Sun. It is true that, monthly, Madame Moon has visited us and shed over the landscape and ice her luminous rays of cold reflected light. But she has done so only when old Boreas has been asleep and he has slept little this winter.

"I have just come in from taking a look outside. In the entrance way to our castle I was set upon by about twenty dogs, all frantic to show me how pleased they were to see me and the light I carried. When the elements war without the dogs crowd into the entrance ways and storage tents, curl themselves into fur balls as close together as possible, and sleep out the periods of storm. But just as soon as the storm is over they hold high carnival that generally ends in a free-for-all fight, and often in the death of a dog unless we are quick to find the murderous creatures and take from them the dog that has incurred the antagonism of the pack."

During the period of darkness we lost eight dogs; three of them splendid, large animals, Nansen, Tochkoff, and Spot, were killed by their companions. The other five either wandered off on the young ice and were blown away or were killed by the pack at a distance from camp. Every dog was known by name. It is a curious fact that when one dog has antagonised the others the only way to save him from destruction later on is to chain him. Then the other dogs let him alone. Unfortunately for us the dogs that seemed to

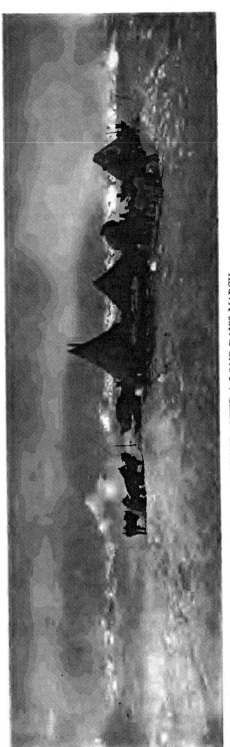

CAMPING AFTER A LONG DAY'S MARCH
Unharnessing the dogs after the tents were pitched

SUN WITH TWO MOCK SUNS
Photographed March 19, 1905

ENTERING THE ROUGH ICE

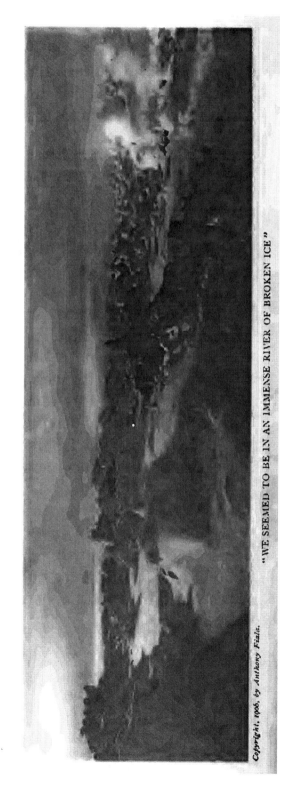

"WE SEEMED TO BE IN AN IMMENSE RIVER OF BROKEN ICE"

incur the enmity of their fellows were the large, strong animals—the bullies and fighters. There seemed to be a degree of justice in their judgments. From close observation, I found that the dogs generally forgave a bite on the head or body, while an attack on the legs seemed to be considered foul play and must be paid for by the life of the offending canine—the whole pack uniting in his execution.

On the departure of the party retreating south in April, 1904, sixty-six dogs were left at Camp Abruzzi. Twenty-three dogs were taken away by Mr. Porter's party on May 9, leaving forty-three in camp. Of these, eight were lost up to the date of my arrival, leaving a total of thirty-five dogs. Of these thirty-five, eight were pups born at camp the winter before and too young for heavy work. From the twenty-seven available dogs remaining two good teams could hardly be picked out. Thirty-three dogs were brought up by my party from Cape Flora, reaching camp November 20th and increased the number of dogs and pups to sixty-eight. During the winter, three good dogs were killed by the pack and five disappeared, reducing the total number to sixty, my dependence for the march north. February 20, 1905, I arranged the dogs in six teams of nine dogs each, being obliged to use some of the pups to make up the required number.

CHAPTER XXI

THE RETURN OF THE SUN

ON MARCH 5th I wrote:

"February has been an awful month for storms. There was but one fairly clear day and we utilised it to make a sledge trip to Cape Auk, where we replaced the meridian mark destroyed by storms during the winter.

"We saw the sun for the first time March the first, shining through a veil of fog on the horizon to the south. Ever since it has been cloudy and stormy.

"We have been busy loading the sledges for the trip North. If it is good weather we may be able to get off next week. The loss of all the ponies and the small number of dogs limit me considerably. I have decided to go with one man and three dog teams—a support of men and dogs accompanying me only a few days as it will be necessary for me to send as many dogs as I can back for use of the party—who are to transport food to Camp Ziegler.

"The man I have chosen is a strong obedient sailor, Duffy by name, who would rather be on the trail than in the house. We will have about 100 days' food for ourselves and about fifty days' food for the dogs. With the limitations before mentioned I have little hope of reaching the Pole and look forward as an achievement to breaking the noble Captain Cagni's record. Both Duffy and I are determined to do our utmost. I intend to use the dogs as long as their food lasts. Afterward we will pull the sledges ourselves."

Duffy had accompanied me on the trip in 1904 to Cape Barentz and formed one of my party from Cape Flora to Camp Abruzzi in the autumn of that year. He had also volunteered to return with me from Cape Flora in June 1904.

I arranged for Mr. Peters to accompany me north in charge of the third supporting party and on his return to camp to remain in command of the expedition until my return from the field. A party of men at Camp Abruzzi were directed to leave for Camp Ziegler after the return of the supporting column and to spend the time from the latter part of March to the end of June, or until the ice broke up, in sledging supplies from Camp Abruzzi and Coburg Island to Kane Lodge and from there to Camp Ziegler, to provide food in the event of the Relief Ship's not reaching that point in the summer of 1905. The teams to be returned to camp from the north were to be divided by Mr. Peters so as to provide one team of dogs to each two men.

A trace of twilight in the southern sky at noon gladdened our eyes during the last days of January. Each day the light became stronger and stayed with us longer. We utilised the twilight of February 15th to make a sledge journey to Cape Auk, where we erected a signal pole as an azimuth mark for the astronomical observatory at camp, the one placed there the year before having been destroyed by the storms of winter. We fortunately chose the only day in the month free from wind or fog. It was a beautiful period of about six hours of twilight. A full moon almost in conjunction with the two blazing planets, Jupiter and Venus, helped to illuminate the scene and added to the strange, almost unearthly beauty of the view revealed to us from the summit of the glacier. The afternoon of Sunday the 12th of February the weather was clear and for the sake of exercise I walked along the high ridge of rocks from the astronomical observatory to Cape Saulen. In the dim light I could see nothing but great sheets of dark coloured young salty ice stretching out toward the horizon north and west till it was lost in mist. On my return I sighted a bear out on the rough ice of Teplitz Bay. With her were what I took to be two dogs.

All three made off toward the thin ice on the edge of the bay. Remembering that our Steward had always wished for the opportunity of a shot at a bear, and just then being in need of fresh meat I ran to camp and told Spencer of my find. He had not been feeling well and was lying down in his bunk, but he brightened up and seized his gun and with Seaman Perry we went out accompanied by a pack of dogs. Their barking soon announced that the bear was discovered. Climbing over the ice cakes we found a female bear, with two cubs, fighting the dogs. The three of them put up a splendid fight and were so mixed up with the dogs that it was a difficult task to shoot a bear without injury to the pack. At last the old bear exposed her head in a desperate charge and Spencer fired and killed her. Then there was a battle royal between the dogs and the cubs. The young bears were quite large and active and fought surprisingly well, each engaging about eight dogs, the centre of a growling, snarling, biting, heap. Perry shot one; the other, pursued by the pack, charged my way and I was obliged to put a bullet through his head.

Sketch by Anthony Fiala

A MILE AND A HALF NORTH IN EIGHT HOURS

The next day another bear appeared and our dogs followed him out in a fog on to the young ice, dangerous because the least wind from the east would break it up and open the sea. Darkness descended before all of them returned from the hunt. Alarmed for their safety I fired a rocket and a number of signal lights which on previous occasions had been effective in attracting them to camp. The absentees came in later, their coating of ice showing that they had been in the water. We thawed them out beside the stove, after which I instructed the men to chain them up. Soon their doleful howls and yelps announced to us their dissatisfaction, the young dogs particularly being distressed at their loss of freedom.

As I have stated, February 1905 was noted for the number of storms, and the return of the sun brought no respite from the high drifting winds that continued to blow through the early days of March. The temperature see-sawed and was often above zero.

On February 21st a little auk was seen swimming in the sea near the edge of the bay ice, and a seal was shot. On the same day Tessem, the carpenter, shot a seal and the Steward a guillemot. Several days later they secured two more seals and three guillemots, while Doctor Seitz killed a large bear. More birds were secured on March the 14th. The presence of the birds so early in the year troubled me as harbingers of an early summer. It was unusual for them to come before June. The warmer weather of which their presence was a warning was unseasonable at this time of the year and was usually accompanied by almost incessant storms and winds which would have the effect of making our road rough and creating numerous lanes of water in the Polar pack.

We used every interval of calm in sledge trips over to Cape Saulen for the purpose of training our dogs and hardening them for the work. I waited anxiously for Porter with his small team of powerful dogs, to arrive with news from Camps Ziegler and Jackson (C. Flora). But the bad weather that prevented our departure for the north also delayed his coming to us. Our sledges had been loaded during the first days of March and we were only waiting for the wind to cease.

The detail of the sledge column was as follows:

First Support: Assistant Surgeon Seitz and Seaman Perry, one team of nine dogs (all poor dogs and pups), one sledge, tent, camping equipment, and rations for ten men and fifty-nine dogs for one day, and three days' rations for two men and one dog team for return to camp. This party was not furnished with a kayak as they were not expected to leave the Island and because it would have increased the weight of the load beyond the power of the team. The three days' food was provided for the return in case of storms.

Second Support: Steward Spencer and Seaman Meyer, one team of seven dogs, one sledge, a two man kayak, a tent and camping outfit, two days' rations for the advance of eight men and fifty dogs, five days' rations for the return of two men and seven dogs.

Third Support: Chief Scientist Peters, Assistant Engineer Vedoe, Assistant Commissary Stewart, and Carpenter Tessem, two teams of eight dogs each, two sledges, two kayaks, two tents and camping equipment, navigation instruments, six days' rations for the ad-

SOFT SNOW AND ROUGH ICE

SLEDGE TEAMS WAITING TO BE ASSISTED OVER A SNOW-COVERED PRESSURE RIDGE. ALL OF THE MEN BUT ONE ARE CON-
CEALED BEHIND THE MASS OF ICE AND SNOW

vance of six men and forty-three dogs and ten days' rations for the return of four men and two dog teams to Camp Abruzzi.

Of course, in addition to the above, each detachment was provided with ice picks, arms, and ammunition, of which I give a detailed account in the appendix to this volume.

Seaman Duffy and myself formed the Advance Party with three teams of nine dogs each, three sledges, one canvas canoe, one tent, camp equipment, and instruments. We were provisioned with food for two men for a hundred days and an allowance of dog food for about sixty days, the dogs to be killed for food as necessity required.

In planning the above I could not allow for more than a week's support all told. I had to keep in mind the need of dogs at camp and the necessity of keeping them in as good condition as possible as, on the return of the three supporting parties to Camp Abruzzi, the dogs (thirty-two in number) would have to sledge stores south to Camp Ziegler. A heavy load of food for the dogs on the return journey was accordingly carried on all the sledges of the supports. Then on account of the open condition of the sea there was the need of carrying heavy kayaks. The few dog teams and the dead weights of kayaks, tents, equipment, and return food, was so great that the party could not carry enough food to permit of a longer period of support. I could depend therefore on but seven days' help in all from my three supports. The third support was so arranged that Peters acted as guide while Stewart helped Duffy and me with our three sledges.

CHAPTER XXII

OUR THIRD AND LAST FIGHT WITH THE POLAR ICE

ON THE 15th of March the wind ceased, the temperature went down, and the air cleared. Next day we hitched up our teams, and at half past ten in the morning left Camp Abruzzi for the ice pack to the north, climbing the glacier in the direction of Cape Rath. Though newly formed smooth, salt ice seemed to stretch north and northwest to the horizon, the continual movement and breaking of the ice and the prevalent open water to the westward decided me to advance from the east of the island in order to insure the safety of my supporting parties on their return.

Engineer Hartt volunteered to remain at camp alone until the return of the First Support. Every other man took part in the advance north. As we left camp that cold March morning, climbing north over the glacier, we could discern on looking back the solitary figure of the Engineer. The only other sign of life on that desolate waste in our rear was "Bruno" a three-legged dog, barking and whining disconsolately because he was not permitted to follow his companions yoked in the sledge teams.

We crossed the summit and then directed our way toward Cape Rath where Steward Spencer and I descended in April 1904. When approaching the eastern side of the island, and while going down the long slope

"OUR TRAIL WAS FROM ICE CAKE TO ICE CAKE"

Sledges waiting while the trail was being cut

"WE WERE ALL OBLIGED TO GO AHEAD OF THE SLEDGES WITH OUR PICKS AND ICE AXES TO LABOUR AT CUTTING THE TRAIL,"

AND THEN RETURN AND ASSIST THE TEAMS AND SLEDGES, ONE BY ONE, OVER THE ROUGH ROAD"

of the glacier nearing the sea level, we saw a bear and
two cubs slowly making their way toward Hohenlohe
Island, and in the channel near the glacier was a water
hole in which birds were swimming and over which we
could see a flock of birds flying.   Just as darkness
came down we reached the edge of the glacier finding
that it had calved since 1904.   About a thousand yards
of the terminal slope had broken off leaving a high
perpendicular face of ice from the top of which a descent
was impracticable.   I ordered camp for the night and
the next morning sent back the First Support.   At
8 A. M., Dr. Seitz and Perry left me with their dog
team and sledge, ascending the glacier on their return to Teplitz Bay, while we directed our course
along the edge of the glacier toward Cape Habermann
where a descent to the channel was possible.   We were
obliged to go a short distance eastward, to round a mass
of icebergs, and then set our faces northward (magnetic)
camping that night on heavy ice that seemed to be
fast to the land and was close to a pressure ridge that
separated us from the moving sea ice.

The next morning we cut our way through hills of
ice, reaching an expanse of young ice broken and under pressure.   From that point I ordered the Second
Support to return and Steward Spencer and Seaman
Meyer left at 3.30 o'clock that afternoon, returning
over the trail we had cut going out.

An odometer brought from camp for measuring
the distance travelled was destroyed in the rough ice
on the outward march that day and abandoned.
Four more days we held our way northward, the trail
bending more to the east as we advanced.   The ice

was very rough, worse than in 1904, and very slow progress was made, as for every few yards gained we were obliged to go ahead of our sledges armed with picks and ice-axes to cut the trail and then return and assist the teams and sledges one by one over the rough road. We seemed to be in an immense river of broken ice that moved under the influence of the wind. Our trail was from ice-cake to ice-cake, while we crossed the separating water by means of ice bridges laboriously constructed at the narrowest points by means of our picks. In other places we traversed monster pressure ridges that splintered and thundered under our feet, frightening the dogs until they whined and whimpered in terror.

It was difficult to find a cake of ice large enough for our small party to camp on. Deep snow and numerous water lanes with a high temperature and attendent fog also impeded our advance. The dogs were often up to their bellies in the deep snow but, urged on by the drivers, hauled our sledges over the most awful ridges and out of deep holes where they had fallen often with runners up in the air. At noon on March 21st I took an altitude of the sun and was disappointed to find that, after all our hard work, our latitude was only 81 degrees and fifty-five minutes North. On March 21, 1895, Nansen was at 85 degrees, nine minutes North and on March 23, 1900, Captain Cagni sent back his ill fated First Detachment from 82 degrees, thirty-two minutes North.

The sledges were standing the hard knocks wonderfully well though ridge after ridge was crossed. A rough trail was first cut then the sledges were hauled

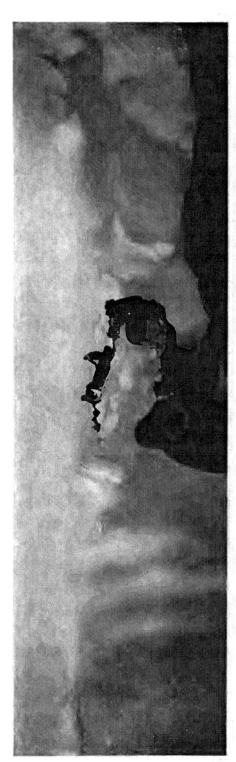

"IN OTHER PLACES WE TRAVERSED MONSTER PRESSURE RIDGES THAT SPLINTERED AND THUNDERED UNDER OUR FEET"

82nd parallel of latitude but found further progress impossible on account of a large open lead filled with broken young ice. From the highest vantage point, nothing was visible but a horrible jumble of ice-cakes on end, mixed small young ice and brash, the whole in motion. To make matters worse the temperature was rising rapidly At last we found a heavy cake surrounded ˙with pressure ice, the only flat block in sight, and on its surface we put up our tents and unhitched our tired dogs.

That evening, Mr. Peters and I freely discussed the outlook. I told him that I purposed pressing north with Duffy after he (Peters) had returned to camp with his party. Peters did not believe that anything could be accomplished by going on, saying that it was an impossibility to break the record in such ice. He pointed out that if six men and five sledges could hardly make three miles a day, two men and three sledges would make still less, as the ice was growing worse as we advanced. He thought our best course was to return to Camp Abruzzi, for should the Relief Ship not arrive that year the three teams of good dogs that I was taking north with me would be seriously missed, and their loss might result gravely for the parties at Cape Flora and Camp Ziegler. He also urged the possibility of a shortage of food and a lack of game at the southern camps. I spent the night sleeplessly and, I may add, prayerfully, revolving in my mind the arguments for and against continuing the advance. It was a bitter disappointment to find retreat inevitable, but I was compelled to admit the cogency of Mr. Peters's arguments and to acknowledge the possi-

up. Shouting at the teams, we bent our backs under
the loads, the heavy work causing the perspiration to
flow copiously in the very lowest temperature we
experienced.

As I recall that trip I wonder what Job would have
done under similar circumstances. Viewed through the
months that have since elapsed, some of the happenings
appear ludicrous, particularly those in which the dogs
took part, but at the time they were serious and ex-
asperating enough. Time and again, just as a sledge
had been laboriously hoisted and poised on a cake in
mid-air, down would rush the dogs yelping with joy
to find their loads suddenly grown so easy, leaving the
driver behind deep in a crevice between blocks of ice.
The sledge crashed down the slope of tumbled blocks,
turning over on its descent and bringing up with its
load of nearly 600 pounds suddenly against a barrier
of ice.

Then the dogs would all sit down happy over the
mishap which gave them a rest while the tired driver
chopped the ice away from his sledge and painfully
lifted it upon its runners again. I often thought that
there was more design than accident in these bursts
of energy on downward slopes.

A number of times we found the drawbars of our
sledges bent flat against a great cake by reason of the
weight of the loads and the speed on the down grade,
but the elastic hickory, on being released, always
jumped back to its form. Stewart, in admiration,
said one day, " Mr. Fiala, these sledges are made of
India rubber!"

On the afternoon of March 22d we reached the

I realised that we had ice and weather conditions un-precedentedly bad, but I hoped for and believed in better ice after we passed the hundred-mile limit from land and got out of the maze of channels and ridges.

But beyond and stronger than pain at heart in being disappointed in my wish to go North, was the reali-sation that the ultimate responsibility was mine and that the right thing for me to do was to turn back and take up the reins of government once more. In the face of possible danger to the lives of those I had left behind, I must not proceed.

Then if it was right to go back it was not right to go any further north and thus chance the loss of men, dogs, or equipment.

The next morning I ordered a return and we set our faces toward the south.

The journey occupied ten days Two days and three nights were spent on a small floating ice-cake, sur-rounded by water and broken, melting ice impassable to boats or sledges. The temperature meanwhile rose to 34 degrees above zero, an abnormal condition since, at that time of the year, it should have registered as many degrees below Our position was made the more perilous by huge mountains of ice that sprang up with the frightful sound of breaking fields and threatened to sweep over and engulf our little camping ground. Once the cake divided and a broad lane opened to within a few feet of us. The following night, with a report like that of a small cannon, a crack appeared directly beneath one of the small tents. Fortunately it did not split the cake asunder.

bility of peril to the expedition party at Cape Flora if unsuccored by the Relief Ship and deprived of the extra dogs needed to haul supplies. Therefore, with our equipment still in perfect condition and with men and dogs in the best of health, I saw that I would have to return and take up the more important duty of the management of the expedition until the arrival of the Relief Ship. I, personally, believed that there was game enough in the Archipelago and that if proper enterprise were shown food in plenty could be secured which augmented by the supplies at the various stations on the islands would obviate all danger of starvation.

If the Cape Flora party, obeying my instructions, placed all their strong men in the field and spent the entire spring and summer sledging supplies from Camp Ziegler to Cape Flora, if they used the whale boats in search of game, making trips to a distance for it if necessary, they would undoubtedly be well supplied for another winter—if they were doomed to another winter in the Arctic But the question arose— "Would this energetic obedience to directions be forthcoming?"

Many bitter thoughts came to me that night as I lay in my sleeping bag.

We had reached only 82 degrees North Lat., but with the food on our three sledges, if Duffy and I could average only five miles a day, we would at least break the record and make some return for the large expenditure of material, supplies, time, and money. We felt ourselves equal in strength, purpose, and endurance to any that had ever been in the field; our equipment was better and our dogs better trained.

"THE ICE WAS ROUGH, WORSE THAN IN 1

In order to extend the view angle so as to include the column of men, dogs and sledges, the pictures were taken as a rule from the summits of high blocks of ice. The high view point had the effect of lowering the ridges and flattening the steep places of which the above photo is an example.

"LOW PROGRESS WAS MADE"

"IT WAS DIFFICULT TO FIND A CAKE OF ICE LARGE ENOUGH FOR OUR SMALL PARTY TO CAMP ON"

"WE FOUND A HEAVY CAKE SURROUNDED WITH PRESSURE ICE, THE ONLY FLAT BLOCK IN SIGHT, AND THERE WE PUT UP OUR TENTS AND UNHITCHED OUR TIRED DOGS"

Of course we lost no time in moving our tent to a more secure location.

We kept watch through the nights by tents, two hours to each of the three tents. There were two men in a tent and one of them, dressed in his furs, kept watch for an hour, at the end of which time he aroused his companion who would dress and, at the expiration of *his* hour on duty, wake up a man in the next tent.

And so a succession of vigilants kept unceasing guard over their sleeping companions.

The dogs lying in the snow chained to picket lines did not know what to think of the unwonted rest. A number of them were pups only a little over a year old and their shrill barks were a ludicrous contrast to the hoarse croaks of the old dogs. At times the whole pack would chorus their emotions in a strange uncanny medley of howls and yelps that we had heard often at camp during the long winter. It was always sung while the dogs were lying down. A musically inclined one would start it by emitting a prolonged howl which was taken up before he ceased by every canine within hearing. It was interesting to trace through their utterances the pedigree of the dogs. Those whose wolf ancestors had been the terror of the lonely Russian Steppes howled dismally, while the descendants of the Fox tribe brought in the treble with their sharp, quick yelps. Each dog lent as much volume as he could, and there was a certain doleful harmony to the flood of sound. Who can say what history of the past, what feats of the hunt, were immortalised by the chant? It ended as suddenly as it began, the last notes usually a few yelps given rapidly and out of key.

The temperature dropped to 4 degrees below zero on the 24th, and, on the morning of the 25th, we made an attempt to cross the newly frozen brash that surrounded our island; but, the temperature rising above zero, we were obliged to retreat again reaching our old ice-cake just in time. The ice was in motion around us and opened into broad lanes and deep holes. On the 26th, the thermometer indicated 10 degrees below zero and under a shining sun we marched toward the island whose dome of ice seemed far away. We crossed ridge after ridge and some of the worst ice seen thus far. The trail we had so laboriously cut on our way out had been obliterated by crushing ice fields, and the thunder of the forces of frozen nature was in our ears as we bent our course south.

We came to a wide lead in which a large iceberg was jammed and with its great solid bulk prevented the two fields from meeting. We spent an hour chopping an inclined plane up its face and then hauled our sledges over its crest to the other side. The tired dogs would lie down at every opportunity and we shouted ourselves hoarse in urging them on. Three English ice-axes we had brought with us were broken early in the march north and in cutting the trail, we depended entirely upon the formidable Collins picks. These tools were manufactured in America for mining prospectors and weighed, with their handles, from four and a half to five pounds each. They were more satisfactory than the Alpine axe and in two years of hard use we never broke one.

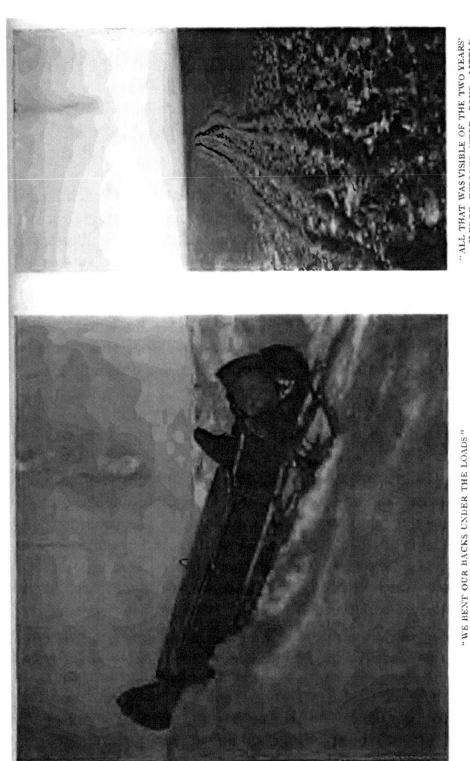

"ALL THAT WAS VISIBLE OF THE TWO YEARS' SLEDGE EFFORTS WERE FOUR LITTLE TRACKS IN THE SNOW THAT COULD BE TRACED UP THE GLACIER TOWARD THE MYSTERIOUS NORTH"

"WE BENT OUR BACKS UNDER THE LOADS"

The dogs had fallen into the water so often while crossing leads that they grew timid as the temperature lowered and the wind arose.

One of my dogs, Isaac by name, was continually causing trouble by slipping his harness when we neared a lead Once loose he was difficult to catch. A commotion invariably arose among the teams when they caught sight of Ike unharnessed, for nothing angered them so much as to see one of their number running free while they toiled in the traces. Once, in crossing a small lane Isaac slipped his collar and started off, but before he got away Duffy's team gave chase and Growler, particularly offended at Ikey's defection, pounced upon him and held him by the throat until I came up and secured him. He received a severe whipping which the other dogs seemed to thoroughly enjoy, and was tied into his harness with a piece of rawhide. He gave no further trouble after that.

We had been obliged to turn four dogs loose— Robert, Grabber, Bugler, and Neddie. The first named we shot later as absolutely useless; Grabber and Bugler were too old and inactive to be of service and little Neddie, a pup, was too young to pull well and needed more training before we could use him successfully. These dogs formed our rear guard. They felt their inadequacy and followed respectfully about twenty yards behind the last sledge At night when we halted, they came shamefaced into camp, their arrival heralded by the barks of the other dogs who snarled and showed their teeth and would have nothing to do with them. We fed all three for I thought they could be used later in hauling loads over the smooth stretches in the channels from Teplitz Bay south to Camp Ziegler.

The winds that blew from the 27th of March to the end of the month were exceedingly cold. The temperature steadily falling reached 45 degrees below zero on the 31st, the day we reached Cape Habermann. Marching was really painful, a ten- or fifteen-mile-an-hour wind, filled with drifting snow particles, striking our faces and turning our cheeks and noses white. We called to each other continually, "Your nose is frozen!" or, "Your cheeks are frozen!" The dogs gave us much trouble by their unwillingness to face the freezing blast. We raised our tents under the shadow of the great mass of rocks and ice discovered and named Cape Habermann by Payer, and there we had protection from the wind.

The Polar traveller on a sledge journey is troubled by an accumulation of ice on his tent, sleeping bag, and clothing. On account of the low temperature the moisture from the body, instead of escaping as vapour, condenses in the cold clothing or sleeping bag. When the cooker is heating the food the interior of the tent is filled with a fog of condensation that whitens every object under cover. Companions in a tent have difficulty in seeing each other by reason of the fog, and the damp atmosphere accentuates the experience of cold. When he camps at night he is obliged to unfasten frozen dog harness that sticks to his fingers pulling off the skin. He must thaw out his frozen sleeping bag by the heat of his body and on awaking in the morning soften his deer skin shoes, which froze

Seaman Mackiernan

Ass't. Scientist Russell W. Porter

"MR. PORTER WAS ON HAND TO GREET ME WITH SEAMAN MACKIERNAN, HAVING REACHED CAMP ABRUZZI ON THE 17th OF MARCH"

as hard as steel during the night, by the warmth of his hands and pull on his frozen outer garments stiffer than an ancient warrior's suit of mail.   All this, however, is gladly endured if only he may attain Success in the end.

On April 1st we crossed the glacier and descended to Teplitz Bay and once again found ourselves at Camp Abruzzi—the place of many hopes and disappointments to me.

As I stood looking northward over the way we had just come, all that was visible of the two years' sledge efforts were four little tracks in the snow that could be traced up the glacier toward the Mysterious North, the Polar explorer's paradise, guarded by the Angels of Cold and Darkness whose flaming swords illumine the skies with auroral splendour during the Polar night.

CHAPTER XXIII

FROM TEPLITZ BAY TO CAMP ZIEGLER

I WAS pleased to find on reaching camp that both supporting parties had returned in safety, and that Mr. Porter was on hand to greet me with Seaman Mackiernan, having arrived at Camp Abruzzi on the 17th of March, the day after I left for the north. Porter's march had been a trying experience, bad weather, with the loss of his sledge and part of his equipment in a snow drift, delaying his progress and preventing his reaching me in time to take part in the sledge trip. He gave me the good news that everyone was alive and well at Cape Flora and at Camp Ziegler and that the winter had passed without accident. Two of the men, Second Officer Nichols and Seaman Kunold, were not in good health, but he thought the return of the sun and warm weather would help them to an early recovery.

Porter also brought me letters from Capt. Coffin and Observer Long at Camp Jackson, and from Mr. Rilliet at Camp Ziegler. They all told of having passed the winter successfully and asked for tobacco and supplies. Porter told me that the men at Camp Jackson suffered considerably for want of tobacco Accordingly I arranged for a sledge party to leave for Cape Flora in early April with two sledge loads of tobacco and food. This party was to go, after delivering the stores, to Kane Lodge and spend the spring and early summer hauling food and supplies from there to Camp Ziegler. I arranged for still another party to work between Camp Abruzzi and Kane Lodge and to move the larger part of the cache on Coburg Island to the latter place. From Kane Lodge both parties would unite in moving the stores to Camp Ziegler

The work of exploration and survey was not completed in 1904, and I instructed Mr. Porter to penetrate the unmapped country known as Zichy Land from the south and east while I rounded the islands from the north and west, mapping as I went down later in the season

We had bad weather at camp until April 9th. On the 11th, Assistant Engineer Vedoe with Stewart and Tessem left for Cape Flora. They had two heavy sledges, each pulled by a team of seven dogs. Mr. Vedoe carried a bag of mail for Camp Ziegler and Cape Flora. Some postage stamps had been designed and printed and, before the departure of the mail, the men found pleasure in writing to their comrades at the southern stations and in pasting on the envelopes the expedition stamps Porter cut a cancelling stamp on rubber and with it the postage was marked in the most approved and regular style.

Doctor Seitz with Seamen Duffy and Mackiernan left at the same time with three teams and sledge loads. Their destination was Kane Lodge, where their loads of food stores were to be deposited. The rest of the season was to be spent by them in transporting stores from the large cache at Coburg Island to Kane Lodge while Mr. Vedoe and his party, on [their return from

Cape Flora, carried the stores from Kane Lodge to Camp Ziegler. After the required amount of pemmican, etc., had been moved to Kane Lodge by Doctor Seitz's party, I instructed him to join forces with Vedoe and together transport supplies to Camp Ziegler, continuing at this work until the ice showed signs of breaking up.

On the 17th Doctor Seitz's party returned to Camp Abruzzi for a second load having successfully deposited stores at Kane Lodge. They reported exciting adventures with Polar bears having killed three large ones in self-defence, the last within a few feet of them. The carcasses of three walruses which they had secured for dog food undoubtedly attracted the other two bears which made a savage attack upon the men who escaped through a fog, having fired their last round of ammunition away. Duffy said, "Shure everywhere you looked, begob, you would see a bear! Shure they were thicker than flies in the summer time!"

The same day Mr. Peters and Perry left for the south with scientific instruments and records, and Messrs. Porter, Spencer, and Meyer left with two sledge loads of equipment for Camp Ziegler.

On April 20th Doctor Seitz, Duffy, and Mackiernan started on their last trip for Kane Lodge, leaving Engineer Hartt and myself alone at Camp Abruzzi. I wished to leave the Camp in good condition, and to that end we transported a rifle, tools, ammunition, and pieces of equipment that could not be taken south to the observatory on the hill, reasoning that under its shelter they could not be injured by streams of glacier water which I feared would run through the camp in

ON THE WAY TO CAMP ZIEGLER, MAY, 1905

Sledge party, transporting food from Camp Abruzzi, nearing Alger Island

Drawn by Russell W. Porter

[Photo: Newstadt Island]

the summer time. A kayak and sledge with fur clothing, a tent, and camping equipment—to provide for the possible visit of a party in years to come when the main camp might be under snow and ice—were also taken to the observatory.

Eleven dogs remained at camp of which Flannigan, Jacob, Yellow, and Timmerman were good strong sledge animals. Malcheska, a splendid dog, was limping from a wound given by a bear, while another dog possessed only three legs, having lost the other by an accidental shot. The others were discarded animals and included in addition to Bugler and Neddie, of whom I have spoken, Thor, Francis, and Grey. I found on the trail that the poor dogs would not pull if hitched up with good ones. They let the willing dogs do all the work. To use the whip was to ruin the hard workers. So I arranged them in two teams of five dogs each, placing all the good dogs in one and all the poor dogs in the other. I found that the indifferent team could not, or would not, haul even so much as 150 pounds the first time I took them out. Gradually, by the exercise of much patience and training, their ability increased until they hauled a load of 400 pounds without my help, Thor, who had never been known to work before, pulling willingly and powerfully and seeming to enjoy the exercise

On May 26th Hartt and I left our northern station for Camp Ziegler. We took our last look at the deserted settlement of Camp Abruzzi and at the icy bay of Teplitz behind us, the most desolate of all sights— an Arctic desolation. On the march south I had the Engineer go ahead while at some distance behind I

followed with the two teams.   I had placed the weaker
team in the lead with its small sledge and load weighing 375 pounds; following came my good team drawing a sledge load and canoe weighing 543 pounds and
an odometer weighing about eight and a half pounds.
This arrangement of teams allowed me to halt when
I wished to plot angles and read distances—the comparatively smooth ice in the channels after we left the
vicinity of the coast permitting a degree of accuracy in
measuring distances on the odometer.

We found much open water on our journey and in
rounding Cape McClintock were obliged to use the
canoe. The heavy weight of canoe, instruments,
equipment, records, etc., prevented our taking sufficient dog food and I depended upon the cache at Cape
McClintock to replenish my stock of pemmican. But
on arriving at the Cape I found that the place had
been visited by a bear and the cache destroyed. We
found only four cans of pemmican. Though we were
thus prevented by lack of [dog food from threading
the new channels through Zichy Land. we yet had
glimpses of that new territory.

We camped on Ziegler and Luigi Islands and later
within a short distance of Cape Clare on Champ Island.

We arrived at Camp Ziegler on June 19th, where I
was glad to find that my instructions had been carefully followed, a great cache of thousands of pounds of
food having been gathered from the different stations
north by the industrious sledge parties and cached at
our summer headquarters on Alger Island.

Very little of the large amount of food left there by
Baldwin had been taken away by sledge parties from

Asst. Eng. A. Vedoe   Asst. Commissary S. W. Stewart   Asst. Surgeon C. L. Seitz, M. D.   Seaman J. Duffy   Seaman D. Mackiernan   Carpenter P. L. Tessem

THE SLEDGE PARTIES FOR KANE LODGE AND CAPE FLORA READY TO LEAVE CAMP ABRUZZI—APRIL 11, 1905

Cape Saulen
"WE LEFT THE ICY BAY OF TEPLITZ BEHIND US."

The Odometer

ON THE MARCH SOUTH ENGINEER HARTT WENT AHEAD WHILE SOME DISTANCE
BEHIND I FOLLOWED WITH THE TWO TEAMS.

Cape Brorak.

THE CAMP AFTER OUR FIRST DAY'S MARCH FROM TEPLITZ BAY

Cape Flora. On inquiry I learned that in March a party of four men, Vaughan and Moulton of the Field Party, and Hudgins and Beddow of the crew, with two dog teams and sledges had made two trips for food from Cape Flora to Camp Ziegler   In April, Hudgins and Montrose, with dog team and sledge, made another journey for food for the ship's company   I learned also that, following instructions, Vedoe and his companions had taken the food stores and tobacco to Cape Flora, arriving there on Easter Eve, and that the men were very thankful for the addition to their stores, especially for the tobacco.

The large Vertical Circle loaned to the expedition by the Christiana Observatory, together with two chronometers and valuable scientific instruments, were transported in safety over the ice from Teplitz Bay to Camp Ziegler, and two observatories were very ingeniously erected under the direction of Mr. Peters.

The Magnetic Observatory, in the construction of which not a nail or a piece of iron could be used, was built of old oars and roofing material, the rolls of ruberoid sheeting serving as walls, the whole fabric lashed together with marline by Seaman Meyer. The astronomical observatory was built of cases (still full of emergency rations), wire netting, and roofing material by Mr. Porter on his return from his trip of exploration.

After the work of sledging was over both observatories were in constant use in a regular routine of work. Porter's mapping trip through Zichy Land had been successful   He had penetrated the region through an uncharted channel, surveying three new islands and four channels and mapping numerous capes and headlands.

CHAPTER XXIV

WAITING FOR RELIEF IN 1905.

ON OUR arrival at Camp Ziegler we found the two little houses there surrounded by great embankments of snow. Much was accomplished in the digging of drains for melting snow water, and it was necessary to cut ice and dig constantly as the rising sun melted the hard packed masses. It was not until the end of July that we had rest from pick and shovel. On July 4th I sent Doctor Seitz, Stewart, and Butland with two dog teams, a sledge and a boat over the fast frozen channel to see if there was any game at Cape Dillon and to report on the condition of the ice south of the islands. The party returned July 11th. Doctor Seitz reported that game seemed plentiful, and that they had secured and cached two walruses. He also gave me the cheering news that a large body of open water which seemed to stretch to the horizon was visible from the highest point of the cape. A week after their return I sent the same party to Cape Dillon with a canoe, sledges, and three weeks' food to keep watch for the expected Relief Ship and to hunt for game to prepare for the winter should the ship not arrive.

On the following day I sent seamen Duffy, Perry, and Mackiernan also to Cape Dillon to assist in the

CROSSING A LEAD IN THE CHANNEL ICE HAULING A TEAM OF DOGS THROUGH THE WATER

CAMP ZIEGLER—JUNE, 1905

"THE TWO LITTLE HOUSES WERE SURROUNDED BY GREAT EMBANKMENTS OF SNOW"

THE ENTRANCE TO THE HUTS AT CAMP ZIEGLER

watch for the ship and hunting of game so that a continual outlook could be kept day and night.

By keeping in the field all spring and summer, the men were in splendid condition physically, but as the month of July drew to its close without a sign of relief anxiety expressed itself on the countenances of my comrades.   The Steward climbed the high hill back of the camp almost every day, taking with him a powerful binocular.   Though the sea was twenty miles away—too far to sight a sail—and the channel was fast with ice, it gave him a sense of satisfaction to look down toward the way of escape and watch for the steamer's smoke.   He was the most successful seal hunter in the party and never was so happy as when he secured one of these wary creatures.   He would drag himself out on the ice imitating the motions of a seal and thus get within shooting distance before the animal was aware of his danger.   I shot one at long range once but he had life enough left to wiggle into his hole.   I never succeeded in securing one or in approaching within killing range.   A seal always lies within a foot or two of his hole, usually situated in the centre of a large clear space free of hummocks behind which his great enemy, the Polar bear, can hide.   The least sound communicated to his sensitive ear through the ice, or the sight of an unfamiliar object is enough to make him disappear.   Unless the bullet is put through the seal's head and instant death results he will use his last breath to sink in the water out of reach.

We lived well at Camp Ziegler on Polar bear steaks and on walrus and seal livers, varying the diet of fresh food with fried brant and guillemots which were really very palatable. At the station we found a large store of Swedish conserves with oatmeal, rice, flour, and emergency ration of which we made use.

Stewart and John Vedoe discovered the nesting place of a pair of brant and secured the eggs, thus proving that they were not hybrids or sterile as has been stated.

After the departure of the six men for Cape Dillon the small party at Camp Ziegler worked hard to put the houses in repair and make things comfortable for the winter. I instructed the industrious carpenter to repair an old walrus boat in which I prepared to take a load of provisions to Cape Flora just as soon as the channel opened, for I reasoned that unless the party at that point had been very active in the search for game they would be short of food in the latter days of August.

Game could be had though we saw very little at Camp Ziegler and found it necessary to make trips to a distance in the search for it.

A bear was secured at Cape Tegetthof, about forty-five miles from camp, by three seamen, Duffy, Meyer, and Perry. Sledge journeys for game were also made to North Island and West Camp and later, as before mentioned, to Cape Dillon—the party there being the most successful, securing sixteen walruses, one large seal, and a bear.

In the last days of July a feeling of depression seemed to possess some of the men and they were harrassed with the fear that we would be left in the Archipelago for another winter. The more optimistic would speak of the dark sky south which could be seen from camp and which indicated open water where before there was nothing but ice   While last year the prevailing winds were from the southeast and had a tendency to lock up the ice in the Barentz Sea, this summer we were favoured with both southwest and northerly winds, the former bringing with them the roll of the western ocean, broke up the ice, while the latter would disperse it.

There was at heart an anxiety felt by all and evidenced in the longing looks that were daily sent down Aberdare Channel.

The sun shining day and night melted the surface snow and ice in the channel, and great lakes of fresh water formed, spreading out as far as one could see, and reflecting the blue of the sky   The ice underneath began to disintegrate and at places the sea water came through   When a wind was not blowing a dense fog usually covered the land and water and often a flurry of rain would make us think of warmer climes.

About half a mile from camp there was a large pool of water, and on Sunday afternoon, July 30th, Seaman Meyer and I launched our little canvas canoe intending to take a sail around the pond. We had dragged the canoe out on a sledge through a fog that concealed shore and camp.   Just as the bow of the boat touched the water I heard the clear notes of the bugle at camp sounding the "recall."   Not since my service in the cavalry in 1898 had I heard that sound It had an urgent meaning   We ceased our preparations for the sail and the same question was in the eyes of both when we looked at each other—News!   Was it relief?   I told Meyer to place the canoe on the sledge and wait and if he heard three blasts on the bugle, to come in with the sledge and boat; if the signal was not given, I would return. Putting on my skees I threaded my way between the water pools to the shore where I saw the teams, sledges, and boats of the Cape Dillon party. Mr. Stewart was awaiting my arrival, and with smiling face told me that the Relief Ship *Terra Nova*, Captain Kjeldsen, had arrived off Cape Dillon at 1.30 that morning with my friend Mr. William Champ on board and in charge.

On entering the house I found a happy party of men. Doctor Seitz handed me a letter from Mr. Champ, my first news from the outside world in more than two years. Mr. Champ wrote that he was on the *Terra Nova* en route to Cape Flora to rescue the men who had wintered there. That accomplished he would return immediately with the ship to Cape Dillon and there await the arrival of my party, as the ice in the channel was still too solid for the ship to force her way through the twenty miles to Camp Ziegler. His letter also informed me of the death of Mr. Ziegler, an intelligence that cast a gloom over me shadowing the happiness I felt in the relief of my men. The experience of the two years with its numerous sledge journeys had given me an insight into Arctic conditions that I believed would be invaluable for future work, and made me feel that with an another opportunity this dearly bought experience might purchase victory. And in addition to my sense of personal loss in the death of a good friend, was the realisation that with his departure possibly the work would cease.

The long strain at last was over! Members of the

Asst. Commissary Stewart.   Fireman Buthard.

SIXTEEN GREAT WALRUSES WERE SECURED BY THE PARTY AT CAPE DILLON

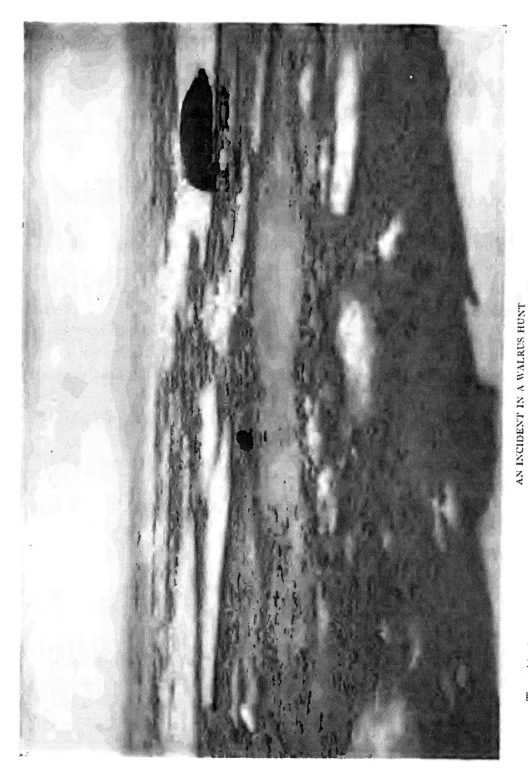

AN INCIDENT IN A WALRUS HUNT

The seal in the centre of the picture put his head out of the water just after the walrus on the ice cake was shot. He seemed quite interested but disappeared on approach of the boat

Cape Dillon party with those at camp talked happily over the prospect of home going. Plans were formed for pleasure trips through Europe en route home.

Many expressed their longing to possess the letters and packages from relatives and friends awaiting them on the *Terra Nova*.

The Cape Dillon party had made a splendid march through fog and bad ice to our camp, every one of them anxious to unburden himself of the good news. They had tramped through miles of surface water, over the channel ice and crossed leads, making the entire distance—a little over twenty miles—in less than seven hours.

While the Steward—his face wreathed in smiles—prepared a meal for the travellers, we plied them with questions. We were all especially amused at Duffy's account of the ship's arrival.

I did not expect the *Terra Nova* to return to Cape Dillon from Cape Flora until late the following day and thought it unnecessary for us to hurry down the channel.

When the sun was low, during the hours we through force of habit called night, the surface water froze over into thin sheets of ice that cut the dogs' feet. I believed it would be better to leave camp near noon and thus allow time for the midday sun and the higher temperature to thaw these sheets, so glass-like and sharp.

The great cache of food stores we had placed on a sand hill was moved down to the camp, and the boxes, barrels, and tins stored in the houses. Messrs. Peters and Porter, with the aid of Assistant Engineer Vedoe, packed up the large transit and magnetic instruments and all the records, and soldered them in tin cases to prevent injury.

A boat or kayak was placed on each of the five sledges and instruments, tools, etc., were packed within, as Doctor Seitz had reported much water on the ice and at least one lead which we would need a boat in crossing.

We had one more night's rest in our old sleeping bags. They had served us well and were now worn from use. On arising in the morning our eyes, nostrils, mouths, and ears were full of deer hairs which the bag had shed overnight.

After the houses and observatories at Camp Ziegler had been locked up, and all provisions carefully stored, sledges were loaded for the last time and, in a thick fog, we started south over the ice of Aberdare Channel on our homeward trail.

Fireman Bulland   Asst. Surgeon Seitz

HAULING A DEAD WALRUS ON TO THE ICE FOOT AT CAPE DILLON

WELLMAN'S HOUSE AT CAPE TEGETTHOFF

Visited during the early summer of 1905 by a hunting party from Camp Ziegler

CHAPTER XXV

RESCUED

MEN and dogs took the water like ducks, though in some places it was over our knees, with rotten ice underneath that gave under the weight of the caravan. A fog obscured the view and I went ahead feeling the way with a skee staff—a precaution that saved me many a bath.

After passing a point of land and changing our course we came to a long open lead across which we were obliged to boat the entire party of sixteen men, five sledges, and fifty dogs.

On nearing Cape Frithjof we heard rifle shots and —the fog lifting while we were crossing the lead—we had a glimpse of our rescuers on the farther side

Mr. Champ, accompanied by Surgeon Mount and a party of Norwegian sailors from the *Terra Nova* and Sergt. Moulton and Assistant Engineer Hudgins from the Cape Flora party, had come to meet us out on the ice. And a memorable meeting it was! It was good to look into the face of our brave rescuer and to hear his voice after the long months of separation. Mr. Champ was overjoyed to learn that only one of the large party that had set sail from Norway two years before was missing.

After the first exuberant greetings, came anxious queries for news of home and of the great outside world. We learned, all at once, of the war between Russia and Japan, the result of the international yacht race in 1903, and of the many disasters on land and water that had marked our months of exile.

But what touched every one of us most deeply was to hear from Mr. Champ's lips the account of the death of Mr. William Ziegler. He had died thinking of and providing for our rescue, and his last spoken words had been a wish that we might be found.

In this intensely commercial age it is well to pause and consider one who though in life a prince of finance had yet for his strongest ambition not the possession of material wealth but a wish to enlarge the geographical borders of the world and to capture the most inaccessible region of the earth in the name of his native land.

We travelled together to the *Terra Nova*, Mr. Champ's party using the two dog teams and sledges I had left at Cape Flora in 1904. A dense fog concealed the ship until we were a very short distance from her.

The trail broken through the ice by the relief party proved of much assistance in guiding us to where the ship lay and over it the dogs could move faster and without cutting their feet.

The *Terra Nova* was a glorious sight as she materialised out of the mist—her form glistening in the sunshine as the fog lifted.

I never experienced such a sense of loss as I did on beholding the splendid vessel; never realised so keenly our ship-wrecked condition.

It did not take us long to go aboard and enjoy once again the luxuries of a warm bath, clean clothing, and

fresh food, and, best of all, to receive the two years'
accumulation of mail, the letters from loved ones and
friends.

Aboard the *Terra Nova* we learned from Mr. Champ
of his efforts to reach us in 1904. He and Captain
Kjeldsen, one of the best ice-pilots of Norway, had
hammered away at the ice in the steamer *Frithjof*
until her bow-plates had loosened and fallen off.
When nearly all the coal had disappeared, a return was
made to Norway and the *Frithjof's* bunkers were filled.
At the end of the season still another and a more dangerous effort was made to reach us, the *Frithjof* returning only when the sea began to freeze on the approach of winter.

The ice in 1905 was bad, and at times the powerful
Terra Nova was helpless to advance against it. It
was only after weeks of patient, courageous hard work
that we were rescued in the last days of July.

Those great bags of mail contained but one letter
with sad news It was never delivered. Fireman
Myhre, to whom it was addressed, was asleep in his
tomb on Cape Saulen's height when his wife died in
Norway.

I found all the members of the Cape Flora company
on the *Terra Nova* and 'was glad to note that their
general health seemed good. I learned later that it had
been necessary to help several of them aboard the
ship when rescued. Hardly twenty-four hours had
elapsed since their relief. Joy is a great physician!
There was not a noticeably sick man amongst the number. They had brought on board with them two
little Polar bear cubs which they had captured

at Cape Flora in the spring. The mother had been shot the same day—May 29th—but "Billy" and "Louise" were fed and kept alive at the station until the arrival of the *Terra Nova*.

The ship's company was increased by still another passenger—"Buster Brown," a cub larger than the other two. He had been captured by the relief party out on the ice in Barentz Sea He was so savage a beast and gave so much trouble that it was necessary to confine him to the constricted space of a heavy wooden cage.

Under Captain Kjeldsen's guidance the splendid *Terra Nova* forced her way through the icy Barentz Sea. It is always easier to leave the ice pack than to enter it; to go south than to go north, and, on Sunday, August 6th, we entered the open sea and felt for the first time the motion of the waves.

In the early morning of August 9th our eyes were gladdened by the sight of land as the green hills of Norway rose before us Steaming through the beautiful fjords we felt that our bond with the human race had not been broken, that sunshine the year round would soon be our experience, and God's Country a reality.

We had lost in our raid to the north, and had been forced to return without our ship or the colours of the enemy. Still hope burned in the thought that, over the bones of our dearly bought experience, some day an expedition might march to Discovery and Victory.

ANTHONY FIALA

WM. S. CHAMP

Photographs taken directly after the meeting of the rescued and rescuer on the ice of Abedare Channel

OUR LAST MARCH

WILLIAM S. CHAMP
Commander Ziegler Relief Expedition, 1904-1905

AN AFTERWORD

AN AFTERWORD

BESIDES the tangible results of the Ziegler Polar Expedition in the discovery and mapping of new lands and the recording of scientific data, the lessons learned by the experience of two years in the ice-fields should be of value to prospective explorers.

Outside the realm of the Arctic there are no camps of instruction for Polar travellers; but each expedition, each reconnoissance or assault in force upon the ranks of the Ice King brings new knowledge of his stronghold, new methods of attack.

Every explorer must evolve a plan, provide an equipment, and engage his assistants, and it is to him —the man who contemplates a venture for the Pole— that this chapter is especially addressed.

THE PLAN

After the experiences of 1903–04–05 it appears to me that the most feasible method of attack would be to use a strongly built drift ship on the plan originally suggested by Admiral Melville from observations taken during the drift of the *Jeanette* and materialised later in the successful *Fram*. I would advocate a small ship as it could be more easily handled and would be less liable to destruction. The party on such a vessel should be no larger than absolutely necessary

Our own expedition ship, the *America*, would doubtless not have been lost had she been constructed so as to rise with the pressure and had been heavily timbered to her keel.

As a result of the squeeze of November, 1903, the ship was raised bodily until the thin skin under her armour was reached and penetrated by the ice. She was not strong enough to bear the enormous weight of engine, boiler, and coal in addition to the outside pressure of the ice-fields. The *America's* bow and fore-foot were well armoured to the keel with tough, old "greenheart," which withstood the strain of the fatal nip of Nov. 21, 1903, so well that the bow was raised without injury high enough for us to touch her fore-foot.

As is the case with most whalers of her class, the *America's* heavy, wooden sheathing ended a few feet below the water line, a short distance aft of the bow. For forcing her way through the summer ice-fields she was well constructed. Her thick sides stood many a tight nip and resisted the ice in Teplitz Bay until it caught her "below the belt" of armour.

Wood is, undoubtedly, the best material from which to construct a drift ship as it is more elastic than metal. However a sheathing of steel over an under armour of greenheart would be valuable as a surface protection.

A ship such as I have described would serve as the expedition's base and from it a small, well conditioned sledge party with dogs and ponies could proceed north. The vessel should be equipped with a complete apparatus for wireless telegraphy. The necessity for economy of space and weight would preclude the possibility of carrying a transmitter with its accom-

THE S. Y. "TERRA NOVA"—ZIEGLER RELIEF EXPEDITION 1905

Painted by A. Operti

A. Operti, 1906
N.Y.

paniment of dynamo and machinery on the sledges, and consequently no messages could be sent from field party to ship. A light receiver, however, could be carried and by means of it the sledge party could be informed of the condition and position of the ship. This communication, sent at a specified hour each day, would be a time signal by which the watches of the sledge party could be corrected. Thus the exact longitude of the party would be assured—another provision for safety

The sledge party should carry a kite for receiving the messages The ship should be supplied with a captive balloon and inflating apparatus, the gas being carried in steel cylinders and a gas compressor used to inflate and deflate. Possibly a hot air balloon would serve the purpose, the furnaces of the ship's boilers providing the necessary heat.

The balloon would be valuable on calm days as a mark for the returning sledge party, its great elevation affording also a position from which observations of the ice could be made. Mirror signals could also be flashed from the car of the balloon.

The drift ship should either enter the ice by way of Bering Sea at the point advocated by the Canadian explorer, Captain Bernier, and drift with the ice-fields across the Polar Sea, or force a passage to Teplitz Bay and there await the opening of the sea north of the Franz Josef Archipelago, in September or October, and then slowly fight her way north

Doctor Nansen's ship, the *Fram*, reached her highest latitude north of one of that group—Rudolph Island— and in the two years we spent at Teplitz Bay both

September and October of 1903 and 1904 were characterised by large stretches of open water to the north of the islands.

Norwegian sealers and whalers speak of a great open sea north of Spitzbergen and between that group and the Franz Josef Archipelago in which they have sailed during certain seasons.

With a drift ship as a base the sledge party would have the advantage of a high latitude from which to start polewards, and would also be favoured with better ice conditions than they would find when leaving a land base. They would escape too the open lanes and pressure ridges that extend north from all Arctic lands. Another advantage lies in the fact that should the sledge parties find it necessary to return to the ship the distance to travel would be materially shortened.

To march from a land base would require a large party, and an expedition leader deciding on the plan of advance from a base on terra firma could do no better than establish his headquarters at a station about one or two hundred miles south of the most northern land at a place accessible to steamers and from which a trail with fairly smooth ice conditions might be made to the northern limit of the land.

Cape Dillon, on McClintock Island in the Franz Josef Archipelago, is well adapted for such a station and is connected by an interchannel route with Rudolph Island, the highest known land on the European side of the globe.

After landing the cargo the expedition ship should return to civilisation where arrangements would be made yearly for her return to the Arctic until the completion of the work.

The spring following the expedition's arrival the leader would take a large party of men, dogs, ponies, and sledges on a journey to the most northern land attainable where a cache would be established and a shelter erected. The cases of food supplies could be made of one size and used for the walls of the house—all covers inside.

The cache placed and shelter arranged, a return should then be made to headquarters. This first journey would serve as a practice march, being at the same time a test of men, animals, and equipment The fibre of the men would thus be proved and only those fitted for the undertaking should be kept for the work the following year, when the real advance north would take place. The Relief Ship arriving in the summer after the practice march would take home all who were discontented or unsuited for a cold climate, and also reinforce the expedition with new men, animals, and supplies.

In the sledge work on the comparatively smooth channels between the islands there are long stretches where a special form of alcohol or gasolene driven motor would serve admirably to help the party to the advance camp the second season. But on the *moving* ice the use of such machines can hardly be recommended for, even if a motor could be constructed to go over the pressure ridges and rough ice of the Polar pack, it would necessarily haul so slowly that from the standpoint of economy a pony or dog team would be preferable, since either could travel on a less expenditure of fuel *

Crossing the Pole with a balloon or a flying machine is advocated by some   To succeed in so doing in the present undeveloped state of aerial navigation would be a miracle almost.   No machine of any construction should be depended upon for use in the Arctic until it has been tried successfully in civilisation.   Even then its success in the ice-fields would be problematical. I believe the only way a balloon could be used would be to construct one large enough to carry two men and an entire sledge equipment north.   So long as the balloon or flying machine kept its northward course, the occupants could depend upon its help and possibly a number of miles could be thus covered with little exertion; but as soon as the wind changed a descent should be made, the travellers continuing their journey by sledge.

All things considered, the drift ship seems to afford the greatest possibility of success.   But the explorer who takes this method should be provided with light boats and be prepared to winter on the Polar pack should he lose his ship.

*While crossing the numerous pressure ridges and lanes in our sledge journey in March, 1905, it occurred to me that a sledge could be constructed from about 40 to 80 feet long and propelled by gasolene or alcohol motors.   The great length and size of the sledge would make the hummocks seem small in comparison and many of the numerous pitfalls, crevices, ridges and lanes would be crossed with comparatively little effort As an ocean steamer is unaffected by the waves that almost swamp a small boat, so this great structure of wood and metal could cross the summits of pressure ridges, in many cases from crest to crest, without the need of descending into the labyrinth of broken blocks between   I drew a plan of such a contrivance on return to camp but could not think of constructing even an experimental sledge on account of lack of suitable material and machinery

EQUIPMENT

The Ponies

The one important point in which our equipment differed radically from that prepared for other attempts over the Polar ice was in the use of ponies. These tough little animals are accustomed to the very lowest temperatures experienced on the Steppes of Siberia— some parts of which are considered the coldest places of the earth. They are also accustomed to forcing their way through deep snows and to cross frozen rivers whose shores are lined with broken ice and deep drifts. They had been used first by Jackson who believed them superior to dog teams and used them in preference to dogs on his trips of exploration and survey through the Franz Josef Archipelago.

In the record of his journeyings,"A Thousand Days in the Arctic," he states his belief that the Pole could be reached by means of ponies. Baldwin followed in the footsteps of Jackson and it was on his numerous sledge journeys over the frozen channels of the Franz Josef Archipelago in 1901 and 1902 that I became convinced of the ponies' worth. On smooth ice the dogs travelled faster than their rivals but just as soon as they struck rough going the ponies out-distanced the dogs easily, at the same time dragging heavier loads. The men driving the dog teams were tired out at the end of a day's march by the constant exertion in helping the dogs pull their loads up grades and over ice-blocks, but it was seldom that the ponies required assistance.

Lucas—one of the pony drivers on the Baldwin-

Ziegler expedition—with five assistants made about six trips over rough ice between Hohenlohe Island and Cape Auk with from ten to twelve pony sledges heavily loaded, while the dog teams made only one trip.

In my own experience the ponies proved of great value. In the unloading of the ship, they were used to the exclusion of the dogs, and during the retreat from our northern base to Cape Flora in the spring of 1904 they dragged the heaviest loads, and instead of requiring help when rough ice was encountered in the British Channel, they often helped their drivers over some of the bad places. The distance travelled over the floating sea ice north of Rudolph Island on our first two attempts north was too short to allow of a fair estimate or criticism of the service of the ponies. On our second sledge journey, four men attended the seven pony sledges while there was a driver to each dog team.

The ponies could hardly be restrained in their wild efforts to keep constantly on the march and in touch with the preceding sledge on the trail. The greatest difficulty was experienced in the constant overturning of the unattended pony sledges. The ponies, continuing to drag their upset loads, often wedged them between ice blocks, and so a number of sledges were broken.

The harness we used consisted of a breast-strap covered with sheep skin and suitable traces and shoulder straps. A collar harness would have been better by far but not knowing the size of the ponies until I reached Archangel I was unable to order that style of harness in America. The only collars procurable in

Russia were made of wood and straw-stuffed leather, altogether too heavy and clumsy for use on the Arctic marches where every extra pound, every ounce, meant so much slower progress, so much more fuel for transportation

The ponies required each about ten pounds of food a day in the form of hay and oats They seemed to prefer the hay and, undoubtedly, in their Siberian home they had little else to eat For their use on the trail we carried nose-bags in which was placed their daily allowance of oats. A leather measure was used to proportion the daily ration

As a protection against wind in the very cold weather each pony was provided with a wool blanket covered with khaki cloth with which, after a day's travel, we always covered our little charges, thus insuring their warm bodies from injury by the chilling blasts.

I believe ponies would work admirably in the rough ice if provided with sledges built with five or six runners around a central load with a swivel bar in front to which the harness would be attached—the loads to be placed in the sledges from the rear

Of the thirty ponies, property of the expedition, fourteen were lost up to April 30th, 1904, the day the retreating party left Camp Abruzzi.

The losses were as follows

Aug 8, 1903—One pony reported by Veterinarian to be infected with glanders Shot   . .   1
Aug 31-Sept 4, 1903—Five ponies lost in stampede by falling into crevasses on glacier .   ..   5
Sept 3, 1903—One pony died of exhaustion from overwork   .   1
Feb 1, 1904—One pony reported by Veterinarian to be infected with glanders Shot   ..   1

Feb. 8, 1904—One pony reported by Veterinarian to be infected by
    tuberculosis. Shot. 1
Feb. 21, 1904—One pony died of catarrh of the stomach 1
April 16, 1904—One pony shot for fresh meat 1
April 22, 1904—One pony reported by Veterinarian to be infected
    with glanders. Shot. 1
April 28, 1904—One pony reported by Veterinarian to be infected
    with glanders. Shot. 1
April 30, 1904—One pony reported by Veterinarian to be infected
    with glanders. Shot. 1
                                                                                       ——
        Total loss up to and including April 30, 1904. 14

Sixteen ponies left Camp Abruzzi April 30, 1904, for Cape Flora. Dur-
    ing the march south, three ponies were shot for dog food and one
    died in harness. 4
May 16, 1904—Ten ponies reported by Veterinarian as infected
    with glanders and farcy. Shot on arrival at Cape Flora. 10
During September, 1904, the two remaining ponies were shot for food
    for the men at Cape Flora. 2
                                                                                       ——
        Total. 30

The Dogs

The dogs gave little trouble as most of them had been
broken into harness and sledge hauling on the previous
expedition. The collars for their harness (furnished
by Abercrombie and Fitch of New York City) were
admirable, never causing abrasions of the skin or harness galls.

Under Doctor Vaughn's direction, dog harness
was made and traces attached to collars after the
mode in use in Alaska. The dogs were placed in pairs,
a method that worked very well, and there was little
entangling of harness on the trail.

On the Baldwin-Ziegler expedition, we had been
much troubled by torn dog traces and chewed harness.
To obviate a repetition of these annoyances, I ordered
a number of light, strong chains, canvas covered, for

use as dog traces. They proved entirely satisfactory and on the second year's trip were used almost exclusively.

Only the incorrigible fighters among the dogs were chained. The others were allowed to run free at camp and the exercise thus received kept them in good condition for the sledge work in the spring. A number were lost in fights and others having wandered to the ice off shore were carried away by the wind.

I believe the best way to keep dogs through the Arctic winter would be to have a stable tent—such as we had—and in addition have, connected with this shelter tent, a large space enclosed by a high wire fence in which, on calm days, the dogs could run free without danger of straying.

When drifting snows raised the level within the enclosure extra wire could be added to increase the height of the fence, long poles or fence standards having been planted in the beginning to provide for such a contingency.

Great stress should be placed upon the importance of every man's knowing his own dogs To effect this the teams should be assigned the first autumn, and, if possible, the original arrangement should stand throughout the time spent in the Arctic.

If the pack is a large one the dogs should be watched constantly to prevent loss by fights. The shelter tent and fence already mentioned would make such surveillance possible.

I had ordered a quantity of Spratt's dog biscuits for food for the pack during the winter. At the suggestion of Doctor Vaughn, who was engaged to take

charge of the dogs, some tons of tallow were also purchased. A box of biscuits and a keg of tallow were
always kept open in the shelter tent. The dogs frequently partook of this "free lunch" and grew sleek
and fat.

Doctor Vaughn constructed an ice melter from the
mixing tank of the gas generator left by the Italian
Duke. It was mounted within the entranceway to the
stable tent and furnished sufficient water for both dogs
and ponies throughout the long dark winter.

On the trail we fed the dogs with pemmican, a one-
pound block of the condensed meat to each animal
at the end of a day's journey. It proved sufficient
and kept the dogs in splendid condition.

The record of the dogs reads as follows:

Taken aboard S. Y. *America* at Trono, Norway 158
Large pups taken abroad same place 27
Taken aboard S. Y. *America* at Solombol, Russia 24
Already aboard ship 1
Pups born at Camp Abruzzi (winter 1903–4) 8

      Total 218

Dogs taken from Camp Abruzzi April 30, 1904, to Cape Flora 65
Dogs remaining at Camp Abruzzi April 30, 1904 66

      Total 131

      Total losses to April 30, 1904 87

From the 66 dogs left at Camp Abruzzi, twenty-three were taken
    South (May 9, 1904) by Mr. Porter and his survey party 23
    Losses to Nov. 20, 1904 8

      Total 31

Dogs remaining in Camp 35
Dogs brought from Cape Flora to Camp Abruzzi Nov. 20, 1904 33
Total at Camp Abruzzi, Nov. 20, 1904 68
Dogs lost during winter of 1904–5 8
Number remaining for sledge trip of 1905 60
Dogs brought from Cape Flora by Mr. Porter Mar. 17, 1905 4

Total number at Camp Abruzzi April 1, 1905 64

There were also about twenty-five dogs at Cape Flora and five at Camp Ziegler. These together with the number at Camp Abruzzi were taken aboard the Relief Ship the following summer. The laws of Norway forbade leaving them upon any Norwegian territory and the disposition of so many dogs became a serious problem The Norwegian members of the party took some of their sledge dogs home, and some of the best pups were given to sealers and whalers. Five were brought home and presented to the Bronx Park. But the vast majority of the animals were too old for further use and had to be shot and thrown overboard. I regretted the measure— for the creatures had served us well—but it was the only thing we could do.

Food Supplies

The food aboard ship, in camp, and on the trail was good, and the great variety in our stores allowed much change in the menu from time to time. Fresh bread, pies, cakes and puddings formed part of our daily bill-of-fare at the expedition base, thanks to the activity and industry of Steward Spencer who had much to contend against, particularly after the loss of the ship when the entire party was housed in the crowded quarters at Camp Abruzzi. In response to an expressed wish of mine, the Steward experimented until he succeeded in producing a fine biscuit composed of nutritious beans, pork, and flour. He cooked and baked 600 pounds of this food during the winter of 1903–04 On the trail the men showed a decided preference for the pork-and-beans biscuits which never grew hard, no matter how cold the weather, and had, in addition to a high food value, a very pleasant taste.

In the large cache left at Teplitz Bay by the Duke of the Abruzzi many delicacies were found that proved acceptable. We have the Duke to thank, too, for the food stores left at Cape Flora which, on the non-arrival of the Relief Ship in 1904, became the chief supply of the party in retreat at that point.

Game was secured at all the camps and the meat of the Polar bear, walrus, and seal, as well as of guillemots, loons, and brant, appeared on our table. Over 120 Polar bears were killed during our two years' stay in the Franz Josef Archipelago. Scurvy was unknown and the general health of the party was good.

The sledge ration used the first year was as follows [the diagram was prepared by our Assistant Surgeon Charles L. Seitz, M.D.]:

THE ARRIVAL OF THE RELIEF SHIP OFF CAPE DILLON JULY 30, 1905

CAMP JACKSON AT CAPE FLORA AT THE ARRIVAL OF THE RELIEF SHIP

RESCUERS AND RESCUED MEET ON THE ICE OF ABEDARE CHANNEL "AND A MEMORABLE
MEETING IT WAS"

THE CAMP AT CAPE DILLON WHERE WATCH WAS KEPT FOR THE RELIEF SHIP—AND
FOR GAME

ONE WEEK'S RATIONS FOR ONE MAN

		1st Day	2nd Day	3rd Day	4th Day	5th Day	6th Day	7th Day
Pemmican (uncooked) 4½ oz	} 10 oz.	4½	4½	4½	4½	4½	4½	4½
" " (cooked) 5½ oz		10		9		10		9
Bovril Meat and Potato			6		6		6	
" Red Ration	} 3½ oz.							
Cracked Wheat and Beef								
Erbswurst				2		2		2½
Corned Beef			6					
Pate de Foi		4						
Mortedello Sausage	} 4 oz.							
Tongue					6		6	
Smoked Beef				3		3		
Vienna Sausage								
Army Bread 6 oz	} 12 oz.	12	12	12	12	12	12	12
Pork and Bean Biscuit		2½						
Oatmeal 2 oz	} 2½ oz.			2		2		2
Cornmeal 3 oz			3		3		3	
Milk	1 oz.	1	1	1	1	1	1	1
Butter	1½ oz.	1½	1½	1½	1½	1½	1½	1½
Sugar	3 oz.	3	3	3	3	3	3	
Salt (taken in bulk)								

ONE WEEK'S RATIONS FOR ONE MAN (*Continued*)

		1st Day	2nd Day	3rd Day	4th Day	5th Day	6th Day	7th Day
Tea 5 dr.	0 oz. 10 1/7 dr.	5 dr.	5 dr.	5 dr.	5 dr.	5 dr.	5 dr.	5 dr.
Coffee 5 1/7 dr.		....	12 dr.	....	12 dr.	....	12 dr.	....
Chocolate	3 oz.	3 oz.	3 oz.	3 oz.	3 oz.	3 oz.	3 oz.	3 oz.
Raisins, Figs, Cranberry Sauce	1/2 oz.	....	....	....	....	....	....	3 1/2
Kerosene	6 1/2 oz.	6 1/2	6 1/2	6 1/2	6 1/2	6 1/2	6 1/2	6 1/2
TOTAL	48 oz., 2 1/7 dr.	48 oz. 6 1/7 dr.	47 oz. 10 1/7 dr.	47 oz. 14 1/7 dr.	47 oz. 10 1/7 dr.	48 oz. 14 1/7 dr.	47 oz. 10 1/7 dr.	48 oz. 14 1/7 dr.

In some cases malted milk was used instead of chocolate, and a small quantity of dried onions was carried for daily use.

OUR LAST SIGHT OF THE ICE

THE RELIEF SHIP ARRIVES OFF CAPE FLORA

The ration was ample and gave good working energy. It was large enough to allow of some saving from day to day and an extra day's ration could be thus gained in a week's time.

Through experience on many sledge trips we found that the quantity of tea should be about double the regular allowance. We also found that cornmeal and oatmeal did not, during the cold weather, satisfy the sense of hunger. They were consequently reduced to a very small amount for use of the party when storm-bound or during the warmer weather of early summer. Smoked beef, beef tongue, and corned beef were eliminated from the sledge-trip bill-of-fare.

We found the sausages valuable in many ways and particularly good in the Erbswurst stew.

Beans when well cooked with pork and dried in an oven to expel the water are valuable as food since they not only furnish considerable energy but also please the palate. I have already mentioned the pork-and-bean biscuit. It is best when prepared in camp and is a food that should be carried on every Arctic sledge trip.

We carried two kinds of pemmican, one prepared in the United States, the other in Europe. The American product bought of Armour and Company consisted of the lean and fat of beef mixed with currants, the whole made to resemble as nearly as possible the original pemmican used by the American Indian during war and on the chase.

The bulk of the American pemmican was sweet, nutritious, and energy producing. It should be carefully watched though during its preparation. Our cans were not uniformly good, some of them being filled with meat that contained gritty particles hard to chew and in consequence difficult to digest It took a longer time to cook, which meant an undue expenditure of oil on a sledge journey

The pemmican prepared abroad was nearly 30 per cent. fat, and we used it for dog food. On account of the one-pound blocks into which it was manufactured it was particularly convenient for this purpose.

The food stores furnished by Beauvais of Copenhagen, Denmark, were particularly well canned and the order for provisions from his firm was honestly executed. Amongst all the stores furnished by Beauvais not one article was found defective.

On all our marches where there were a number of men, a separate cook tent was used and it proved a great convenience as well as a great economizer of oil, food, and time. During the retreat to Cape Flora two warm meals were cooked each day for the whole party of twenty-five men, at which coffee or tea, and drinking water were furnished. After the column had marched four or five hours, a halt was usually made and hot coffee served. On several occasions I timed the duration of the halt and found that within one hour from the time the signal to stop had been given each of the twenty-five men, having received two cups of coffee and all the water he wished to drink, was on the march again. Within that hour, the cook tent was unlashed and raised, the ice cut and melted, and coffee prepared and drank without hurry. There was also the necessary readjustment of the cook tent.

For convenience in handling, provisions and stores

should be packed as far as possible in cases not weighing over fifty or sixty pounds gross.

All tins of provisions should have paper labels removed and be heavily lacquered or painted to preserve them from rust. The cans should be stamped or embossed with numbers as a key to their contents, all cans containing the same food article being marked with a similar number.

Petroleum should not be carried in barrels as it soon evaporates through the wood. Small steel tanks containing about ten gallons each are a convenient form for shipment.

Clothing

The clothing to be selected for wear in the Far-North is a most important matter. A number of Arctic explorers are strong advocates of woollens; others believe in furs.

From my own experience and from observation I have come to the conclusion that the lightest and most serviceable clothing is that made from the skins of the domesticated deer—young animals from two to five months old. The skins tanned by the native Samoyede or Esquimaux are vastly preferable to other varieties.

The suit should consist of a shirt rather long in the skirt to be worn over the trousers—the fur side, of course, turned in. It should be so made that the neck opening could be extended when the wearer desired to expose his neck or upper chest to the air.

I wore a separate fur cap because it gave more freedom

of movement; but a hood could be attached to the shirt. That is a matter to be decided through personal preference.

The shirt should not weigh more than two and a half pounds at the outside.

The trousers, made of heavier fur, should go just below the knee, and should be worn with the fur side out. They would be too warm otherwise.

The fur stocking should be made of the thin skin of the two-month-old deer and worn with the fur inside. Over it could be worn either the Lapp shoe, made of the hard skin taken from the head or leg of the adult deer and stuffed with senne grass, or the sealskin shoe made after the pattern in use among the Greenland Esquimaux.

I take this opportunity to recommend a light felt boot as a style of footwear admirably adapted to feet accustomed to the leather boots and shoes of civilisation.

I had a number of pairs made of this material for use in sledge work.

Mr. Frederick Simpson, of Rogers, Peet and Company, New York City, spent much time and thought in their manufacture. They were well made and warm and proved to be the most serviceable footwear we had. As an instance of their durability I will quote my own experience. I wore a pair of these felt shoes on sledge trip over the glacier of Rudolph Island in October 1903. The same pair did service on both attempts north in March 1904, on the retreat south in May 1904, and on the advance north from Cape Flora which occupied parts of the months of September and November and all of October 1904 I also wore the same boots around camp at Teplitz Bay and at Cape Flora.

Two pairs of these boots were furnished every man in the expedition

In addition to the articles of apparel already mentioned, a fur coat to be worn during-halts should be added to the sledger's outfit This coat properly constructed of fur not too heavy would not weigh over five pounds and would slip easily over the fur shirt.

For protection from wind and flying snow, we wore loose coats of Pongee silk and long trousers of the same material. The latter were provided with tapes at the bottom by means of which they were secured around the ankles Pongee silk is far better than canvas or sheeting made from cotton or linen It does not absorb moisture readily and if wet dries quickly. It is in every way more desirable than canvas or the thin cotton sail and tent material erroneously placed upon the market under the name of silk.

On entering a tent or shelter for rest, we always removed our silk wind coats and trousers and shook out the snow and ice particles before placing them in a corner of the tent where they would be at once accessible and out of the way

A fur suit properly cared for and worn correctly is the most comfortable garment for Arctic travel A good plan would be to adopt the Esquimaux fashion of wearing the fur next the skin.

While travelling in a low temperature a large part of the moisture given off by the body condenses in the clothing. By removing all garments worn during the day on entering the bag—another Esquimau practice—the sleeper will be warmer and the bag will not become charged with moisture so quickly.

Mr Porter's fur suit, which was a trifle heavier than my own but might stand as a fair average, weighed as follows:

Reindeerskin trousers	2¼	pounds
" shirt.............................	2¼	"
" stockings and shoes................	2¼	"
" mittens...........................	¼	"
Total	8¼	pounds

With this fur was worn a thin wool union suit the weight of which was a pound and a half. The silk trousers weighed about three-quarters of a pound and the wind coat about one and a quarter pounds.

While travelling over the Polar pack there is the necessity for being always ready for an immediate exit from the sleeping bag on account of the unstable condition of the ice. So to disrobe entirely before retiring would not be the safest thing to do. It would be well to have a separate sleeping suit of thin fur. The wearer would then always be ready to leave his sleeping bag or tent if an emergency arose without danger of freezing. I suggest that such a garment be made in one piece—a sort of union suit—with stockings attached.

Our woollens were furnished by Jaeger and by Morley of London. We had an abundant store and the majority of the party preferred them to the furs for field work. Wool garments were used by all of us when in camp as they were more easily cleaned than furs. The close skins would have been too warm for indoor wear.

The chief recommendations of the fur as a travelling suit are its warmth, lightness, and simplicity, and the ease with which it regulates the body's temperature.

The proper construction is to have the shirt loose with an adjustable draw-string opening at the neck. The skin being almost impervious to wind prevents the escape of air warmed by the body. If the wearer becomes overheated and perspires unduly, the opening at the neck may be enlarged and the belt loosened or taken off and strapped underneath. The larger part of the moisture given off by the body thus escapes through the openings instead of condensing in the clothing as is the case when a wool suit is worn. A man dressed in woollens on a sledge journey has his clothing soaked with perspiration, the porous material allowing the moisture to come to the surface of the outermost garment where it quickly solidifies into hoar frost. The wet clothing robs the body of heat. This is particularly true if the sledge worker wears his damp garments in the sleeping bag. A garment of any material worn during the day becomes wet if slept in and thoroughly uncomfortable.

It requires some courage and resolution to disrobe in a temperature of from thirty to fifty degrees below zero in a cold sleeping bag; but it is the safest and most comfortable thing to do in the long run.

The worst possible order of dress in the Arctic is a heavy wool suit under furs. The fur soon becomes ruined by the excessive amount of moisture absorbed from the perspiration-soaked woollens.

The first year of our sojourn in the north many of the men wore their furs over heavy Jaeger suits. No wonder that their fur shirts became moisture laden and froze stiff.

It is a mistake to wear too much clothing of any sort on a sledge trip as it induces perspiration. During periods of labour a well-made fur suit with a silk wind coat should be sufficient in the very coldest temperatures. The fur coat should not be added except during halts. As may be seen, I am an advocate of furs and recommend their wear from the double standpoint of comfort and economy. The fur suit I wore on all the sledge trips of my two years' stay in the Arctic I left at Camp Ziegler in good condition on my departure from that point in July, 1905. A partial list of clothing furnished to each member of the Expedition follows:

Vodmal suit, coat and trousers
One sheepskin jacket
Two suits of medium weight underwear
Two suits of heavy weight underwear, Jaeger
Two pairs of heavy knitted drawers, Jaeger
Two sweaters, Jaeger
One Jaeger woollen vest
Two pairs medium weight socks
Five pairs heavy weight socks, Jaeger
One pair long blue wads, woollen
One pair long German stockings, woollen
Three pairs long Jaeger stockings
One pair horschide mitts
Two pairs fleece lined Jaeger mitts
Two pairs felt lined Jaeger mitts
Two pairs blue woollen mitts
Two pairs long woollen mitts
One woollen cap, Jaeger
One camelshair cap, Jaeger
One woollen comforter, Jaeger
One pair police suspenders
Web belt and knife
One suit overalls

Two gray woollen shirts
Two large camelshair blankets, Jaeger
Two pairs felt boots
One pair felt slippers, Jaeger
One pair buckskin moccasins
One pair sea boots
One pair Samoyede boots, remade
Fur clothing or fur sufficient for coat, shirt, trousers, and stockings
    was issued to each man, also silk trousers and wind coats or silk
    for same
A sleeping bag and pair of goatshair sleeping socks were furnished
    to each man
Additional clothing was furnished to each member according to his
    personal needs
Oilskins and rubber boots were furnished to those needing them

On every Polar expedition a generous supply of footwear should be carried, each member being required to bring two pairs of long hunting boots, a size larger than those usually worn, and several pairs of shoes, for use in summer when melting snows and running water make wet travelling. Buckskin moccasins, Finn schu, Esquimau winter boots, felt boots, and the Norwegian "Komager" should be provided in large numbers in the expedition stores, for the way footwear disappears—particularly if the men are inclined to be careless—is most astonishing.

Cotton canvas, wool cloth—close woven like the winter khaki furnished the U. S. Army—and Pongee silk for manufacture into clothing should be taken along.

To secure the native tanned deerskins—which are preferable for Arctic work—the expedition ship would have to visit the Esquimau settlements before entering on her voyage proper.

Hand sewing machines and a plentiful supply of

pins, needles, thread, tapes, buttons, etc., should form part of the equipment.

Sleeping Bags

No sleeping arrangement on the trail affords so much comfort as the one-man sleeping bag made of the skin of the adult deer. It should taper down from the shoulders to the feet. A piece of soft skin sewed to the edge of the opening of the bag can be drawn close about the neck and shoulders, insuring warmth and comfort. I found that the one-piece flap in use on the bags when wet with escaping breath dropped down on the head and face of the sleeper almost suffocating him. To obviate this unpleasant experience, I devised a form of fastening which I liked better than any in use to date. I cut the overflap of my bag down the centre and instead of one flap I had two. To the cut edge of one I sewed a four inch strip of fur so that one flap overlapped the other. While one piece folded down in front of my face and neck the other fitted over my head. This arrangement permitted the entrance of fresh air and prevented the condensation of the exhalations in the bag. It also made entrance into the bag easier and saved weight, as that sort of flap could be made smaller.

Tents

Our tents of Pongee silk were small and pyramidal in shape and had floor coverings of khaki or light weight canvas.

First Officer Haven, to whom I explained the tent plan, volunteered to make the tents and constructed twelve of them during the first winter. They proved comfortable and strong and were used on all the sledge trips of 1904, some of them doing service until the departure for home in 1905. They were 7½ feet high and 7½ feet square at the base and weighed with khaki floors 8½ pounds. Those with canvas floors weighed 13 pounds. The poles weighed 3 pounds and the pins for each tent one pound. Sleeping bags were always carried in the tents and rolled up with them when lashed on a sledge—the tent serving as a protection for the bags.

Lighter material than that needed for large tents may be used with satisfactory results in the construction of small tents and so considerable weight may be saved.

As a rule two men only occupied each of our little Pongee pyramids. While one of them put down or took up the tent his comrade cared for the dogs, and much time in pitching and breaking camp was saved.

On his sledge journey the Duke of the Abruzzi carried the following weights in sleeping bags and tents:

Two 3-man tents—complete weight	66 lbs.
One 4-man tent—complete weight	46 "
One 3-man sleeping bag and jackets	83 "
One 3-man sleeping bag and jackets	86 "
One 4-man sleeping bag and jackets	112 "
Total 10 men	393 lbs.

For the same number of men our weights were as follows:

Five 2-man tents, with poles and pins .... 87 lbs.
Ten 1-man sleeping bags, with blankets and sleeping
    socks.... ;..................................... 181 "
                                                      _____
            Total 10 men......................... 268 lbs.

This was a saving of 125 pounds. Thirty pounds more could have been saved if we had been able to place khaki floors in all the tents; but we had run short of that material and were obliged to substitute canvas.

One objection can be urged against the pyramid tent—under the pressure of wind, its walls curve in and constrict the interior space. To obviate this we attached guy ropes to the corners of the tents. They helped but there was still a loss of space on the windward side.

Profiting by the experience of 1904 the following year I designed a new form of two-man tent. Its base, a seven-foot square reaching three feet above the ground, was surmounted by a rather flat pyramidal peak. The whole structure was raised on one pole. The floor was smaller each way by six inches than the other tents but the increased wall space gave a roomier interior. An adjustable opening at the peak allowing the escape of all cooking vapours and a door with a draw-string opening were other improvements. The entrance to a tent is a very important feature. Many devices were tried for closing the opening through which we went in and out. At last I adopted the following plan: A three foot circle was cut in the wall,

THE S. Y. "TERRA NOVA" AT TROMSO, NORWAY AUG. 11, 1908

"LOUISE"

"BILLY"

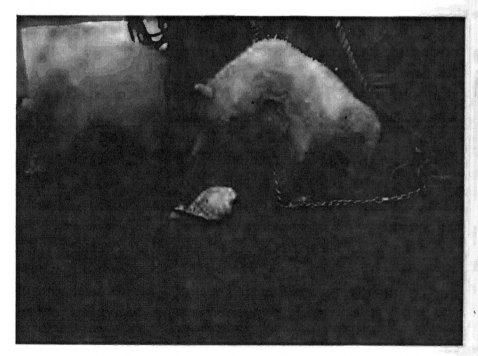

"BILLY" AND "LOUISE," PASSENGERS ON THE S. Y. "TERRA NOVA" ON HER
HOMEWARD VOYAGE

to the edge of which a strip of the Pongee silk about
two feet wide was sewn   A draw-string was then
run through a hem on the other side of this strip.   On
entering the tent a pull at the draw-string and the
door was made fast   The ends of the cord were then
tied around the bunch of silk—a task not so delicate
but it could be performed with mittened hands—and
our door was locked and we were safe from the blasts
and snow that whirled and drifted on the other side of
our little pyramid.

Sledges

The dog sledges we used were constructed of second
growth American hickory on a modification of the
plan advised by Admiral Melville and in the two years
not one sledge broke down through fault of design.   I
do not recall a single stanchion broken or a runner
turned under.   The material of which the runners
were made gave way on the trip north in 1904 on account of bad ice conditions and improper placing of
loads.   In loading a sledge for travel through rough
and hummocky ice care should be exercised that no
heavy weights rest on or forward of the first stanchion.   A load so placed will deprive the sledge of
elasticity in the forward end—the part that receives
all the heavy blows, and the front bows and curves of
the runners will break—our own experience in March,
1904.

I made the mistake of shoeing the runners with
lignum vitæ from observation of its splendid wearing qualities on some sledges of the expedition of
1901–2.   I could not purchase the wood in strips

long enough for the entire length of the runners and it had to be spliced on in two sections. This weakened the runners. During the winter of 1904–5, I had all the lignum vitæ taken off and hick-·ory put in its place. The sledges then proved wonder-·ful in their powers of resistance and were in the field from March to July 1905 without breaking. The hickory of which the sledges were built was chosen in the tree while growing on dry hilltops, as such wood is tougher than that grown in moist low soil. T. A. Cook of Callicoon, N. Y., built our sixty sledges during the spring of 1903 and shipped them in sections to the *America.* We put them together aboard ship and at Camp Abruzzi, where the joints were lashed with raw-hide.

In cold weather the wooden runners go smoothly and are better than metal on the hard snow; but for summer and fall work, when the surface of the ice and snow is wet, the wooden runners drag hard. I would suggest that the explorer carry extra runners of phosphor bronze or aluminum bronze, the edges of which could be turned up so as to slip over the wooden runners when needed.

Captain Cagni and Doctor Nansen provided metal shoes to their sledge runners and wooden underrun-ners were lashed on. These underrunners gave trouble when the lashings wore off and the weight of the sledges was increased by the metal. Only a few of the sledges can return from a long Polar dash so it is not necessary to have them all metal shod. The special form of sledge for use with the ponies I have already described under another heading.

Boats

A serviceable boat is an absolute necessity on a Polar dash, particularly so on the return journey. We had two canoes of five sections each and a number of two-man and one-man canvas kayaks all of which were used. The sectional canoes weighed 250 pounds each, entirely too much for northern sledge work. Kayaks are easily injured and are not adapted for carrying heavy loads My idea of a serviceable Arctic boat is a strong elastic frame made of many thin small ribs of tough wood covered with canvas or thin aluminum and silk and thickly coated with marine varnish. We built such a craft at Camp Abruzzi in 1905 It was covered with canvas and weighed when completed ninety-one pounds. It was large enough for two men and could carry a heavy load in addition. The canoe had two covered compartments, one fore, the other aft. The man-holes to these compartments were covered with hinged canvas hatches that fitted tightly over combings and were held down with one little toggle each. I kept instruments and cooking untensils in these covered places which proved a great convenience on the sledge trip. A mast and sail, three paddles, two cane seats, a pump, and two harpoons and lines were provided for the craft. Wooden sheathing is not advised for a light boat as it is too easily injured in the rough ice while on the sledge and is difficult to repair.

Cooking Apparatus

Like Doctor Nansen and Captain Cagni I found the Primus the best form of petroleum burner for Arctic use. We also used the Khotal burner, made and sold as an improvement on the Primus. As long as the temperature did not fall lower than twenty degrees below zero, the Khotal worked well and was easily regulated. But in extremely low temperatures the valves would sometimes leak and we were obliged to take the burners apart for repairs. Instead of replenishing the oil in the tank permanently attached to a Primus burner by pouring through a funnel from other oil tanks—to which cold and troublesome operation is added the danger of spilling the precious fluid— a good plan would be to have all the petroleum tanks carried on the sledges arranged with screw threads so that burners and air pumps could be screwed on. Then when the oil became exhausted in a tank it might be thrown away, the burner and pump having been first unscrewed and attached to a full tank.

Our cooking untensils were of pressed aluminum, which proved admirable for the purpose.

Arms

A modern military arm of simple construction built for hard usage is the best weapon for a sledge journey. We carried the Mannlicher carbine of eight mm. calibre. It has a very simple bolt action for the breech and can be taken apart and put together in a few minutes. The rifle proved a strong and accurate shooter It loads with a clip of five cartridges. By taking one of the cartridges out of the clip the magazine of the weapon can be kept loaded with the barrel of the piece empty and harmless Each rifle was placed in a case of canvas and leather to keep out the snow. I had a little pocket of canvas sewed on the outside of the case in which a full clip of ammunition was always carried. Thus with the charges in the magazine there were nine rounds of ammunition ready for use with each rifle. These clips could be handled with the mittened hands —another recommendation. The rest of the ammunition was kept packed away in one of the compartments of the canoe. We also carried 12-guage double-barrelled shot guns on our sledge trips. But it was always a question to me whether it was not a needless weight on our sledges. I believe a very light twenty-two calibre rifle or pistol would be more effective for killing fowls, as they are usually shot when swimming in a pool or sitting on the rocks where they nest. A hundred rounds of twenty-two cal. ammunition would not weigh more than a few rounds of twelve guage and the rifle would be lighter than the shot gun and more accurate and effective at long range. Combined rifles and shot guns are not recommended because of their very delicate construction.

Navigation Instruments

For determination of position a light strong theodolite should be carried, so arranged that it could be attached to the tripod before being removed from its case. This could be accomplished by having the instrument permanently attached to the bottom board of the case with its levelling screws, etc., above. After screwing the bottom board to the tripod the upper part of the case could be removed leaving the instrument clear and ready for use. This could all be done with the mittened hands which would prevent many

a frost bite. A light sextant should also be carried
for use when travelling by boat. Odometers are of
very little use on the sea ice for the trail is usually so
zigzag and so many miles are made out of the required
direction that their ·readings would be misleading.
It would also be almost impossible to build an odometer that would last longer than two or three days
on the rough ice.

Personnel

Most important of all to an explorer who essays the
leadership of an Arctic expedition, is good material
in the personnel of his party. The Arctic is a field
that will try to the utmost men's souls. Many a man
who is a " jolly good fellow " in congenial surroundings
will become impatient, selfish, and mean when obliged
to sacrifice his comfort, curb his desires, and work
hard in what seems a losing fight. The first consideration in the choice of men for a Polar campaign should
be their moral quality. Next should come mental
and physical powers. If possible a leader should take
his candidates for Polar work on a two months' journey
in the mountains the winter before leaving civilisation.
The trip should be made purposely hard. It would
be a good plan to go without food one or two days at
a time so as to thoroughly test the endurance and tem-
per of the men. The man that shows the slightest
inclination under the test to find fault or complain
should be discharged. · Even after the expedition party
is complete, and the ship ready to sail, should any one
of the party (no matter how valuable he may seem at
the time!) give evidence of dissatisfaction he should ·

be sent home. The same disposition should be made of any who show a tendency to question orders.

The assistants should be young, for as men grow older they become overcautious. They should be of good personal habits and not addicted to the use of either tobacco or strong drink. The men should be paid a fair salary in return for their work, and should express themselves as perfectly satisfied with the amount on signing to go with the expedition. A sum of money sufficient to cover all expenses should be placed in a bank at the disposal of the leader or his representative on the return of the expedition.

The men should look to the leader of the expedition for everything.

There are two methods of government. One is the Paternal where the leader is King and keeps himself separate from his men issuing his orders through an Executive Officer; the other is of a rather democratic form, the leader taking the attitude of a friend among friends, joining with them in work and play, and depending entirely upon their sense of honour and gentlemanly deportment for obedience and success. To the man who believes in the Golden Rule the latter appears not only the true Christian method but also seems to offer the best chance of success. It is quite possible, however, for a leader who began his campaign in the optimistic confidence that leaden instincts would somehow wind up in golden acts to end by taking an entirely opposite position. The Arctic is no Utopia! Alas for human nature! In its present unregenerate state, the "brotherly love" plan—however desirable—is apt to fail.

The leader of an expedition could do no better than have one of two officers of known ability for assistants, the rest of his party being forecastle hands or men occupying the same relative position toward him as the crew to the Master of a ship, or privates in a military organisation to their Commanding Officer.

The Executive Officer and Second in Command should be responsible for no duty other than the executive work of the expedition He should be a man of action and of few words The scientists should be enlisted men as on the Greely Expedition and be given special opportunities for work A scientist interested in his work is a valuable member of an expedition and should be relieved as far as possible from other duties

In Arctic research—as in all undertakings—Christian character is the chief desideratum. The Polar field is a great testing ground Those who pass through winters of darkness and days of trial above the circle of ice know better than others the weaknesses of human nature and their own insufficiencies. They learn to be more tolerant of the mistakes of others and read more understandingly the words of the great Master of Life.

POLAR PHOTOGRAPHY

THE sun shines day and night through the short Arctic summer, revolving like the hour hand of a great clock in the dome of the sky not far above the circle of the horizon. With the blazing luminary and the vast white stretches of snow and ice there ought to be no lack of light—a veritable paradise for the photographer.

At first sight it would seem that with all this dazzling brilliancy, over-exposure would be the evil to guard against and that comparatively small openings and quick speeds would be the rule for lenses and shutters. But no! Though the Arctic explorer may travel in danger of snow blindness in a flood of light direct and reflected, he soon finds that the actinic value of sunlight is less than in lower latitudes, in fact, surprisingly little, and he is obliged to use his very quickest lenses and that with their widest openings use the slowest speed consistent with the movement of the men and animals he photographs on the crystal fields.

On my first Arctic expedition I took colour screens but only used them or tried to use them a few times. I soon found that, instead of giving colour and character to the views, they flattened and deadened the pictures of ice and snow and lengthened the exposure to hopelessly long intervals of time. The reason for this is the low altitude of the sun and the consequent high refraction which gives more of the yellow and red rays than of the blues as is the case with an evening sun in our own latitude.

With so much reflected light the pictures would suffer for want of shadows and I soon found that to get good values in ice pictures it was necessary to photograph with the sun in such a position that the long shadows cast between the ice blocks by the low orb could be used to accentuate the high lights and give character and contrast. To that end, it was necessary to have the sun either at the right or left hand, and often I exposed a film pointing the lens directly at the sun.

The artist who attempts to photograph the ice-fields after the time honoured custom of always having the sun behind his back will generally be doomed to flat, insipid negatives and almost meaningless pictures unless he can find shadows enough in the foreground to give character to the view.

In regard to apparatus and material—around the ship and hut any good camera can be used. I had several sizes. On the first expedition I took a number of glass plates but was unfortunate enough to break some of my best negatives, so when I went into the field again, I took nothing but films. On the sledge journeys where the question of weight is of great consequence the lightest form of camera is sure to be the favourite. In my last trip over the moving Polar pack, I found that a kodak was about the most convenient and took with me a panoram kodak (which weighed with its leather case only four and a half pounds) and a small supply of films in water-tight tin tubes.

On a sledge journey the camera and films were always kept in the outer air, usually in a compartment of the canoe that was lashed to one of the sledges. During low temperatures, the interior of a tent is not the place in which to load a camera. The little difference in temperature between the air of the shelter and of the outside is sufficient to cause condensation of moisture and the cold lenses and metal work of the instrument coat with a film of ice. Often, as I stood with my back to the sun in an endeavour to shade the camera as much as possible with a temperature of from 30 to 40 ° below zero, I have struggled with the little catches of the kodak and have had my fingers stick to the cold metal of the tin tubes containing the films while taking out an exposed roll and reloading the camera with a new one. Care had also to be exercised to keep the instrument from being frosted by the vapour from hands and body. It was always with a feeling of thankfulness and relief that the camera was made ready and I could slip my half-frozen hands into mittens and by swinging the arms and performing a sort of Indian war dance restore circulation. On return to camp the films were all developed in an improvised dark room with a small alcohol lamp to keep the developer at about 60 degrees temperature. I believe the new tank developer would be just the thing for explorers and particularly good for developing films exposed in the Arctic where long development is absolutely necessary to insure good results   Part of the outfit comprised a bioscope, a form of moving picture camera, with which I hoped to secure views of men, dogs, and ponies moving over the ice fields, the advance of the *America* through the ice, and, if possible, a bear fight. Of all my photographic apparatus, the bioscope gave me the most trouble, particularly in the low temperatures of spring and early autumn. The long celluloid film upon which the numerous little negatives were made (twenty to a second) became very brittle under the influence of the extreme cold and would fly to pieces when the mechanism of the instrument was started and pieces of celluloid would clog the gear wheels and jam between moving parts After many failures, I hit upon the plan of warming the machine and wrapping it up in hot blankets just before taking a picture The heating and wrapping up was done in the hut at camp. I was thus enabled to secure some valuable films, a few of them reaching a length of 300 feet. But always, as soon as the instrument became cold, the films broke like fragile glass It was impossible to warm the bioscope on the trail so I was limited to views near the ship and in the vicinity of camp.

We shot a number of bears for food. A bear fighting for his life surrounded by a biting, snarling pack of dogs would have been a splendid subject for a motion picture camera; but I was never so fortunate as to have camera and fight at the same time.

The pictures which show the ponies and dogs hauling their loaded sledges over the ice bring back in vivid reality the cold white fields and the struggling men and animals fighting their way over the frozen wastes.

The explorer with a camera has gone over very nearly all the earth and has brought back as part of his record, views of life and land in the far-off parts of the earth. There is still land to be conquered. And it is good to know that when these unknown places are found and the flags of discovery are planted, that, with the help of the sun and modern chemistry, we will all be able to view with the explorer what had once been forbidden and mysterious territory.

ANTHONY FIALA.

APPENDICES

APPENDIX NO. I.

FORMATION OF THE SLEDGE PARTIES IN THE THREE ATTEMPTS NORTH 1904-1905

FIRST SLEDGE PARTY NORTH

MARCH 7th-11th, 1904

26 men; 16 ponies, 16 sledges; 117 dogs, 9 sledges

MAIN COLUMN

Reserve	*1st Support*	*2nd Support*	*Advance*
4 men	8 men	8 men	6 men
1 pony sledge	4 pony sledges	6 pony sledges	5 pony sledges
1 dog sledge	1 dog sledge	5 dog sledges	6 dog sledges

Reserve—4 men, 1 pony sledge, 1 dog sledge.

2 Days' rations for 26 men, 16 ponies, 117 dogs. Four men to return after 2 days' advance from land; 5 days' rations for return of 4 men, 1 pony, 9 dogs.

First Support—8 men, 4 pony sledges (2 ponies to be used for food), 1 dog sledge (dog team to return).

6 Days' rations for 22 men, 15 ponies, 108 dogs (12 teams). Eight men to return after 8 days' advance from land; 10 days' rations for return of 8 men, 2 ponies, 9 dogs.

Second Support—8 men, 6 pony sledges (ponies to be used for food), 5 dog sledges.

16 Days' rations for advance of 14 men, 11 ponies, 99 dogs. Eight men to return after 24 days' march north; 26 days' rations for return of 8 men, 5 dog teams (provision made for return of the ponies in place of dogs if necessary).

Advance—6 men, 6 dog sledge teams, 5 pony sledge teams.

82 Days' rations for advance and return of 6 men. Ponies and 4 dog teams to be used for food. (The dogs had not been figured in as food and would mean so many extra pounds dog food. The final party could remain out 120 days without danger.)

———

106 Days

SECOND SLEDGE PARTY
MARCH 25th-27th, 1904
14 men, 7 pony sledges, 9 dog sledges

1st Support	*2nd Support*	*3rd Support*	*Advance*
4 men	3 men	2 men	5 men

First Support—4 men, 1 pony sledge "G", 2 dog sledges No.1, No.2
4 Days' rations for 14 men, 9 dog teams, 7 ponies. Four men to return after 4 days' march north; 10 days' rations for return of 4 men, 2 dog teams, 1 pony.

Second Support—3 men, 1 pony sledge "A", 1 dog sledge No. 3.
4 Days' rations for advance of 10 men, 7 dog teams, 6 ponies (ponies to be used as food as loads disappear). Three men to return after 8 days' march north; 14 days' rations for return of 3 men, 9 dogs.

Third Support—2 men, 4 pony sledges "B", "C", "D", "E" (ponies to be used for food), 1 dog sledge No. 9.
19 Days' rations for advance of 7 men, 6 dog teams, 5 ponies. Two men to return after 27 days' march north; 30 days' rations for return of 2 men; 25 days' rations for return of 9 dogs.

Advance—5 men, 5 dog teams, 1 pony sledge.
53 Days' rations for advance and return of 5 men, 5 dog teams, 1 pony, with the possibility, if occasion demanded, of reducing size of party on return of 3rd support to 3 men, and increasing the time limit.

80 Days

THIRD SLEDGE PARTY NORTH
MARCH 16th-APRIL 1, 1905

First Support—2 men, 9 dogs, 1 sledge "Y"
1 Day's rations for 10 men and 59 dogs   Three days' rations for return
to camp of two men and one dog team

Equipment—

Sledge	80	lbs
Tent with equipment and two sleeping bags .	60	"
1 Cooker filled with oil .	20	"
Can of petroleum, 5 quarts	14	"
Hatchet	2	"
Clothing bag	25	"
6 Signal poles and flags	20	"
Rifle, ammunition, etc......	25	"
		—— 246 lbs.

Food—

Sausages, Erbswurst........ .	9	lbs
Emergency ration... .	7	"
6 Tins of condensed coffee	6	"
1 Bag of bread	15	"
6 2-lb Cakes of pemmican	12	"
Meat chocolate.	3	"
Compressed tea	1	"
1 Bag sugar .	2	"
Butter. .	5	"
8 Squares Lazenbury's soups	2	"
		—— 62 lbs
Dog pemmican	70	"

Total weight	378 lbs

Second Support—2 men, 1 dog team, 7 dogs and sledge
2 Days' rations for the advance of 8 men and 50 dogs   Five days'
rations for return of two men and one dog team

Equipment—

Sledge "X", weight .	78	lbs
2 Man kayak and paddles	82	"
Picket chain	3	"
Tent, 2 sleeping bags, etc	60	"
Cooker and equipment	20	"
Rifle and ammunition .	10	"
Clothing	25	"
		—— 278 lbs

Food, 4 bags containing each—

Pemmican	4	lbs.
Pork and bean biscuit	2	"
Bread	2	"
2 Erbswurst sausages	1½	"
Cracked wheat	2	"
Sugar	1	"
Milk (condensed)	2	"
Butter	1	"
Coffee	1	"
		72¾ lbs.

One bag for return of party—

Pemmican	12	lbs.
Pork and bean biscuit	4	"
Bread	6	"
6 Erbswurst sausages	5	"
4 Tins of cracked wheat	4	"
1 Tin of bovril red ration	1	"
Sugar	2	"
Butter	2	"
Condensed milk	1	"
Coffee	1	"
Tea	½	"
		41½ lbs.

1 Tin alcohol	4½	lbs.
1 Tin petroleum	14	"
Dog food for advance	113½	"
" " " return	40	"
		172 lbs.

Total weight		564¾ lbs.

Third Support—4 men, 2 teams of 8 dogs each, and 2 sledges.
5 Days' food for advance of 6 men and 43 dogs. Ten days' rations for return of 4 men and 2 dog teams to Camp Abruzzi.

Sledge "A"

Equipment—

Sledge "A"	84	lbs.
2 Man kayak and paddles	82	"
Tent, 2 sleeping bags, etc	60	"
Ice pick, No. 8	4	"
Cooker and equipment	18	"
Theodolite and tripod	20	"
Clothing and repair kit	30	"
		298 lbs.

Food, 3 bags containing each—

Pemmican	8	lbs.
Pork and bean biscuit	5	"
Bread	5	"
Sausage	2	"
U. S. A. emergency ration	3	"
Erbswurst	2	"
Bovril red ration	1	"
Butter	2	"
Onions	½	"
Borden's coffee	2	"
Tea	½	"
Chocolate	2	"
Milk	2	"

$115\frac{1}{2}$ lbs.

Tin petroleum	24	lbs.
" alcohol	4½	"
Dog food	153	"

$181\frac{1}{2}$ lbs.

Total weight.......... $594\frac{3}{4}$ lbs.

Sledge "B"

Equipment—

Sledge "B"	85	lbs.
1 Man kayak and paddles	65	"
Tent, sleeping bag, etc	60	"
Oooker and equipment	18	"
Rifle and ammunition	10	"
Shovel (steel)	2½	"
Picket line	3	"
Clothing	30	"

$273\frac{1}{2}$ lbs.

Food for return, 2 bags containing each—

Pemmican	10	lbs.
Sausage	3	"
U. S. A. emergency ration	3	"
Erbswurst	3	"
Red ration	1	"
Sugar	2½	"
Butter	2	"
Onions	½	"
Tea	½	"
Borden's coffee	2	"
Milk	2	"
Chocolate	2	"

$88\frac{1}{2}$ lbs.

Pork and bean biscuit . ...   6 lbs
Bread   .   ...   6 "
Pemmican .   .. .   211¼ "
                                                    ———— 223½ lbs

       Total weight   . ...   585½ lbs

Advance—

100 Days' Rations for 2 men, 3 dog teams of 9 dogs each, 3 sledges

Sledge No 1

Equipment—
Sledge No 1   .   . ..   86 lbs
Ice pick ..   . .   4½ "
Small shovel (steel) ....   2¼ "
Canvas cover over load and lashing.   7   "
Picket line   .   ...   .   .   2¾ "
                                                    ———— 102½ lbs

Food, 3 bags containing each—
Pemmican   .   ..   .. 10 lbs.
Erbswurst sausages   5   "
U S A emergency ration   2   "
Bovril red ration   ....   1½ '
Onions   .   ...   ¼ "
Tea .. .   .   6 ozs
Borden's coffee   ...   ..   2 lbs
Sugar   2   "
Milk   2   "
Butter   .   1   "
   "   (peanut)   1   "
Chocolate   2   "
                                                    ———— 88¼ lbs

3 Bags pork and bean biscuit .   22½ lbs
3 "   bread   ..   19½ "
1 Bag sausage.   .   5   "
Cornmeal.   2   "
Cranberries .   . .   2   "
Extract beef   1   "
Ground coffee.   ...   1¼ "
11 Blocks pemmican .   154 "
10 "   "   .   ..   150 "
1 Tin petroleum .   ...   24 "
1 " alcohol .   . ..   4½ "
                                                    ———— 385¾ lbs.

       Total weight. . ...   577¼ lbs.

Sledge No 2

Equipment—

Sledge No 2	85 lbs.
Picket line	2¾ "
Clothing bag (belonging to 3rd support)	15 "
Tent, sleeping bag, etc	60 "
Rifle and case	9 "
Pair snow shoes	3 "
Canvas cover for load	7 "
Ropes, etc	4 "
Ice ax	3 "
Harpoon	1 "
Thermometer, case, etc	5¼ "
	——— 195 lbs.

Food—

Pemmican	175 lbs
Erbswurst	23½ "
Pork and bean biscuit	35 "
Swedish bread	30 "
U S. A. emergency ration	10 "
Bovril red ration	5 "
Sugar	16 "
Butter	8 "
" (peanut)	8 "
Onions (evaporated)	3 "
Flour	3 "
Cornmeal	3 "
Tea	1½ "
Borden's coffee	8 "
Chocolate	12 "
Milk	2 "
Horlick's malted milk	2 "
Cranberries	2 "
Extract beef	2 "
Sausage	5 "
Pâté de foi	5 "
Salt	1 "
	——— 372¼ lbs
Petroleum	23½ "

Total weight	590¾ lbs

Equipment—   *Sledge No. 3*

Sledge No. 3	85 lbs.
Canoe	91 "
Rifle and shot gun	17 "
Ammunition—150 rounds 8 mm	11¼ "
" 100 rounds 12 guage	12¾ "
Sail, harpoon, and line	4 "
Pump	1 "
Can Rubberine for repairing	2 "
3 paddles	7 "
Picket line	2¾ "
Bag with ephemeris, etc.	4½ "
Clothing	10½ "
Medicine case, barometer, compass	10½ "
Camera	4½ "
Repair outfit and photo films	11½ "
Sextant and artificial horizon	11½ "
Cooker and fry-pan	13 "
Spare clothing	18 "

317¾ lbs.

Food—

7 Tins pemmican	140 lbs.
Bag pork and bean biscuit	21 "
2 Bags bread	27 "
Sausage	5 "
Lazenbury's soups	5 "
Emergency rations in tins	6½ "
" " " bag	6 "
Butter	8 "
Onions	2 "
Flour	5 "
Oatmeal	5 "
Tea	2 "
Borden's coffee	4 "
Chocolate	7 "
Cranberries	3 "
Extract beef	1 "
Evaporated eggs	1 "
Extract coffee	1 "
Horlick's malted milk	1 "
Condensed milk	3 "
Salt	1 "
Sugar	11 "

265½ lbs.

Total weight .... 583¼ lbs.

APPENDIX NO. II.

REPORT OF SCIENTIFIC WORK DONE ON THE ZIEGLER POLAR EXPEDITION 1903-1904.

[The following report was presented to me at Camp Abruzzi by Mr. W. J. Peters before our third sledge journey north. Considerable work was accomplished after that time, and the full scientific record is published in a separate volume under the auspices of the *National Geographic Magazine* of Washington, D. O.   ANTHONY FIALA.

Sir: Camp Abruzzi, Feb. 5, 1905.

The action of the National Geographic Society selecting a representative to the Ziegler Polar Expedition was followed by the appointing of a Committee of research to consider the possibilities of scientific work to be executed under the direction of its representative. The Chairman of this committee, Prof. G. K. Gilbert, submitted a plan of work to the President of the Society from which the pertinent matter is copied as follows:

GRAVITY

" It is recommended that a determination of gravity be made by Pendulum observations at the winter camp. With the assistance of Mr. Hayford and other officers of the Coast Survey Mr. Peters is now making preparation for that work.

TIDES

" It is recommended that systematic tidal observations be made at the base camp, a continuous record being maintained through a complete lunation and so much longer as may be necessary to eliminate any irregularities occasioned by storms. For this work Mr. Peters is receiving instructions from Doctor Harris of the United States Coast Survey

MAGNETISM

"It is recommended that systematic observations of the usual magnetic elements be made at the base camp. It is important that the declination be observed if possible at some point where a previous record has been made, and also that the magnetic station of the present Expedition be definitely marked and recorded so that at any future time it may be possible to reoccupy the station The determination of declination will have immediate importance in connection with the main purpose of the Expedition, because if the Pole is approached the compass will afford the most trustworthy means for orientation and for the determination of the proper route to be followed in returning. Conversely, the traverse of the journey on the ice taken in connection with astronomic observations, will throw light on the position and curvature of the magnetic meridians in the Polar region, a field of inquiry which has heretofore been occupied only in a theoretic way.

AURORA

"In connection with systematic magnetic work it is desirable to make systematic observation of auroras, recording phenomena with some fulness. The question whether the aurora is ever accompanied by sound is one to which attention may well be given.

METEOROLOGY

"It is the opinion of Professor Moore that in the present state of meteorologic investigation the regular observation at Franz Josef Land of pressure, temperature, and surface wind, while desirable, is less important than the determination of the height, drift, and velocity of clouds. Professor Moore has undertaken to prepare instructions for such a determination.

SEA-DEPTH

"In the judgment of Admiral Melville it is very desirable that soundings be made on the northward journey, especially as the results of such soundings on the outward journey may aid in the determination of position during the return journey. They will of course make contribution to the general body of geographic information, and supplement the important determinations made by Nansen. Whether it will be practicable to carry on the sledges any apparatus adequate to reach considerable depth is a question which may advantageously be considered on shipboard.

OTHER OBSERVATIONS

"It is not recommended that any special preparation be made for observations in geology, zoology, or botany, although the geologist will welcome samples of prevailing rocks, and especially any fossils which may be found, and the zoologist will be glad to have records of birds and mammals seen, so far as the members of the party may be able to identify them."

PENDULUM OBSERVATIONS

In regard to pendulum observations. The apparatus taken on the previous expedition was sent back to Washington to be repaired and tested, but its late arrival did not allow sufficient time, so the instrument was not taken.

TIDES

An attempt to register tides was made in October 1903 at the ship's winter quarters, no nearer place being available owing to the thickness of the ice. The gale of October 22d and the subsequent pressure which destroyed the ship frustrated this plan.

Observations commenced April 1, 1904, at Camp Abruzzi. These observations were taken by Mr. Long and Mr. Stewart until April 30, when Mr. Long left to return south. From this date to the close they were taken by Mr. Stewart, Mr. Tafel, Mr. Vedoe, and myself.

As the season advanced the disintegration of the ice revealed a strong current close to shore which may have produced flexure in the wire attached to the sinker. I think it therefore very desirable to obtain another month's observation in the coming spring with a special view to guard against this effect.

Mr. Long was instructed to establish a gauge at Cape Flora and there resume observations. This he did with very satisfactory results, and was assisted by members of the expedition of whose names I have no record. The observations at Cape Flora extend over several months and were discontinued upon my arrival September 1.

MAGNETISM

Upon the completion of the magnetic hut September 23, 1903, which was delayed by the necessity of immediately constructing living quarters for the fast approaching winter, observation for declination were made with but few interruptions up to my departure from Camp Abruzzi in July 1904. The scheme arranged by Mr. L. A. Bauer, Magnetician of the U. S. C. & G. Survey was followed. The severe blizzards of the winter caused several breaks in the continuity of intensity and dip observations. The declination observations were principally by Mr. Tafel and myself, assisted later in the season by Mr. Vedoe. Doctor Newcomb continued observations during the short absence of these observers on journey north.

In the early part of July 1904 the instruments were carefully packed in their cases and original shipping boxes and taken south in order to observe at Cape Flora and then ship them to Washington. Transportation to Eaton Island was effected by canoe. Further transportation being impossible the instruments were carefully cached on the island together with the records.

An unsuccessful attempt to reach the island again was made on my return to Camp Abruzzi.

I cannot praise too highly the brave perseverance of Messrs. Tafel and Vedoe in facing the blizzards when the wind was often blowing at sixty miles or more per hour and the drifting snow and intense darkness made the walk to the hut, short as it was, quite unsafe.

AURORA

Observations of the aurora are meagre because of the prevailing stormy weather and because of the lack of observers sufficient to keep a continuous series. Some notes made in connection with the magnetic work and sketches made by yourself are available for publication

METEOROLOGY

Before leaving Norway Mr Francis Long had set up the instrument shelter house, anemometer, and single register aboard the steam yacht *America*, and immediately after commenced the meterological record. The barograph and thermograph were operating. This has been continued without interruption to date.

On arriving at Teplitz Bay the instruments were installed on land. The anemometer was set up on the astronomic observatory and the wind vane erected at the shelter house

Mr. Long left the station April 30, 1904, to return home. At Cape Flora he set up the thermometers, barometer, anemometer, and wind vane, and began a record which is to continue until the arrival of the Relief Ship. After his departure from Camp Abruzzi the weather observations were noted by Mr. Stewart.

It has been found impracticable to use the nephoscope during the winter on account of darkness and during the period of daylight on account of the lack of clouds of definite form.

SEA-DEPTH

The suggestions regarding soundings on the northward journey have been considered   It is now impracticable to carry the necessary weight for such determinations.

ASTRONOMIC OBSERVATIONS

An observatory was built on the high land west of the house at Camp Abruzzi soon after our arrival in Teplitz Bay, 1903. A brick pier was erected inside on which was mounted the vertical circle loaned by the Christiania Observatory through the kindness of Professor Geelmuyden. Mr Porter made observations for time throughout the winter of 1903–4. He made twenty-six observations of moon culminations. Some observations for latitude and anomalies in refraction were made but the number was restricted by weather conditions.

On his departure time observations were made principally by myself until June when the instrument was taken down, packed in its case and an additional covering of painted canvas was sewed over the whole.

On my return to Camp Abruzzi in November, 1904, the circle was again mounted on the pier and observations made for rating the chronometers.

The chronometer and watch record was kept by Mr. Porter during his stay at Camp Abruzzi. Later it was kept by myself until I left when the record was discontinued. The chronometers were wound by Mr. Stewart until my return to Camp Abruzzi when I commenced a new record.

The chronometers have been running since leaving Trondhjem.

During the winter of 1904–5 I have prepared an ephemeris of the sun for the coming summer in which I have been ably assisted by Doctor Seitz.

OTHER OBSERVATIONS

On the way to Teplitz Bay in 1903 the limited time at our different landings and afterward our late arrival precluded any collection relating to the subjects under this head.

During the summer of 1904 Mr. Porter verbally reported having seen Ptarmigan and having secured some specimens, also of having found coal.

Some of the members of the expedition have collected mineralogical specimens, but nothing of scientific value, except possibly the fossils collected at Cape Flora.

RECORDS AND INSTRUMENTS

The weather records in duplicate together with the instruments are in the custody of Mr. Long excepting those at Camp Abruzzi.

Astronomical records are in two books labelled respectively "Transits 1904" and "Repsold Circle, description and constants." The Repsold circle remains mounted on the brick pier in the observatory and is protected from ice particles falling from the observatory roof by cardboard housing.

Of the three sextants two are available for the sled journey. The index glass of the Cary sextant which was found to be unreliable was taken out to replace an imperfect one in the large K. & E. sextant.

Of the fifteen watches four have defective winding mechanism.

The magnetic records are to be found in thirty consecutively numbered books labelled "Mag. dec." and on loose forms of the U. S. C. & G. Survey labelled "Oscillations," "Deflections," and "Dip." All magnetic records are filed in a black tin box.

· The magnetometer and dip circle are securely packed in their cases and original shipping boxes and cached on Eaton Island.

Chronometer and watch records are in two books labelled respectively "Chrono. errors and comparisons" and "Watch rates."

A complete list of the instruments with their ownership is found in book labelled "Instruments, Ziegler Polar Expedition 1903-4."

This book also contains the record of distribution of instruments.

In conclusion I would say that assistance has been cheerfully given by various members of the expedition and I take this opportunity of making grateful acknowledgments of many obligations.

Very truly,

To Mr. Anthony Fiala.   W. J. PETERS.

EXECUTIVE REPORT, MAY 1 TO SEPTEMBER 30, 1904

Dear Sir:

After your departure, May 1, for Cape Flora there remained at Camp Abruzzi, besides myself, Messrs. Porter, Tafel, Rilliet, A. Vedoe, J. Vedoe, and Stewart, of the Field Department, Mr. Hartt, Chief Engineer, Mr. Spencer, Steward, and five of the ship's company —Mackiernan, Tessem, Myhre, Meyer, and Perry.

Mr. Porter left Camp Abruzzi May 9th to continue

the survey begun in March and to connect it with the Astronomic Station at Teplitz Bay and also with Cape Flora.   His party included Mr. Rilliet, A. Vedoe, Spencer, and Mackiernan.   The last two whom you expected to remain here, became discontented with the prospect, and could not be persuaded to remain

Meyer and Perry were detailed to assist Mr. Porter in altering his outfit.

Mr. Hartt was engaged up to my departure on the conversion of one of the whale boats into a steam launch.   In this work he was assisted at different times by Tessem and Perry

On May 4th Myhre and Tessem were reported sick. Myhre had a cough.   They were assigned rooms in the main building where the remaining sailors were soon afterward quartered.

On May 6th Myhre's cough had disappeared but he had not recovered sufficiently to come to table for meals. Tessem had fully recovered by May 11th   On May 12th Myhre was feeling better, but. weak, taking only liquid nourishment in bed.   Apparently he was in no trouble and I could not get him to describe or locate any pain

On May 13th he was assisted out near the stove where he sat wrapped in blankets for half an hour or so, when he returned to bed apparently better.   From this time on his mind wandered and he finally died at 1.30 P. M., May 16th, apparently without pain.

Tessem and Meyer immediately made a coffin and on May 18th Myhre's body was placed in it and taken up to the Astronomic Observatory, where it remained until the burial on May 20th.

Myhre's grave consists of a large stone cairn on

which is erected a cross bearing his name and date of demise   It is located on the high land west of the Astronomic Observatory overlooking Teplitz Bay.

Myhre's room was cleaned and washed and his effects were searched for articles of either personal or intrinsic value.   These few things were taken with me on my way south to turn over to you but on account of the difficulties of the last stages of the journey they were placed in the cache at Eaton Island

During May and June the party at Camp Abruzzi was variously employed and accomplished the following

The old galley was renovated and turned into a store room.   A small cooking stove was set up in the large room where bench and cupboard and shelves were constructed for galley use.   Snow was removed from around the house and runways were dug to carry off the water.   Various articles of dress left in the different rooms were bagged, labelled, and stored in the tent.   During this time the scientific observations were taken by myself, Messrs Tafel, Vedoe, and Stewart, all of whom also cooked the meals

As the snow disappeared stores were recovered and promptly taken care of.   Those not immediately needed were stored in a cache near the Astronomic Observatory.   Two kayaks were repaired for immediate use and a large keel was attached to the sectional canoe so that it might be dragged over the ice without injury.

The old storehouse adjoining the workshop and the one adjoining the old galley were torn down and sails which had been used for roofs were dried and stowed away.

The Italian quarters were cleared of snow and the ice was penetrated at two or three places to the floor in the hope of finding coal.

The first thaw occurred May 28th, but water did not appear in quantity until June 24th. On the morning of this day we awoke to find the machine and work shops flooded with a foot of water. This was drained off by ditching in the snow. Finding water in the horse and store tents we again resorted to ditching. In fact the whole of that day was spent in draining off the water, which persisted in avoiding the channels we had constructed at an earlier date with considerable labour. On June 25th a great stream burst down the old horse trail which extends to Capes Saulen and Fligely. Coming with a roar it again filled the machine shop and old galley. This was at first led off by a deep cut in the snow bank, that stood on the south side of the old galley and afterward diverted above the machine shop into ditches leading to the Italian tent, in hopes that it would cut away the ice and disclose the coal.

In this our attempts were only partially successful. It was not until later in the season, when I had left, that the Italian quarters were fully exposed

On July 4th preparations to take Messrs Tafel and Vedoe to Cape Flora were completed, but no opportunity offered until July 8th when I sailed away with them in the portable canoe, leaving Mr. Hartt in charge. The voyage to Eaton Island was marked by the usual vicissitudes incident to travel by boat at this season of the year in the Polar regions, fogs, rains, windstorms, alternating with fine weather; long hours of utmost

"A BLANKET OF THICK, DAMP, ARCTIC FOG OBSCURING THE VISION"

exertion in paddling or hauling over the ice following days of enforced idleness.

On August 4th we landed at Eaton Island, where on account of ice conditions no further progress with the load of instruments was possible. I waited here until August 24th for a favourable change in conditions. This not having taken place and the food supply reduced to eight days' half rations, I made a cache of instruments and records and proceeded with party to Cape Flora, where I reported to you on Sept 1st, having gained a day somewhere in my calendar.

Very truly
W. J. PETERS.

To Mr Anthony Fiala

Camp Abruzzi, Feb 5, 1905.

APPENDIX NO. III.

THE orders of Mr. Fiala, issued to me at "The Tombs" in the fall of 1904, were to the effect that I join him at Camp Abruzzi by March 10th of the following year. This early rendezvous at a station some hundred and seventy miles away required my leaving Cape Flora by the 20th of February and this alone is reason for two men going forth into the night from a starvation camp.

With considerable difficulty were my dogs carried through the winter. "Spot" disappeared in the fall; later "Tibus" ran foul of a bear, suffering an ugly tear to one of his hind legs. "Ostiak" was badly bitten by Bismark in January. In fact Bismark alone came through the night skin whole. The sailors at the log house were kind enough to allow the invalid dogs a chance to convalesce in an empty bunk and for the last month before starting I kept them chained up in the snow observatory fearing to lose some of them either in dog or bear fights.

With the hauling power reduced to four dogs but one man could accompany me. The selection was made on the eve of our departure and fell to one of the firemen. Duncan Butland was a native of Newfoundland, had spent a winter with the Esquimaux of Northern Greenland, and could take care of himself

258

in a tight place. We found the tight place later on and Duncan did not disappoint me.

The loads came up to one hundred and twenty-five pounds to a dog, and while we took a silk tent along, we had experimented on building snow huts or igloos before starting, and thought they would be much the more comfortable to live in. We had to leave the kayak behind.

The eighteenth of February found us saying good-by to some of the men at the little caboose where they had helped Duncan lash the loads and hitch up. A fresh wind from the south enveloped us in the drift and in a short time we were alone in the storm running along the shore toward Peace Point, the wind at our backs, dogs pulling well, and a keen sense of satisfaction that at last the dull life of inaction was broken, and there was a hard definite purpose ahead to work for.

It was a short day's run as we were late in getting started and the twilight was only a few hours long. The sun had not returned and remained below the horizon even at noonday. The snow hut went up nicely and when the capstone was finally dropped into place, the joints between the blocks chinked up, and the interior cleared out we went inside with our sleeping bags and stove and felt at once that huge relief that comes in getting out of the wind. It is hard for one who has not travelled all day in those drift storms at low temperature to realise what this sense of shelter means. And we found that once the snow door was set in place one could hardly tell whether a storm was raging outside or not, so solid and tight this igloo proved to be. Then again you felt a certain sense of

proprietorship in your new home and caught yourself
admiring the way you made the snow blocks tip in
over the dome to the capstone, or criticised this or that
detail of its architecture. Duncan had told me that a tent
was not in it with an igloo for comfort, and the first
night's experience attested the fact. In fact the drift
held us in our first hut the next two days and we frequently remarked how warm and quiet it was there
in our dry bags, the yellow candle light transforming
the snow vault into glistening marble.

The drift went down the third night, the sky cleared,
and a nearly full moon hung over the upturned shield
of Bruce Island We were not long in starting and
found travelling by moonlight through the channel ice
a weird and uncanny thing. By breakfast time Camp
Point was rounded and we stood over "The Tombs."
The drifts of the winter had completely blotted out
our settlement of the fall before. A bread tin only
remained to mark the spot. By sounding the surface
of the glacier the cavern below was located and a hole
knocked in the roof, through which Duncan descended
with the revolver, for we were not sure but the bears
had taken up quarters there

Then I lowered the stove and food and followed and we had breakfast, the cold blue light shimmering through the ice of the glacier, bringing up a
clear vision of our long incarceration here in the fall.
Everything was evidently just as it had been left; the
hay strewn over the floor, the improvised tin blubber
lamps reposing in their niches in the wall. In the
next room the roof had bulged in to such an extent
that each block seemed hanging by itself

By one o'clock we were well out across DeBruyne
Sound and going into camp, picking out a fine hard
drift which had been formed during some big winter
storm to the leeward of a large hummock. This was
the twenty-first and we had made a good run.

Washington's Birthday we completed the run
across the Sound, finding it full of good heavy ice but
always open stretches here and there that made progress steady, though tortuous. Just before noon a
blood-red spot appeared on the southern horizon and
moved slowly toward the west. I was ahead picking
the course and shouted to Duncan, pointing to the sun.
He vouchsafed only a wave of his arm in recognition
of the event, then returned to the sled upstanders,
guiding the sled in its erratic course among the pressures. I never saw him let go those upstanders once;
he seemed glued to them.

It was monotonous work relieved only by the thought
that this sound, this Rubicon of the fall before, was
being so easily crossed. Though clear overhead, fog
covered Northbrook Island, so there was constant
reference to the compass to keep us on our course.
We travelled well into the night, wishing to make the
land before camping, but were forced to camp among
the pressures with our object unattained. And so
tired were we, and so little light remained, we thought
of the advantage of just setting up the tent and turning in, instead of a weary hour and a half or two hours'
work spent in building an igloo.

It was a miserable night! It seemed as if we were
no sooner asleep than the wind awakened us, the tent
walls slatting, setting the air in the tent into violent

motion, and chilling us to the bone so that further sleep was out of the question. The bags were already wet with accumulated moisture. How we maligned the fate that found us in a silk tent with the worst wind yet! How we longed for the cozy interior of the igloo, with its quiet and—yes, its warmth, for we had found that no matter what the temperature outside was, or how hard it was blowing, the inside of a snow hut remained up around zero and the air absolutely quiet.

We hardly waited for sufficient daylight before we were out in the drift throwing up a hut, and felt well repaid when it was done and we were inside beating the snow out of our bear skin trousers. It was well the hut was built, for the drift kept us prisoners there for three days. When Duncan came in from feeding the dogs the last day he said: "I broke the alpinestock to-night." "Well," I replied, "I can match that. The hatchet's gone: handle broke off square against the head."

We burned a little extra candle that night trying to get the wood out of the hatchet head. I improved matters by shutting my clasp knife over the end of one of my fingers, nearly taking it off. Sometime in the night Duncan woke me up showing me the hatchet nicely fitted to a tent peg.

I remember that night we discussed our prospects.

"We've been out over a week now and over half our grub's gone (but ten days' food supplies were taken from Flora)."

"Well," Duncan inquired, "how far is it before we can get some more?"

"I should say forty miles."

"And how far have we come?"

"A little over thirty."

"Oh we can make that all right. It's been bad weather."

And so it had!—six days out of the eight. Certainly no one had any business to be out in such weather as this after six months starvation diet. It was just this weakness of the body that was worrying me and the hundred odd miles to Rudolph Island loomed up very big ahead of us.

The next day we pulled out with clearing weather, a light head breeze frosting our faces and requiring frequent applications of melting snow to the affected parts. From this day on the temperatures were lost. The minimum thermometer was out of service, the column was separated and could not be united again until we reached Camp Ziegler.

Looking over the dome of Hooker Island, as we passed through Mellenius Sound and by the towering rock of Rubini, past the summer camping ground of the surveying party the year before, I hesitated a moment. Should I cross the island over my old trail and cut off some two or three miles or stick to the shore and go around it, keeping on the bay ice? Perhaps the recall of an admonition of my father's years before, as I was just leaving for the Arctic, to "Keep off the Glaciers" decided me to hold to the latter course. We little imagined that there, up on the dome of the island, in the dusk of an October afternoon the fall before two men of our expedition had plunged into the bowels of the glacier.

The day proved satisfactory, both overhead and

under foot, and when the short daylight was gone found us in our snug hut perched on a snow terrace lying against the island and giving us a clear view down Allen Young Sound. We had done fairly well; were still behind our schedule, but thought that better weather was due us (it couldn't have been much worse, only two quiet days out of the week) and the going ought to improve.

But good weather had not arrived to stay. The morning of the twenty-fifth was stormy, the drift combing down over the slope behind us in a veritable snow fall. It had started in the previous night soon after camping. After breakfast Duncan went out to free the dogs and came in to say that he had hard work getting down to the stake line. So we let the poor animals come into the igloo and they were soon busy cleaning their coats of the snow that had driven into them. They seemed to thoroughly appreciate the change, putting themselves on their good behaviour and giving us no trouble at all. These dogs had all been with me the year before and one of them, "Bismark," a powerful gray animal had been my constant companion on the previous expedition.

It was around noon that misfortunes fell thick and fast. The alcohol stove refused to burn. The daylight, which filters through the walls of a snow hut, faded rapidly. The dark line of the drift outside was moving slowly up over the roof. "We'll wait until it gets up to there," and I pointed to a joint on the dome some two-thirds the way up, "then we get out." When it reached that point we broke through the roof and Duncan got on to my shoulders and forced his way

through the drift   I handed out the dogs and followed   We went down among the heavy pressures
at the ice foot and by nightfall had succeeded in throwing up another shelter.   After that we returned to the
submerged camp   Duncan descended and handed me
everything there was in the igloo.   It wasn't much,
only our bags and a small bag of food and the rifle.
While he was doing this there was an ominous slumping
sound around the hut and I told him to catch hold of
the rope and haul himself out   He said he was going
to try to break through the side of the hut by the door,
where he thought the harnesses were.   After some time
there came another slump and I ordered Duncan to
come up or he would be buried.   But he either did
not or would not hear me, and when he passed out
the four harnesses and came up after them, hand over
hand, through the burrow, the fact of seeing him there
alive again was one of unspeakable relief   Before
leaving the place a skee was jammed into the roof of
the hut and another, as a marker, set up farther down
the terrace, and we groped our way to the new hut,
hardly realising what had actually happened.

There was no let up through the night and returning
dawn found us criss-crossing the slope of the glacier,
vainly searching for the old site.   The terrace had
disappeared.   Not even the point of a skee protruded
The snow was showering down over the glacier, giving out a sharp hissing sound   It was quite impossible
to stand up against the stronger blasts, and so, after
a minute or so, while we tried to yell to each other
that it was no use, we returned to the shelter down by
the ice foot, called the dogs in after us, closed up the

door and warmed up some tea. And while we drank the tea we sized up the situation and took account of stock.

"There's about four days food in this grub bag," I said, after counting the broken pieces of pea sausage and estimating the amount of crumbled up hard tack mixed in with a plentiful supply of bear and caribou hairs.

Duncan lifted the alcohol stove and shook it.

"Seems to be about half full," he commented. "Good for about two meals isn't it?" ,

"Not more." Then I let my eyes run over the rest of our belongings—sleeping bags, a small bag containing a change of underwear and stockings, rifle, revolver, the mail bag, and a "diddy" bag. The "diddy" bag held our sewing kit and ammunition.

"That's all," I said despondently. "Sled gone, man food, dog food, fuel, skees, shovel—all gone.

Duncan ventured that I had forgotten one thing.

"What's that?" I asked.

"The dogs."

And sure enough, the old faithfuls that finally brought us through, our biggest assets, I had ignored entirely.

"But there's no food for them, Duncan, and they can't work long in this temperature without food."

Duncan's answer to this damper was that we had saved our guns and it was about time a bear showed up anyway. "And," he went on, "If you're thinking of turning back to that hell at Cape Flora, I'll take chances and go on alone." He delivered this with more energy than I thought him capable of, and it was the first pleasant sound I had heard since the disaster.

"THE CUB WHEELED AND MADE STRAIGHT INTO THE SOUND, BUT ONLY A SHORT WAY
WHEN HE CAME TUMBLING DOWN WITH BULLETS FROM BOTH RIFLE AND REVOLVER"

BUILDING AN IGLOO

R. W. PORTER.

"IT IS A CASE OF MAKING DOGS OUT OF OURSELVES"

Drawn by R. W. Porter

"Well, Duncan, you won't lack company. I have no desire to take the back trail. Now it looks as though there were two other ways open to us—to wait here until the drift lets up and see if we can recover the sled. The top of that skee which I jammed into the igloo is fifteen feet above the sled if an inch, and the Lord knows how much more. And you can figure out for yourself how long it will take us, using the fry pan and that agateware plate, to dig down to it."

"But we don't even know where to dig."

"Then the only thing to do is to push on and take our chances. There's a cache of emergency rations on an island across Young Sound some twenty miles from here, or was, for I saw it landed there four years ago, but I have only a dim idea just where it was placed and it may be, probably is, buried under the snow.. The next grub is as far again beyond there."

And so we crawled into our bags and talked the rest of the day through, planning how we could best conserve our precious hoard, how the sodden, saturated bags could be best tied up to offer the least resistance to the snow, for they must be dragged from now on.

At dawn we were outside the hut, our gear laid out for inspection. The wind had gone down. While absorbed with the aggravating problem of the bags I looked up and saw two bears coming right in among the pressures in front of us. They were a mother and cub, and had sneaked in on us while we weren't looking. I jumped for my rifle and scared Duncan speechless by exploding into his ear, "Get your revolver."

Duncan even then didn't see the bears and I can

remember him, revolver in hand, eyes fairly popping out of his head, looking up and down the shore, up the glacier back of us, everywhere except right beside us where they were.

Perhaps the bears took us for some animals good to eat. Surely we looked more like beasts then men in our bear skins, and with our long hair and grease covered faces. At sight of these bears the savage man rose dominant within me and in my hair and down my spine ran an indescribable prickling sensation and I knew why the hair on the wolf's back bristles when he hunts.

On they came. The report of my Winchester rang out sharp and clear in the frosty air and the old bear fell not fifty feet away. The cub wheeled and made straight into the Sound but only got a short way when he came tumbling down with the bullets from both rifle and revolver.

We didn't stop to argue on who shot that cub. As was common between Duncan and myself when greatly pleased at anything we gave vent to our feelings in the Esquimau tongue; there was a hearty handshake, and forthwith the two bears were skinned and cut up, the meat finally reposing under the two skins among some rocks by the shore close under the cliff.

A big slice had already been cut out of the working day when we finally started. After much shifting, repacking, and relashing, the cumbersome burden of our paraphernalia was ready, the front of it bent up like the bow of a toboggan, guns, snow knife and snow saw dangling on top, dogs pulling from well down under the front. Between the bags was the dogs' food (thirty pounds of the bear meat, we couldn't carry more) and ours. For a hundred yards or so after getting clear of the pressure along shore, our bundle slid along very respectably. The wind coming off the island had blown the Sound ice free of snow. Sharp points of rubble protruded from this ice and soon made trouble, for, hearing a suspicious tearing sound, the bags were overturned and found already partly torn and wearing away.

"This will never do," we both exclaimed at once; "we must save the bags."

But we could see no way of improving matters, and started again, one of us picking out a trail that became very snakey.

All of a sudden we ran into deep snow. "Good" was our verdict this time. "The bags can stand this sort of going indefinitely," but in fifty feet the dogs came to a halt. We started the bundle and the dogs pulled it perhaps twenty feet and then stopped, and so on a few times more when they refused to pull at all.

I knew my dogs and knew they would not act this way unless the resistance to their pulling force was really formidable. Those bags were half submerged in this snow that had evidently come with the last storm, and our skees were gone.

"It is a case of making dogs out of ourselves, I guess, Duncan. One of us will have to get into harness and the other break a trail. We will change places from time to time."

In this way progress became possible but that was about all. Up to dark I don't suppose we made two miles out in Young Sound, and when the igloo was up we were very, very tired. I wrote in my diary, "A rather discouraging day notwithstanding the bears." This was the last day of February.

March first was one long drawn out three-mile drag, from early dawn when Duncan would prod and harass me into getting up and starting the stove, until nightfall in another hut three miles farther on. The snow had grown deeper and we were wading through it to our knees. The dogs could hardly get along at all and the leaders, "Tibus" and "Porridge," were continually fighting for the chance to walk in the tracks of the trail breaker. When we reached Jefferson Island, a huge rock rising out of the middle of the Sound, we were about ready to give up.

There was no drift, but it was the coldest day I ever experienced. Probably our exhaustion made the cold penetrate. Before the hut was done three of the fingers of my left hand were frozen and Duncan's face had a white patch on it as big as the palm of one's hand. It was touch and go whether we could finish the hut. But we did—we had to.

Our bags by this time had become so saturated that they froze soon after we got out of them and in lashing up the bundle it meant quick work to get the end turned up while it was still limp. On the other hand our work was cut out for us: getting back into them again the next night, they were so hard and stiff. So the next morning after breakfast we made everything ready inside the hut, then Duncan went out and harnessed the dogs, the pull rope was passed in and tied to the bundle, I knocked two or three blocks out of the wall to get a clear way, and off we went.

THE S.S. "MAGDALENA"
TRIP TO THE NORTHEAST COAST OF GREENLAND

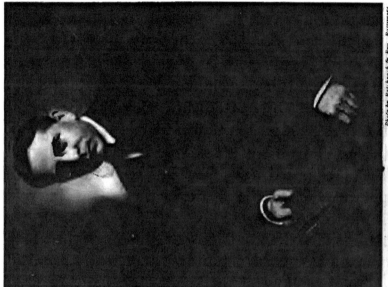

OLIVER L. FASSIG
Commanding Relief Expedition to Greenland, 1905

Photo by Barsbroul & Bro., Baraverst

Oliver L. Fassig

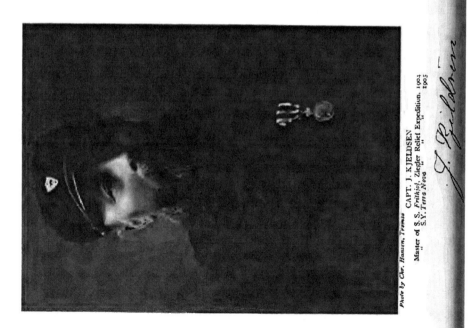

CAPT. J. KJELDSEN
Master of S. S. *Frithjof*, Ziegler Relief Expedition, 1904
"   "   S.Y. *Terra Nova*   "   "   1905

Photo by Chr. Hansen, Tromsø

J. Kjeldsen

This camp by Jefferson Island we called Sun Camp for on that day we saw the whole of the sun for the first time in four months. We always named our camps, usually the day after when the history of the camp before had been made and some distinctive feature could be given to it. Where we lost our outfit was "Camp Calamity," but after the bears showed up it was changed to "Salvation Camp" by mutual consent.

The three miles on the second were in every respect like those of the two days just passed. Late in the afternoon we reached the shore of the island where I had seen food landed in 1901.

"Keep a sharp lookout now, Duncan, right along this shore and not over a hundred feet away from it. Imagine boxes, yellow boxes. Get that fixed in your mind's eye and don't see anything else."

Very soon I described something yellowish sticking up out of the snow and went over to it. A band of strap iron crossed it. No more than three inches of an emergency case was exposed to my view. I let out a yell. Duncan stopped hauling and came ploughing over. We kicked away some of the loose snow and then gave vent to several "penkshuas." The hut was built right there.

While Duncan was under fitting his blocks and passing them to me, he said, "Let's name this camp now."

"All right, what shall it be?"

"Thank God Camp."

As the dome rose, ready for the capstone, I asked Duncan to go up on a neighbouring hill after a slab of stone, for I intended to try some of the wood from the emergency ration box for fuel. When he had gone I proceeded as usual to chink up the joints of the igloo, cut and fit the door.   The dogs had gone inside to get out of the wind.   Then I crawled up over the dome and started fitting the capstone, when the entire structure collapsed inward, myself with it, on top of the dogs.

It was a sorry sight—so much hard labour all for naught and all to be done over again.   I knew it would so depress Duncan that I had it pretty near finished again when he returned, carrying a broad, flat slab of red sandstone.

I felt more like changing the name to "Calamity Camp" again when it tumbled in.   But I suppose we ought to be thankful the dogs weren't hurt.

We could not be downhearted, however, for there was food now aplenty.

"We'll cook the rations over a wood fire," I said. But somehow the wood refused to burn.   We opened the vent in the roof, took the snow plugs out of the three peep holes in the walls, even opened the door, blew the embers until we were purple in the face: we coughed, tears ran down our faces, all to no avail.   We were compelled to fire the whole thing out of the door.

Duncan's resourcefulness came to the rescue.   He overhauled the bear meat and managed to clean off about a plateful of the blubber.   Taking a small strip of canvas, he rubbed it well into the grease, frayed one edge, and applied a match.   Slowly the flame ran along the wick and the canvas placed along the edge of the plate, the pieces of fat nearly covering the canvas. It made a clear, hot flame five or six inches long and cooked us a most delicious stew of the newly acquired rations.

"There's only enough fat left for breakfast," said Duncan as he gazed with an envious eye on what little remained, even after we had finished the second pot of stew

Before leaving "Thank God Camp" we carried three emergency ration cases, all we could find, back from the beach on to higher ground among some wind swept rocks   One of the cases had been opened and in an empty tin inside was a note from Mr. Peters dated October of the fall before, stating that his party at that time were all right but were having a pretty hard fight with the young treacherous ice floes   I took up this note, leaving a copy and left a message to whom it might concern, telling of our mishap and that we were trying to push through to Camp Ziegler: that my hands and Duncan's face were badly frozen and that we were pretty well pulled down.

The following day the going was much better and much worse   For four miles, until we reached Cape Charles Beresford, the ice was swept smooth and glassy. The bags needed only one of us to guide them between the hummocks. We felt quite elated with this let up from the drag ropes when, on rounding the cape, we plunged into very soft snow that was deeper and softer than any yet encountered. We were the entire afternoon making less than a mile and acknowledged ourselves beaten

"But there's no snow here we can use for the igloo," said Duncan, probing the drifts with the murderous-looking snow saw. That saw was a savage instrument. It was a home-made affair about two feet long from a steel tank found at Flora, with teeth half an inch long, like a relic of barbarous or prehistoric times.

So we "hiked" at the dogs and slowly worked in toward shore again. In my exhaustion the lavender light, that floods the snowscape in this land when the sun returns, would suddenly strengthen to a deep purple. Through it, as in a dream, I saw the mountains on the different islands rise and fall in perfect rhythm with my laborious strides. We changed places breaking trail every hundred feet and so made land.

By dint of much teasing a pot of hot water was secured, burning a board from an emergency box, but it was completed in the dark somewhere around nine o'clock. Into the pot we crumpled pea sausages.

Duncan was doing most of the lashing and unlashing now, for my left hand, now covered with blisters from the frosting two days before, was useless. About all I could do was to bounce on the bags as he drew the ropes tight.

From where we had built the hut, some hundred feet up among the rocks, Alger Island, on which Camp Ziegler was situated, could have been seen had it been clear weather. During the night "Tibus" freed himself and tore down part of the door trying to join us inside. The other dogs, jealous of his freedom, woke us up with their infernal barking.

The next morning, the fourth, the last remaining candle was cut up into four pieces. They were all lighted and the pot suspended over them—our last fuel. They looked very festive and made us think of Christmas trees and birthday cakes. They just about melted the snow and warmed the water. We literally used a part of our house for cooking. It was so easy, just to reach over with the snow knife, and with a twist of the wrist slice a cone of hard snow out of the wall and drop it into the pot. And when stopping in the same hut several days the walls became honeycombed. As Duncan remarked, "we were eating ourselves out of house and home."

We had lashed up, ready to harness the dogs, when on opening the door, the drift came pouring into the hut like flour. There was nothing to do but unfasten the load and crawl back into the frozen bags again. We lay there shivering all day. The worst had come. Stormbound and no fuel.

"Duncan," I chattered along toward evening, "if ever I get out of this scrape alive, I'll make a bee line for the tropics and not go ten degrees north or south of the equator for the rest of my days."

His only answer was, "New York for mine."

Some time in the night after cudgeling my brains in vain I said, "Duncan, are you awake?"

"Awake? how can one sleep on an empty stomach in this temperature?"

"Can't you think of something we can use to burn?"

"We ought to have brought more boards from the cache."

I protested at this criticism saying we couldn't have pulled five pounds more through that deep snow if it had been a bag of diamonds. After some time he said:

"There's your butter box."

"By Jove!" I ejaculated, "you are right. It's just soaked with butter."

We were at once all enthusiasm at the thought of

something hot. The little box which had held my butter "Whack" or weekly ration through the winter at Flora was carefully chopped and whittled into suitable pieces. Strange to say it blazed up beautifully without suffocating us. And how good the hot food tasted and felt, notwithstanding the bear and deer hairs.

Some time along in the early morning Tibus woke us up again, tearing down the door. It was drifting as hard as ever.

"Let's let all the dogs in, Duncan, it may warm up the place a little." We didn't need to go out to release them. When the dogs saw the door open and Tibus disappear inside, they gave a frantic bound, tore up the stake chain and came at us "en masse," jamming themselves in the doorway in their eagerness to get out of the storm.

Either the temperature outside rose or the dogs gave off an appreciable amount of heat. Certainly by afternoon our bags began thawing out and we fell asleep, awakening again about midnight craving food and water, principally water. Duncan had eaten a part of a pea sausage raw and it was very salty.

On account of my deafness Duncan usually kept me posted as to the weather outside. He said he always knew when it was drifting by a sound that resembled rustling silk; and just before dawn on the sixth he told me he thought the storm had stopped. It didn't take me long to remove the snow plugs and find out. The wind had not only gone down, but it was clear and I could see Alger Island fourteen miles away.

We were not long getting ready. Our thirst hounded us on. To our great surprise and joy the Sound ice was found swept almost clear of snow; or else packed hard from the last storm. The bags behaved beautifully. It was fortunate we had been able to keep the dogs on nearly full rations. They needed no help and by morn we were at the West Camp furiously tearing up Ruberoid roofing for a fire, whereby we could melt some snow and quench our thirst.

"Shall we try to make the East Camp, Mr. Porter? I think we can do it if it is not over six miles. Just think of getting inside a warm, dry room."

"If we do, Duncan, we break through the roof. We've not strength enough to shovel the place out. The drift around that house in spring is on a level with the roof. I think we'll chance it."

So we put some coal into a sack, against our not finding any at the house, and pushed on, finding the going still good. It was a very anxious two hours. There was a little drift, that raised the surface of the morning snow about a foot. It looked like a sea of milk flowing over the snow. I didn't know it at the time, probably Duncan didn't know it, but the big toe of his left foot was already frozen. The dogs seemed to know we were nearing the end and maintained the pace. By the Basalt Spires, past the huge rock called the Haystack, we came up over the great flat. Far away we made out a pole with a flag on it. On arriving the pole and the top of a stove pipe were all that could be seen of the camp.

But no. There by the pole was a black hole in the snow that seemed to lead into the bowels of the earth.

And beside the hole, lying on the snow, was a gun! Instantly there flashed through my mind the thought that the Relief Ship had reached this place the year before and left here some men.   We slid down through the burrow, colliding with a dog, groped our way through what I knew to be the stable, into the vestibule between the two houses.   Involuntarily I felt for the latch of the door to the east, found it and pulled the door open.

Never shall I forget what I then saw as long as I live. Two soot begrimed faces peering at me in wonder out of a void, made all the darker by the light of a slush lamp sputtering against the wall.   They were Quartermaster Rilliet and Mackiernan, though I did not recognise them at first.

"Hullo, fellows, how are you?"

"How do you do, Porter?   You didn't think to see us here?"

"No, I thought you must be from a Relief Ship. What are you doing here?   What has happened?" I felt there had been some serious accident, for finding two men here was not in the programme.

"Mr. Fiala and the Steward fell seventy feet down a crevasse on Hooker Island last fall."

"Is Fiala dead?"

"No; they were pulled out more dead than alive and brought on here, where we found Mr. Peters's party. They all went on to Camp Abruzzi later in the night and left us two here to hold down the grub. 'Mac' froze his toe on the way over, and had to lay up here.   It's all right now."

We had forgotten all about our own woes in the thirst for news.

Then it was Rilliet's turn.

"Any deaths at Flora?"

"Strange to say, they're all alive," I answered, "though two or three are in pretty bad shape. Two parties will be over here later after food."

"How did you stand the trip over? Gad, look at Smokey's face." "Smokey" was Duncan's nickname among the sailors.

Then we told of our misfortune on Hooker Island and our long fight to reach a place of safety.

"Hooker Island is a sure enough 'Hoodoo'," Rilliet commented. "From your description of the place it was not three miles from where Fiala and Spencer fell in."

They went outside and inspected our ludicrous bundle, told us to go back inside and make ourselves comfortable while they brought in our effects. So the ordeal was over.

I remarked in my diary the second day at Camp Ziegler that Duncan and I had slept hardly two hours since arriving. We were forever prowling about with a candle in the west house after good things to eat. There seemed no end to our appetites and surely no limit to our capacity. When we did finally retire it was to sleep the clock around.

Our arrival was very timely. The next day it was drifting again badly and I began at once getting ready to push on. It was now the seventh of the month and the rendezvous at Abruzzi was on the tenth. We were away behind our schedule. For the three days while it was storming outside our bags were slowly drying out over the stove.   A "trailer" sled was made ready and food put up for a few days.   Duncan's toe was very painful and when Rilliet held a candle back of it you could see a sharp line of demarcation between the live and affected flesh.   I deemed it imprudent for him to go on, though he was anxious to do so, "to get on to good feed and tobacco again" as he expressed it.   So I arranged with Rilliet that Mackiernan take his place.

It was a joy to find myself travelling once again with a sled, that the dogs could look after, to make good time and only to have to speak to the dogs once in a while.   Mac and I walked or trotted side by side, talking over old times and gossiping over the winter's events at Camp Ziegler and Flora.   He said a lot of bears had been around their camp, walking over the roofs of the stable and houses, and that they had shot up through the roof at them to scare them away.   They hadn't killed any but the bears had killed some of their dogs.   Rilliet had been sick and the winter had been very long.   They got very tired of each other's company and would go along for days hardly speaking, although they were always on the best of terms.   He hoped he would never have to put in another Arctic winter with just one man.

We made Camp Abruzzi in just five marching days which we thought pretty good considering the distance, one hundred miles, and our physical condition.   Mac was captivated with the igloos.   At Kane Lodge we found a new saw and iron shovel that greatly facilitated the work of building.   Our longest run was twenty-five or thirty miles to Kane Lodge, where I knew I had left tobacco the summer before. It was this that spurred us on long into the darkness in a blinding drift storm—the thought of a good smoke. Sure enough the tobacco was there just where I had left it, though half gone, The party the fall before had used a little, and in the box was a note to me from Mr. Fiala, telling of their progress to that point.

We ran across a bear at Coal Mine Island. He was coming down the shore by a water hole following some seals that were floating in the current. I shot him but he slid into the water and I tried to spear him with my ivory harpoon using the tent pole for a shaft. But although I threw well and struck him, the line was yanked out of my left hand, and bear, harpoon, and tent pole went floating away beyond reach. At Cape Auk I shot another bear.

On the morning of the seventeenth we crossed the young ice of Teplitz Bay and arrived at the station just one week late. The place seemed absolutely deserted. "Gone" I thought, "we're too late, they're gone."

Soon a black dog, limping on three legs, emerged from the snow and began barking. Then we saw smoke ascending from the stove pipe. I entered the house and found one man, the chief engineer. The main party had left only the day before for the north.

RUSSELL W. PORTER.

APPENDIX NO. IV.

TRIP TO THE NORTHEAST COAST OF GREENLAND

In order to provide for the probability of a return of the Ziegler party by way of Greenland, Mr. Champ organised a second relief expedition with instructions to proceed from Norway to Shannon Island and Bass Rock, off the northeast coast of Greenland. In 1901 a large supply of food, clothing, ammunition, and other necessities for the maintenance of a considerable party, was stored at this point with the hope that they might be utilised by members of the Arctic party sent north in the summer of that year. Shannon Island is just off the east coast of Greenland in latitude 75° north, almost the extreme northern limit of the mapped portion of the east coast of Greenland; Bass Rock is a small island about twenty miles to the south of Shannon Island.

Earlier observations, and particularly the experience of Nansen's party in the drift of the *Fram*, demonstrated the existence of a westward movement of the surface water and the ice of the Arctic across the group of islands known as Franz Josef Land and to the north of the Spitsbergen group, toward the northeast coast of Greenland, the drift changing to a well-defined southwest current along the Greenland coast. Had the Ziegler party attained a very high latitude and concluded to take advantage of the westward drift in returning, there would have been a very good chance of their reaching Shannon Island and Bass Rock, where they could have relied upon finding everything necessary for the comfort of the party for a considerable time. There was sufficient probability of the return of the Arctic explorers by the Greenland route to warrant the fitting out of the second relief expedition, especially in view of the fact that no word had been received from them for two years, and the urgency of relief was increasing.

The vessel chosen for the Greenland journey was the *Magdalena*, a Norwegian sealer of about 350 tons, a good sailer, but rather slow steamer, strongly built, and comfortably fitted up for a small party. The officers and crew of eighteen men were Norwegians, and most of them were familiar with the North Atlantic waters. Captain K. Tandberg had made many trips into the ice-field off the coast of Greenland, and had twenty-five years' experience as a sealer and whaler in the North Atlantic. The writer accompanied the expedition at the request of Professor Willis L. Moore, Chief of the U. S. Weather Bureau, and President of the National Geographic Society, and of Mr. W. S. Champ, representing the Ziegler Estate.

The purpose of the expedition being primarily one of rescue the instructions were to proceed from Sandefjord, Norway, directly to Shannon Island and Bass Rock for the relief of any member of the Ziegler party who might have reached those points; and, after inspecting the condition of the supplies laid down in 1901, to return to Norway. Incidentally, opportunities would probably be afforded for gathering observations of some value concerning the meteorological and ice conditions in the North Atlantic, especially in the little known ice-fields off the northeast coast of Greenland. In the original contract between Mr. Champ and the owner of the vessel, the writer was to accompany the captain and crew on a sealing trip in the North Atlantic waters during the month of June, and at the close of the catch, early in July, when the chances of open water were likely to be very good, to proceed northward through the ice-field to the base of supplies before mentioned. An unusual opportunity would thus be afforded for a study at close range of the modern methods of seal and whale catching. A change in the plans, however, became necessary at the last moment and but little opportunity was afforded during the journey for observation along these lines. However, a daily record of conditions of the weather and ice, and of temperature of the water was maintained, with some additional notes of a miscellaneous character which may prove to be of interest.

The *Magdalena* left the port of Sandefjord, Norway, with the writer aboard on the 22d of June, 1905, about a week after the departure of the *Terra Nova* from Tromso with the main relief party under the direction of Mr. W. S. Champ. After leaving Sandefjord, we proceeded directly to Bass Rock and Shannon Island without stopping at any intermediate point.

On June 30th, we sighted the Fãroe Islands, just north of Scotland, and from this time on, owing to almost continuous fog, we saw no land until we reached the coast of Greenland in latitude 75° north, on the

21st of July in view of one of our objective points, namely—Bass Rock

The conditions encountered and the brief duration of the journey (the entire trip covering less than two months) do not warrant a classification of the data recorded, or a systematic discussion The following pages contain only a chronological arrangement of extracts from the daily journal, showing the character of weather and ice conditions experienced in the North Atlantic in mid-summer, with an occasional reference to matters of more general interest to those unfamiliar with the regions visited

June 22, 1905 Left Sandefjord, Norway, at 10 30 P M yesterday, a high southwest wind prevailing. About midnight a defect was discovered in the boiler, making a return to port advisable Left port again to-day at 5 30 P. M and made good headway down the southeast coast of Norway with a fair wind and tolerably smooth sea

June 23 Made about 100 miles in the first 24 hours out of port As wind and current were in our favour we did not use steam A fine clear day Some of the crew understand a little English, the Captain and First Mate speak the language well enough to make them companionable

June 24 A bright clear day with a fresh northwest wind Used sails nearly all day, making a course a little south of west An exceptionally quiet sea, can scarcely detect the motion of the vessel Averaging about 3½ knots per hour

June 25. A quiet fair day, with a favourable wind Course northwest to north The air temperature has been remarkably uniform, varying less than 1° F from 11 A M to 9 P M The humidity has been high, varying from 92% to 97% of saturation Cloudy in the morning, clearing by noon, with a wind from north to northeast

June 26 A fine day, bright and warm, with a smooth sea Active preparations have been going on all day for the expected bottle-nose whale catch off the northeast coast of the Shetland Islands The decks are covered with coils of rope, the guns and harpoons are in order, and the small boats prepared for action

June 27. A foggy day with occasional short intervals of sunshine. Light head wind. Steaming north, one half east; just east of the Shetland Islands.

June 28. Off the northeast coast of Shetland Islands at noon. A raw northeast wind, with rain nearly all day, and atmosphere near saturation point. The sea is high but the *Magdalena* is remarkably steady and comfortable under sail. Making but slow headway, averaging only three knots an hour. Guns and harpoons are in readiness for whales. Two guns are mounted in the bow and two in the stern of the boat.

June 29. High northeast winds all day with rain all the forenoon. Heavy swell and much rolling. Saw two or three bottle-nose whales, but we were not near enough for a shot. Made but 85 miles in preceding 24 hours.

June 30. A bright day but plenty of swell and roll. Three knots an hour seems to be our limit of speed with the aid of engine alone, and burning three to four tons of coal per day. In sight of the Färoe Islands all day. Passed the *Sunbeam* on her way to port, and requested her captain to report us.

July 1. A cloudy day with a southerly wind, enabling us to make a fair headway under full sail; averaging four knots an hour. Spoke the *Margarite* early this morning, a whaler from Tonsberg, Norway. Her captain reported having caught 28 bottle-nose whales during the past three months, and that he hopes to get ten or twelve more before returning to port.

July 2. A cloudy and foggy day, with a light northeast wind. Air temperature from 48° to 50° F, and water about 46° F. Heavy swell from southwest to northeast. Boat rolling violently. Caught our first bottle-nose whale this evening. Saw a number during the day but did not take time to follow them. Most of them were moving southward. The Captain shot a harpoon into one of three passing about 150 to 200 feet from the stern of the boat. These harpoons, made of wrought iron, are about 5 feet long, and weigh about seven or eight pounds. To the end of the harpoon is attached a manila rope about seven-eights of an inch thick, and about 200 feet long; this rope is in turn joined to a heavier rope of about 2 inches diameter and 700 or 800 feet long. On being harpooned the whale disappeared with a loud "snort," and did not again come to the surface for about half an hour. All the rope had been paid out and another length of about 800 feet attached. In the meantime one of the small boats, equipped with a harpoon gun and several hundred feet of rope, was manned and lowered; the crew rowed in the direction of the line in the water and waited for the reappearance of the harpooned whale. On rising to the surface about 40 yards distant another harpoon was sent into his flank. The rope parted and once more the whale disappeared. On reappearing about half an hour later, a third harpoon ended the frantic struggle for freedom. The pull on the first rope which was made fast to the upper deck of the *Magdalena* was so great as to bodily move the vessel backward for a short distance. The prize was now towed alongside the *Magdalena*, and by means of knives with long handles (6 ft. to 10 ft. long) the blubber was removed, hoisted on deck, cut into pieces of about two to four square feet, and stowed away in one of the thirty-five or more large iron tanks in the hold. The carcass was left to float in the sea and was soon the centre of a noisy bunch of hungry sea gulls.

The whale was one of medium size for these waters, being 21 ft. 6 in. in length, with a middle circumference of 10 ft. 6 in.; around the head (across the eyes) 8 ft. 6 in.: length of upper snout 1 ft.; length of lower snout 1 ft. 10 in. The average thickness of blubber was 3 inches. The Captain estimated the total weight of blubber removed at about 1200 lbs., valued at about $75. The whale "spouted" 3 or 4 times between "soundings." The "spout" had the appearance of a cloud rather than a spray. The "blow" was distinctly heard at a distance of about 800 ft.

July 3. A cold disagreeable day. The vessel rolled badly all night, being without sails to steady her. The first mate reported having seen a bottle-nose early this morning entirely out of the water, clearing the surface, he estimated, over a fathom. The captain tells me they frequently rise entirely out of the water. Making good progress northward, about five knots per hour. Air temperature and the surface water, 44° F.

July 4. A wet, cheerless day. Brisk to high west winds, and a heavy sea. Swell from north-northwest. Making good progress northward, however, under full sail; averaging over 6 knots per hour. The water is 2° warmer than yesterday. Air temperature 39° to 43°.

July 5. Another raw, disagreeable day, with southerly winds in forenoon, and northerly in afternoon, increasing in force. Heavy swell from the northeast. Air temperature 45°, water 45°.

July 6. Creeping slowly northward in a zigzag line, tacking into a northeast wind; made only 20 knots in preceding 24 hours. A dull cloudy day, with light and occasionally dense fog. Have had no sunshine since July 1st.

July 7. Cloudy all day, with a brisk northeast wind. We are somewhere in the neighbourhood of Jan Mayen Islands, but exact location unknown as we have had no good sun observation for three or four days. The air is not clear enough to see more than a few miles. Between noon and 6 P. M. there was a fall in temperature of 2°, without a change of wind. The temperature continued to fall to 11 P. M., making a change of nearly 6° since noon. We must be near the ice fields. There was also a fall of 2° in the temperature of the water. This would indicate that we are farther west than indicated by our calculations. Temperature at noon 43°, at midnight 37°; water 45°.5 and 43°.4 at the same hours.

July 8. A cloudy day with occasional fog. The atmosphere and water growing rapidly colder. We are probably just to the east of Jan Mayen Islands, hidden from view by the dense fog. The first mate reports seeing three or four fin-back whales to-day.

July 9. A cloudy day, with frequent patches of dense fog. Light to fresh northeast wind and a comparatively smooth sea. With a humidity of 98% to 100% fog areas form and disappear very quickly. One moment it is comparatively clear and in the next we are surrounded by a fog so dense that we can not see more than a ship's length about us. Tested our speed to-day; with 60 revolutions per minute the best speed we could get out of our engine was 3¼ knots per hour. The first mate reports seeing a school of about 16 large blue whales early this morning.

July 10. A cloudy day with light and occasionally dense fog. Air temperature from 29° F. to 32° F.; water temperature varying between 31° and 32°. Entered the southern edge of the drift ice early this morning. It is a scene of marvellous beauty. Honeycombed ice in the most fantastic shapes, in pure white and transparent greens, floating on all sides of us. About a mile or two to the west of us is the white line of pack ice, apparently without an opening through which we could force our way. The captain thinks it advisable to go farther north, about latitude 74°, before attempting to enter the thick ice. Saw a number of seals in the water about 8 A. M.; five or six of them in line were swimming a hundred yards or so ahead of us keeping a sharp lookout on our movements. Birds are here in abundance, mostly the auk and the gull. The air is at times filled with fine needles of ice. The clouds are thin and low, much like lifted fog. In the afternoon the fog increased, becoming quite dense. Went gunning for seals in one of the small boats with the first mate and three sailors. We rowed over to the edge of the heavy pack ice, where we saw hundreds of seals on the larger floes. The roar and splashing of the water as the floes were tossed about by the swell is somewhat alarming on first acquaintance, but the excitement of the hunt readily over-balanced the thought of danger. We succeeded in getting but two seals. Two or three jumped into the water after being shot and sank before we could reach them. We lost many of them in a similar manner later on. There were scores of them in the waters about us but it is useless to shoot them under these conditions as they sink within two or three minutes after being mortally wounded   The movements of the seals are exceedingly graceful in the water, but very awkward on the ice   Their antics are sometimes grotesque in the extreme, following one another in a long line, turning complete somersaults, sometimes forward, then sideways or backward, and sometimes leaping far out of the water   Took a few pictures of small ice floes as they moved slowly past us   Some of them are extremely graceful and beautiful in shape, and have the most delicate shades of blue or green by transmitted light, and pure white by reflected light   They are particularly imposing as they float quietly by the ship on a smooth sea and in a light fog   So far the floes have been small, not more than six or eight feet high, and very much honeycombed—evidently in the last stages of dissolution   The fog is bothering us a great deal again   We have not been free from the troublesome and dangerous element for seven or eight days   To-day we are in latitude 72° north, a little to the north and east of Jan Mayen Islands apparently.

July 11.   Another day of fog and slow progress toward the coast of Greenland   The fog lifted for a few hours later in the morning, and I accompanied the ship's carpenter, an experienced sealer, in the small boat on another seal hunt.   We brought back only two seals   It was difficult to get within a reasonable distance of them before they discovered us and took to the water   The ice floes to-day are flatter—evidently an earlier stage than those we saw yesterday   It seemed to me we had considerable difficulty in pushing our way through the ice, but when I expressed this opinion to the Captain he consoled me with the remark that we would soon find the floes forty to fifty times as large   The fog lifted late in the afternoon revealing a closely packed band of drift ice just to the west of us, too thick to think of attempting to push our way through at this point   Saw a large seal jump out of the water, the entire body being at least three feet above the surface.   Air temperature 34° to 36°, water 33° to 34°.

July 12   This morning we found exceedingly dense ice just west of us, utterly impossible to get through at this point (73° N)   Later the fog became dense and the wind rose, making it dangerous to push ahead   The Captain left up just enough sail to prevent drifting, so we remained nearly stationary all day   Just to the north of us the edge of the ice took an eastward trend as far as we could see   A long and weary day, we have not had bright sunshine, even for an hour, since July 1st.

July 13. Another foggy day. The fog lifted somewhat about noon and we found ourselves almost surrounded by compact ice floes, too thick to risk a forced passage. The captain concluded we had gone far enough north and turned southwestward along the edge of the thick ice looking for a promising opening to push westward into the ice field. About 3 P. M. we found a favourable opportunity and started in; steering a course northwestward, and making fair progress toward Shannon Island, but bumping into large floes most of the night. We anchored to a floe long enough to fill our water tanks with delicious fresh water from the numerous pools of melted snow found at this season of the year on all of the larger ice floes.

July 14. Another foggy day. Making fine progress through the ice to-day. The floes are much larger than any we have seen thus far, one of them measuring four or five miles in length, but the open water between the floes is growing in extent. We have presumably been in the region of the midnight sun for some days past, but owing to fog and cloud we have scarcely seen the sun at any time of day. Caught a glimpse of the sun for the first time at midnight, but the break in the clouds was of short duration. In the afternoon the captain saw a large polar bear on one of the ice floes and ran the ship to the edge to permit us to give chase. Four of us followed him through soft snow and pools of water for an hour or so but he swam to another floe before we could get a shot at him. Later we saw another bear on a nearby floe but did not feel justified in taking the necessary time to give chase. We are now in latitude 73° 30′ north, and longitude about 3° 30′ west. With a clear atmosphere we would be able to see Shannon Island to the west and north of us. Air temperature from 34° to 35°; water varying from 32° to 34°.

July 15. A little sunshine to-day. Fog lifted for a short time revealing alto-cumulus clouds in the morning; in the afternoon upper and lower cirrus visible at times. Wind light to fresh southeast. We have had practically open water most of the day; here and there we met a cluster of small floes, but none to give us any trouble. Failed again to get a good sun observation at noon, but we are not far out in our calculations. The water showed a considerable change in temperature from 9 A. M. to 3 P. M., a rise of 2°. There is very little animal life to-day—only a few sea gulls. Sunshine after 8 P. M., but foggy on horizon. A fine exhibition of "trailing cirrus" clouds at 11 P. M., apparently converging from the zenith to a point in the west-southwest. About 11 P. M. we passed a floe on our port side (steering northwest by west) which was larger than any the captain has seen in his twenty-five years' experience in North Altantic waters, it was at least ten miles long from the crow's nest (135 ft above deck) the end could not be seen Got a sun elevation at midnight, the first reliable observation possible since June 30th It is lighter at this hour (midnight) in my stateroom than at any time, day or night, during the past fifteen days The ice floes are getting larger and more rugged, the surface being covered with a network of ridges from 5 to 10 feet high

July 16 A bright, clear day—the first of the kind since June 30th when we were off the Fãroe Islands. Fog set in again from the southeast toward evening, and disappeared at intervals to midnight The sea was remarkably smooth, and the temperature surprisingly uniform for a clear day, varying less than 3° between morning and noon Air temperature about 36° and water about 35° The ice was heavier to-day—the floes were large and numerous with rough hummocky surfaces, but we had no difficulty in picking our way through them Came upon a small sealing schooner from Tromso, Norway, about noon. The harpooner came aboard the *Magdalena* and took dinner with us He stated that they had been in these waters since April and had a catch of about 600 seals and 19 polar bears, three of the bears were alive as we saw when we returned the visit a little later in the day. As the Captain of the schooner was on his way back to Norway we all sent letters by him He had neither chronometer nor sextant with him and seemed to have very little idea as to where he was or just how he was to get out of the ice Captain Tandberg gave him our latitude and longitude and advised him to take a southeasterly course out of the ice It is astonishing what some of these Norwegian captains accomplish every year in these dangerous waters with their small sailing vessels and scant instrumental equipment Saw three polar bears on one of the ice floes but lost sight of them before we could come to a convenient anchorage to follow them Latitude 74° 35′ north, longitude 10° 30′ west

July 17 We got into a tight place to-day. We are now lying in a narrow lane between two immense ice fields and surrounded by a dense fog We can see only a few hundred feet about us. The day has not been wasted, however, as we secured four bears I was the first to see the bear we got this morning, and had the first shot at him as he was swimming toward the boat from one of the ice floes We lowered one of the small boats and headed him off as he turned back toward the ice There were too many hunters in the game and we riddled the hide with our bullets Later in the day, as we were anchored to one of the large floes waiting for an opportunity to push forward, two bears approached to leeward When they were within 150 or 200 yards of us we opened fire.   Before we could reach them a third bear appeared out of the increasing fog and we soon added all three to our stock.   We are now anxiously waiting for the fog to lift in order that we may see where we are, and how to get out of the dangerous position between two large ice floes. The floes about us are from 7 to 8 feet in thickness, judging by some of the smaller ones which we have run into and overturned.   We are now in a narrow lane, not over 50 feet wide, where the ice has been jammed by the grinding of two very large fields, several miles in extent.

We built a fire on the port floe and put a lot of seal blubber into it in order to attract any bears to leeward that may be lured by the odour of the burning blubber.   The air temperature ranged from 34° to 37° during the day, and the water temperature from 30° to 33°.   The fog has been dense and persistent to-day, lifting only at intervals and then only partially.

July 18.   We are hemmed in on all sides by immense ice floes.   To add to our difficulties the narrow channel, in which we have been at anchor since yesterday, began to close up astern.   We could move neither forward nor backward.   The two large floes were grinding, and we were in a dangerous situation.   About noon the *Magdalena* was nipped and lifted 4 or 5 feet out of the water.   She very soon righted herself, however, and we found to our great relief that the damage had been small.   The rudder chains were torn from their moorings on the upper deck and the screw socket was somewhat loosened.   About 4 P. M. the fog lifted and revealed open water just ahead, but the channel leading into it was practically closed up with small pieces of recently crushed ice.   We found on investigation however that the channel was widening, and in a couple of hours we were enabled to push our way through.   Beyond the channel we found comparatively open water and made excellent progress the balance of the day.   The intense whiteness of the ice fields and the reflected light from snow covering of the past ten days caused a severe inflammation of the eyes, accompanied by a slight fever and headache.   By remaining in the darkened state-room for a few hours my eyes improved and the fever disappeared. We are now probably within fifty miles of Bass Rock, but the incessant dense fog has prevented our seeing any great distance.

July 19.   Sighted land at about 4 P. M. in the northwest, probably the mountain peaks on Sabine and Pendulum Islands, just south of Shannon Island.   The water was comparatively open and we made good progress after the fog lifted, about 8 A. M.   At noon we were in latitude 74° 12' north, and longitude 16° 12' west. Spent a large part of the day in the "crow's nest," about 135 feet above the deck, trying to identify the mountain peaks along the Greenland coast   The ice we passed through to-day was largely last year's ice, very thin and soft, offering very little resistance to the boat's passage   The floes of this year's ice were also much smaller   From present appearances we shall be able to get close up to shore in open water

July 20   A dense fog all day   Late in the afternoon and evening the fog lifted for short intervals   About 4 P M we found that we were about ten miles off the eastern coast of Wallaston Foreland   Owing to dense fog the captain was not willing to take any risk, so we remained in practically the same position for twelve hours or more   The water is practically free from ice as far as we can see along Wallaston Foreland and Sabine Island   At noon to-day I witnessed a complete double fog-bow from the crow's nest, with my shadow in the centre.   The outer bow had slight colour, and the inner one a decided colour.   There seemed to be some good-sized glaciers on Wallaston Foreland, and a number of high mountain peaks, probably 4,000 ft to 5,000 ft high.   Since June 30th we have had but one day without troublesome fog   Air temperature 35° to 37°, and water 32° to 33°

July 21.   We reached our destination to-day, visiting both Bass Rock and Shannon Island.   The day was bright and the atmosphere remarkably clear, so clear that we were constantly deceived as to distances   A light northeasterly wind prevailed in the morning, and a southerly wind in the afternoon with a temperature varying from 33° to 37°   The temperature of the water ranged from 32° to 35°   The humidity was remarkably high for so bright a day, being 98% at 8 A M and decreasing to 94% by 10 P. M   The humidity has been uniformly high during the entire month, only occasionally falling below 95% and then only for a few hours at a time   During the preceding night we anchored to a large floe on account of the dense fog.   At 4 A M the fog having lifted, we set out for Bass Rock and Shannon Island, both of which now appeared very near   We found the ice conditions much better than we had expected   There were some large floes, but the captain found no difficulty in threading his way through channels of open water to within a mile or two of Bass Rock   Accompanied by the first mate and three or four sailors I left the *Magdalena* at about 9 A M and we made our way through the rough ice to the two octagonal sheds on Bass Rock, which contained the stores laid down in 1901 for the earlier Ziegler party   There were no evidences of anyone having visited the island since Captain Kjeldsen's trip in the summer of 1903   The supplies and the sheds were in good condition, with the exception of the petroleum which had practically all evaporated from the barrels. The stores had not been disturbed. After leaving a note to the effect that our pary had inspected the station, and wishing to take advantage of the bright day, we returned to the *Magdalena* in about four hours, and immediately moved northward toward Shannon Island, about 20 miles distant. We reached our destination at about 5 P. M. without much hindrance from ice. Here we were even more fortunate as we were able to get one of our small boats close to shore. We remained on the island only about an hour. The shed and the stores were in excellent condition, none of the supplies apparently having been disturbed. The only evidence of the visit of any human being was a note by Captain Ole Nasso of the ship *Severn* of Tromso, stating that he had been here two weeks ago, and that he had been on the lookout for the Fiala–Ziegler party.

Bass Rock and Shannon Island, like the rest of the Greenland coast in this region, are bare rugged rocks, with only a small amount of snow in protected places. We found a few small willows, about three inches in height, and clusters of a small white flower, name unknown. At 7 P. M. we embarked and the captain headed the *Magdalena* homeward. We were all greatly relieved and rejoiced to accomplish the purpose of our journey with so little difficulty and in so short a time, and celebrated the event with a feast of good things. A little later the crew gathered in the bow of the boat and their spokesman (the carpenter) made a speech congratulating me on the successful attainment of my object and thanking me for the refreshments, closing with three cheers for the "Doctor." Not understanding the language I was for a time unaware that the ceremony was in my honour as I stood on the upper deck watching their movements. The first mate, who was standing at my side, interpreted their remarks and I hastened to acknowledge their attention.

Some of the smaller ice floes seen to-day along Pendulum Island were between 15 feet and 20 feet in height—the highest we have seen thus far. The water is much more open along the coast in this latitude than we had expected to find it. All the larger floes have a very rough, hummocky surface, the ridges of crushed ice being from 5 feet to 8 feet high. The only level ice we saw was the fast shore ice in the channel between Shannon Island and the mainland. The current between Shannon Island and Bass Rock is very strong, setting southward with a velocity of about half a mile an hour. Along the main Greenland coast several glaciers are visible in the distance, some reaching down to the water's edge. We have not seen a single iceberg during our journey.

July 22. Homeward bound. Dense fog until 11 A. M. Took a course southwest during the morning but soon came to impenetrable ice and changed to south, following the coast, where the sea was comparatively open. Cloudy, with light fog, changing late in the afternoon to a light mist. The highest floes seen to-day were about 25 feet in height. No evidences of life on the ice to-day with the exception of one large seal reported by the second mate early this morning, and a couple of sea gulls. Ran into heavy ice again about 6 P. M. Air temperature 35° to 37°; water 32° to 36°. Heading for the Jan Mayen Islands.

July 23. Another foggy day, with rain at intervals. The wind was fresh from the northeast in the forenoon, changing to southerly in the afternoon. Made but little progress since yesterday owing to frequent delays on account of dense fog, and the zig-zag course made necessary in order to dodge large ice floes. Fresh east to south winds. Air temperature about 35°; water, 34°. We expect to reach Iceland about the close of the week, where I hope to find a more rapid means of locomotion back to England or the Continent.

July 24. Passed through the thickest ice of the return trip to-day, about half way between Shannon Island and the Jan Mayen Islands. Fortunately found a narrow lane of open water. The day was foggy with light rain after 8 P. M. Fresh southerly winds.

July 25. Dense fog lifted about noon. A great deal of open water with only an occasional large floe to divert us from our course E. S. E. Wind southeast in the morning, changing to east-northeast in the afternoon, and increasing in force. Air temperature 35°; water 33°.

July 26. Another day of dense fog, with light misting rain in forenoon. Very little progress since noon of yesterday. A solid belt of ice ahead of us, which we are skirting to northward to find an opening. Found open water in our course about 8 P. M.

July 27. Dense fog most of the day. The sea was remarkably smooth, with a mirror-like surface. Passed through small and moderate sized slack ice all day long, steering a south-southeast course, with a speed of about 3 knots an hour. The waters abounded in seal, and birds were unusually numerous. Speaking of seals the Captain stated that he and his crew of thirty men killed 999 seals in twelve hours on one of his cruises. I tried to persuade him to make it an even thousand but he refused to yield. A light misting rain fell in the morning. Filled one of the ship's tanks with fresh water from a large floe early this morning. Air temperature, 36°; water, 34°.

July 28.   Passed out of the ice about eleven o'clock last night.   I am convinced we entered the ice too far north, and that we would have found more open water just north of Jan Mayen Islands, and saved three or four days, instead of making for 74° north before attempting to enter.   Dense fog all day, but we made fair progress aided by wind and current.   A smooth sea with a slight swell.   Air temperature, 38°; water, 39°; northwest winds.

July 29.   A day without fog.   The crater of Mount Beren on Jan Mayen Island was clearly visible this morning above the clouds; we were about thirty to forty miles south of the islands when the fog lifted about us.   The cone is apparently covered with ice and snow. The base of the mountain was also visible, and surrounded by ice. The presence of so much ice at this season would indicate that the past winter was unusually severe.   The captain claims that he has never seen so much ice on the mountain even in March and April.   A rise of 8° in the temperature of the air since yesterday indicates that we have passed out of the influence of the ice fields. Saw two large fin-back whales this morning, moving northward.

July 30.   Brisk northeast winds prevailed all day, enabling us to make fine progress toward Iceland without the use of the engines.   Made about ninety miles in the preceding twenty-four hours, nearly as much as we made in three days in this region on our outward voyage.   We are making an effort to reach Miofjord, on the east coast of Iceland, by the 2nd of August in order to catch the steamer *Kong Inge* which leaves that port for Leith, Scotland, on the 3d.   This will enable me to reach England two or three weeks earlier than I could by going with the *Magdalena* to Reykefjord, Iceland.   Saw four or five large fin-back whales to-day, all spouting vigorously.   The spouts resembled so many jets of steam rising from the surface of the water, gradually dissolving and disappearing entirely in three to five seconds.   The captain estimated the length of these whales at 70 to 80 feet.

July 31.   A cloudy day with steady and brisk northeast wind, and a rough sea.   Making excellent progress toward Miofjord, using sails only.

August 1.   A bright sunshiny day with brisk north to northwest winds, and high seas.   Anchored in Miofjord on the east coast of Iceland about sunset.

Taking leave of the captain and crew of the *Magdalena* on the 2d, I took passage on the Danish steamer *Kong Inge* on the 3d and reached Leith, Scotland, early in the morning of the seventh of August.

August 11.   London.   The daily papers yesterday announced the great news of the safe return of Mr. Champ and his party bringing with them, from Franz Josef Land, all but one of the Ziegler Arctic party.   OLIVER L. FASSIG.

APPENDIX NO. V.

WINDS AND TEMPERATURES RECORDED AT
CAMP ABRUZZI, RUDOLPH ISLAND, FROM
SEPTEMBER, 1903, TO APRIL, 1904

FOR MONTH OF SEPTEMBER, 1903

Date	Max. Temp.	Min. Temp.	Mean, Max. and Min. Temp.	Total Daily Movem't of Wind in Miles	Date	Max. Temp.	Min. Temp.	Mean, Max. and Min. Temp.	Total Daily Movem't of Wind in Miles
1	36	26	31	361	18	18	8	13	132
2	35	24	30	729	19	19	5	12	185
3	35	30	32	548	20	21	17	19	312
4	35	22	28	196	21	20	3	12	462
5	35	22	28	349	22	7	1	4	92
6	34	26	30	435	23	12	0	6	159
7	32	26	29	260	24	12	— 4	4	184
8	30	25	28	293	25	8	0	4	368
9	29	23	26	148	26	22	7	14	501
10	25	19	22	110	27	26	22	24	593
11	25	18	22	281	28	28	18	23	147
12	32	21	26	394	29	24	15	20	121
13	31	17	24	298	30	20	6	13	563
14	24	19	26	234					
15	21	13	17	96		Mean Temp. +25.2	Mean Temp. +15.2	Mean Temp. +20.3	Total 9,070
16	27	13	20	293					
17	34	14	24	226					

Aggregate amount of calm weather in month, 3 hours. Maximum hourly velocity of wind for month and direction, 60 miles, southeast. Average temperature for month, +40. Average wind velocity for month, 302 miles a day. FRANCIS LONG, Observer.

FOR MONTH OF OCTOBER, 1903

Date	Max. Temp.	Min. Temp.	Mean, Max. and Min. Temp.	Total Daily Movem't of Wind in Miles	Date	Max. Temp.	Min. Temp.	Mean, Max. and Min. Temp.	Total Daily Movem't of Wind in Miles
1	22	13	18	620	18	5	—12	— 4	173
2	27	16	22	299	19	— 9	—18	—14	294
3	20	5	12	242	20	Zero	— 9	— 5	419
4	16	3	10	84	21	3	—11	— 4	94
5	13	1	7	180	22	8	— 2	3	615
6	17	10	14	689	23	10	4	7	1,249
7	18	— 5	6	227	24	11	4	8	451
8	— 9	—17	—13	71	25	13	4	8	174
9	— 8	—16	—12	49	26	20	12	16	615
10	4	— 4	Zero	234	27	16	5	10	551
11	4	— 7	— 1	427	28	17	11	14	144
12	5	— 1	2	471	29	16	6	11	80
13	13	5	9	256	30	6	— 1	2	73
14	16	4	10	135	31	8	— 3	2	359
15	17	4	10	109					
16	4	— 5	— 1	54		Mean Temp. +10	Mean Temp. Zero	Mean Temp. +6.7	Total 9,932
17	9	Zero	5	494					

Number of calms in month, none. Maximum hourly velocity of wind for month and direction, 72 miles, east. Average temperature for month, +10. Average wind velocity for month, 320 miles a day.
FRANCIS LONG, Observer.

FOR MONTH OF NOVEMBER, 1903

Date	Max. Temp.	Min. Temp.	Mean, Max. and Min. Temp.	Total Daily Movem't of Wind in Miles	Date	Max. Temp.	Min. Temp.	Mean, Max. and Min. Temp.	Total Daily Move't of Wind in Miles
1	Zero	—18	— 9	192	18	—21	—34	—28	128
2	—14	—20	—17	242	19	—21	—28	—24	141
3	—18	—28	—23	189	20	— 4	—25	—14	497
4	—17	—28	—22	145	21	+25	— 8	+ 8	553
5	—15	—27	—21	77	22	+19	—16	+ 2	552
6	—11	—22	—16	86	23	+18	—16	+ 1	636
7	—18	—26	—22	54	24	+21	+10	+15	783
8	—25	—33	—29	85	25	+10	Zero	+ 5	422
9	—31	—42	—36	42	26	+10	— 2	+ 4	1,023
10	—31	—43	—37	111	27	+12	— 1	+ 5	919
11	—38	—47	—42	52	28	+18	— 2	+ 8	870
12	—20	—40	—30	162	29	+11	+ 6	+ 8	1,079
13	+ 9	—36	—14	754	30	+ 9	+ 2	+ 5	398
14	+27	—19	+ 4	407					
15	—11	—25	—18	289		Mean Temp. — 9	Mean Temp. —21	Mean Temp. —14.7	Total 11,422
16	—17	—30	—23	303					
17	— 9	—23	—16	231					

Number of calms in month, none. Maximum hourly velocity of wind for month and direction, 76 miles, east-southeast. Total amount of wind in miles for month, 11,422. Monthly mean temperature, —28.4. Average wind velocity for month, 381 miles a day. FRANCIS LONG, Observer.

FOR MONTH OF DECEMBER, 1903

Date	Max. Temp.	Min. Temp.	Mean, Max. and Min. Temp.	Total Daily Movem't of Wind in Miles	Date	Max. Temp.	Min. Temp.	Mean, Max. and Min. Temp.	Total Daily Move't of Wind in Miles
1	+ 2	— 6	— 2	523	18	— 5	—18	—12	467
2	— 6	—13	—10	233	19	—15	—28	—22	579
3	+ 2	—16	— 7	413	20	—17	—32	—24	851
4	+ 5	— 6	— 1	276	21	—19	—27	—23	279
5	— 6	—15	—10	83	22	—18	—25	—22	870
6	— 8	—36	—22	135	23	—16	—22	—19	633
7	—22	—35	—28	201	24	—18	—30	—24	353
8	—15	—24	—20	251	25	—14	—29	—22	516
9	—15	—21	—18	882	26	—15	—26	—20	283
10	— 9	—20	—14	734	27	—12	—22	—17	752
11	— 3	— 9	— 6	1,087	28	—16	—21	—18	1,761
12	— 4	— 8	— 6	1,523	29	—11	—20	—16	390
13	— 4	—14	— 9	373	30	—14	—21	—18	128
14	— 8	—23	—16	555	31	— 4	—14	— 9	758
15	—18	—25	—22	773					
16	—16	—25	—20	937		Mean Temp. —10.4	Mean Temp. —21.3	Mean Temp. —15.8	Total 18,280
17	— 6	—21	—14	681					

Number of calms in month, none. Maximum hourly velocity of wind for month and direction, 84 miles, south-southeast. Average temperature for month, —31.5. Average wind velocity for month, 590 miles a day. FRANCIS LONG, Observer.

FOR MONTH OF JANUARY, 1904

Date	Max. Temp.	Min. Temp.	Mean, Max. and Min. Temp.	Total Daily Movem't of Wind in Miles	Date	Max. Temp.	Min. Temp.	Mean, Max. and Min. Temp.	Total Daily Move't of Wind in Miles
1	−4	−18	−11	467	18	+14	Zero	+7	515
2	−6	−31	−18	234	19	+14	+8	+11	467
3	−14	−28	−21	362	20	+22	+9	+16	747
4	−15	−32	−24	226	21	+31	−6	+12	762
5	−19	−38	−28	257	22	+26	−10	+8	1,015
6	−8	−40	−24	321	23	−5	−15	−10	342
7	+4	−27	−12	399	24	+8	−18	−5	687
8	−17	−27	−22	742	25	+3	−7	−2	462
9	−15	−24	−20	358	26	−7	−19	−13	478
10	−22	−31	−26	262	27	−15	−25	−20	119
11	−28	−46	−37	391	28	−22	−28	−25	112
12	−45	−51	−48	287	29	−20	−27	−24	788
13	−48	−52	−50	102	30	−21	−27	−24	484
14	−40	−50	−45	34	31	−21	−30	−26	302
15	−23	−42	−32	237					
16	+12	−24	−6	451		Mean Temp. −8.8	Mean Temp. −24.9	Mean Temp. −16	Total 12,518
17	+12	−1	+6	108					

Aggregate amount of calm weather for month, 9 hours. Maximum hourly velocity of wind for month and direction, 75 miles, south. Average temperature for month, −34. Average wind velocity for month, 404 miles a day.　　　　　FRANCIS LONG, Observer.

FOR MONTH OF FEBRUARY, 1904

Date	Max. Temp.	Min. Temp.	Mean, Max. and Min. Temp.	Total Daily Movem't of Wind in Miles	Date	Max. Temp.	Min. Temp.	Mean, Max. and Min. Temp.	Total Daily Move't of Wind in Miles
1	−25	−31	−28	160	18	+4	−37	−16	478
2	−20	−27	−24	259	19	−25	−45	−35	126
3	−12	−25	−18	876	20	−6	−25	−16	983
4	−15	−21	−18	897	21	−1	−17	−9	619
5	−11	−20	−16	443	22	+15	−6	+4	981
6	−10	−17	−14	498	23	+16	−28	−6	387
7	−14	−21	−18	146	24	+23	−32	−4	773
8	−4	−24	−14	166	25	+5	−17	−6	413
9	−4	−18	−11	312	26	+26	−17	−4	707
10	−10	−17	−14	378	27	+24	−25	−1	349
11	−9	−37	−23	280	28	−4	−16	−10	142
12	−37	−44	−40	59	29	+30	+4	+17	684
13	−11	−43	−27	304					
14	+4	−24	−10	464		Mean Temp. −4.5	Mean Temp. −26.0	Mean Temp, −17.8	Total 12,791
15	−24	−43	−34	205					
16	−33	−44	−38	182					
17	−5	−40	−22	920					

Aggregate amount of calm weather for month, 2 hours. Maximum hourly velocity of wind for month and direction, 66 miles, south-southeast. Average temperature for month, −31. Average wind velocity for month, 441 miles.　　　　　FRANCIS LONG, Observer.

Date	Max. Temp.	Min. Temp.	Mean, Max. and Min. Temp.	Total Daily Movem't of Wind in Miles	Date	Max. Temp.	Min. Temp.	Mean, Max. and Min. Temp.	Total Daily Move't of Wind in Miles
1	+23	− 9	+ 7	217	18	−29	−50	−40	122
2	+10	−29	−10	295	19	− 2	−29	−16	241
3	− 9	−37	−23	465	20	− 8	−36	−22	522
4	+17	−24	− 4	786	21	+ 8	− 9	− 1	1,093
5	−10	−36	−23	406	22	+ 9	−13	− 2	349
6	+ 2	−12	− 5	242	23	−13	−25	−19	513
7	+ 1	−16	− 8	360	24	−25	−37	−31	363
8	−16	−24	−20	181	25	−20	−33	−26	78
9	−18	−23	−20	159	26	−20	−30	−25	102
10	−23	−32	−28	72	27	− 6	−31	−18	182
11	−13	−31	−22	189	28	+25	− 6	+10	367
12	−15	−45	−30	110	29	+26	+10	+18	255
13	−41	−47	−44	51	30	+10	−24	− 7	484
14	−33	−44	−38	51	31	+ 5	−25	−10	236
15	−38	−48	−43	95					
16	−41	−51	−46	37		Mean Temp.	Mean Temp.	Mean Temp.	Total
17	−36	−47	−42	49		− 9.0	−25.5	−20.4	8,672

Aggregate amount of calm weather for month, 42 hours. Maximum hourly velocity of wind for month and direction, 72 miles, south-southeast. Average temperature for month, —37.8. Average wind velocity for month, 280 miles a day.　　　　FRANCIS LONG, Observer.

CPSIA information can be obtained at www.ICGtesting.com
Printed in the USA
LVOW11s1552081113

360565LV00004B/630/P